LUTHERANS AND CATHOLICS IN DIALOGUE I–III

I The Status of the Nicene Creed as Dogma of the Church

II One Baptism for the Remission of Sins

III The Eucharist as Sacrifice

Edited by
Paul C. Empie and T. Austin Murphy

LUTHERANS AND CATHOLICS IN DIALOGUE I—III

I The Status of the Nicene Creed as Dogma of the Church

II One Baptism for the Remission of Sins

III The Eucharist as Sacrifice

EDITED BY
PAUL C. EMPIE AND T. AUSTIN MURPHY

AUGSBURG PUBLISHING HOUSE
Minneapolis, Minnesota

LUTHERANS AND CATHOLICS IN DIALOGUE I-III

Published by Augsburg Publishing House
for
U.S.A. National Committee
of the Lutheran World Federation
and the
Bishops' Committee for Ecumenical
and Interreligious Affairs

For information address
Augsburg Publishing House, 426 South Fifth Street,
Minneapolis, Minnesota 55415

MANUFACTURED IN THE UNITED STATES OF AMERICA

I

THE STATUS OF THE NICENE CREED AS DOGMA OF THE CHURCH

CONTENTS

FOREWORD

The coming together of Lutheran and Roman Catholic theologians in the City of Baltimore, Maryland on July 6-7, 1965 for the first of a series of theological dialogues, may be considered as something of an ecumenical milestone in the relationships between these two communions in the United States. To the best of our knowledge this was the first occasion upon which representatives officially designated by agencies of their respective church bodies convened to examine systematically their distinctive understandings of basic elements of the Christian faith.

After nearly two years of negotiations such conversations were officially approved by the U.S. Roman Catholic Bishops' Commission for Ecumenical Affairs and the U.S.A. National Committee of the Lutheran World Federation. A joint Steering Committee met in the offices of Lawrence Cardinal Shehan in Baltimore on March 16th at which meeting it was agreed that conversations should begin with an examination of the role of the Nicene Creed as dogma in the church. The Nicene Creed was chosen because it is a basic statement of faith for both traditions, arises out of the post-Apostolic period, and affords some clues to an understanding of the development and position of dogma in the life of the church. It was also hoped that this first meeting would serve to further mutual acquaintance and communication, to expose sensitive essential issues which might be explored at future meetings, and to understand better the general context within which the several representatives approach apostolic tradition and Holy Scripture in explicating the Christian faith.

The papers prepared as a basis for discussion are printed in their entirety in the pages which follow. Appended to them is a summary statement, the text of which was composed by a drafting committee and, after revision and refinement, was approved unanimously by the entire group. It should be clearly understood that this summary statement represents the judgments of those who participated at the meeting and must not be construed as having the character of an official statement by any of the churches which have sponsored the conversations.

Necessarily lacking in this pamphlet is a transcript of the discussions themselves, which were both intense and fascinating. The issues raised in both of the papers are so fundamental that little more than a beginning could be made at these first sessions. For example, there was little disagreement that the church has a magisterial function, but the question of the basis of authority for the certification of doctrine as dogma was not followed through in depth. The fact of progression was recognized, e.g., from the speaking God to the Word of God to the faith of the church, to dogma, to theology; but the difficult problem of development in theology and its relationship to dogma could not be fully explored. The question was asked whether there are hierarchies both of authority and of dogma and if so what would be the implications of this fact, but examination of these issues was left for a later meeting. The fragmentary character of dogma was emphasized over and over again as well as the fact that although no human phraseology can satisfactorily capture and explicate divine mystery, the necessity to defend the church against error made the formulation of dogma a necessity. How far can one push this recognition of the inadequacy of human words as doctrine attempts to make dogma understandable? This, too, was laid on the table for future consideration. Also deferred for later examination is the question as to exactly what is implied when a group "accepts" a creed—the eternal problem of semantics must be dealt with.

We who were privileged to participate in this dialogue experienced a mutual sense of the guidance of the Holy Spirit, and acknowledge this fact gratefully. The climate of the meeting was conducive to a deepening recognition of the inseparable bond which unites us—our one Lord Jesus Christ—and to a growth in respect and friendship. In his opening devotions Bishop Murphy made use of the Lutheran Service Book and Hymnal, a copy of which had been presented to him by the Lutheran representatives at the March meeting of the Steering Committee.

We are aware of the deep-seated disagreements which divide us and do not underestimate the difficulties of overcoming them. At the same time, neither do we underestimate the powers of the Holy Spirit, and are content as Christian brethren and in obedience to Him to bear testimony to each other regarding our understanding of the Christian faith, trusting His promise that He will ultimately lead us into a mutual understanding of truth.

Paul C. Empie

William W. Baum

September 15, 1965

AGENDA

THEOLOGICAL CONSULTATION BETWEEN THE
U.S.A. NATIONAL COMMITTEE OF THE
LUTHERAN WORLD FEDERATION
AND THE
CATHOLIC BISHOPS' COMMISSION FOR
ECUMENICAL AFFAIRS

Catholic Center, 320 Cathedral Street, Baltimore, Maryland
July 6-7, 1965

July 6 (Tues.)—The Most Reverend T. Austin Murphy, Auxiliary Bishop of Baltimore, presiding

10:00 A.M. Devotions (led by Bishop Murphy)
Adoption of Agenda and Procedures
- Appointment of Recorder
- Appointment of Drafting Sub-Committee
- Appointment of Future Topics Sub-Committee
- Policy on Release of Publicity

Questions Seeking Clarification of Texts of the Papers: "Status of the Nicene Creed as Dogma of the Church"

10:45 A.M. Consideration of the Substance of the Papers
- Comments by the Authors on Counterpart Papers
- General Discussion

12:00 Noon Recess for Lunch

2:00 P.M. Continuation of General Discussion

3:45 P.M. Coffee Break

4:00 P.M. Continuation of General Discussion

5:30 P.M. Closing Devotions (led by a Catholic representative)

6:00 P.M. Dinner followed by Informal Conversation
(The Drafting Sub-Committee to meet separately to prepare the text of a recommended summary statement. The Sub-Committee on Future Topics also to meet.)

July 7 (Wed.)—Dr. Paul C. Empie, presiding

9:00 A.M. Devotions (Dr. Warren Quanbeck)
Report of the Drafting Sub-Committee
Discussion of the Report

10:30 A.M. Coffee Break

10:45 A.M. Continuation of Discussion of Summary Statement

12:00 Noon Recess for Lunch
(Drafting Committee to meet)

2:00 P.M. Second Report of Drafting Sub-Committee
Discussion of the Report
Adoption of a Summary Statement

3:45 P.M. Coffee Break

4:00 P.M. Consideration of Report of Sub-Committee on Future Topics
Date and Place of Next Meeting
Closing Devotions (Dr. Warren Quanbeck)
Adjournment

5:00 P.M. Press Conference

Position Papers

THE STATUS OF THE NICENE CREED AS DOGMA OF THE CHURCH:

Some Questions from Lutherans to Roman Catholics

Part I

by

THE REV. DR. WARREN A. QUANBECK

Luther Theological Seminary, St. Paul, Minnesota

The Nicene Creed is one of a series of confessional statements of the Lutheran church. To understand its place and function in the Lutheran church it must be seen in the context of these statements.

A. *The Scriptures.* It is the Word of God which calls the church into being, maintains and preserves her, and the church lives in loyalty and obedience to this Word. The prophetic and apostolic witness to Jesus Christ the Word of God is found in the Scriptures, which for this reason have a primary place in the church. The authority of Scripture is the authority of the Word of God, that is, the authority of the God who speaks in and through them. This authority must not be understood in a literalistic, legalistic or atomistic way, but is to be seen in the light of three factors.

1. The Holy Spirit. God is sovereign in His church. He is not the God of the Deists, but the living God who uses the things of His creation to confront man with His message. He is present and active in His church, and uses the human testimony to His mighty deeds to further His redeeming work among men. It is the work of the Holy Spirit which enables men to hear God's voice in the Scriptures.

2. The Ministry. God has bestowed the gift of ministry upon His church. It accomplishes its task of serving God and men through the proclamation of the gospel. God uses this proclamation in sermon, sacrament, teaching, counseling and service to effect His saving presence among His people.

3. The Problem of Interpretation. The Scriptures require interpretation, a task which has literary, historical and theological dimensions. The interpreter is concerned to discover what the biblical writer intended to communicate to his readers, and for this work he avails himself of the lexical, literary and historical information which illuminate the text in its historical setting. He is also concerned with theological questions such as the relation of prophecy and fulfillment, the relation of the divine demand (law) to the divine offer of life (gospel), and the problem of the unity of Scripture. The Bible is a record of the saving deeds of God, an interpretation of the significance of those deeds, and also an instrument through which God speaks in the life of the church today.

B. *Creeds and Confessions.* The events of the sixteenth century evoked from the churches of the Reformation a series of theological statements designed to clarify the event of God's saving presence among His people. The Lutheran Confessions may be divided into two main groups:

1. Affirmations of the catholic character and purpose of the Lutheran reformation. These include the three ecumenical creeds, the Augsburg Confession and its Apology (1530), the Schmalkald Articles (1537), and Luther's two Catechisms. Here the Reformers deny the charge that they are innovators, schismatics or heretics, and assert their loyalty to the catholic tradition and their rejection of what they considered to be late medieval deviations from it.

2. As the hope for the unity of Christendom faded, the churches were faced with the task of selfunderstanding in the new situation. The Formula of Concord (1580) seeks to provide a basis for unity within the Lutheran churches, defining their position with respect to current controversies and also in relation to traditional doctrinal disputes.

C. *The Function of Creeds.* Creeds and confessions have a threefold significance in the Lutheran church: Doxology, Self-identification, and Interpretation of the gospel.

1. Doxology. In keeping with the biblical understanding of confession, affirmation of the Nicene Creed is first of all a liturgical act. In its confession of Jesus as Lord and Son of God the church praises God for the deliverance accomplished in the mission of Jesus Christ. The secondary sense of confession as confessing one's sins is not in opposition but tributary to this. By confessing one's sins one acknowledges that God is right when He judges, and adds the voice of the repentant sinner to the chorus praising the Redeemer. When, as happens even in the pages of the New Testament, the primitive confession "Jesus is Lord" is expanded by qualifying expressions, this does not mean the abandonment of the liturgical viewpoint, but seeks to make more precise the identity of Him who is worshipped, and so prevent the assimilation of the Christian faith to Gnosticism or the mystery cults of the ancient world. Confession of the Nicene Creed is therefore first of all assertion of faith in God, of participation in the life offered in Christ, of obedience to the Spirit who reigns as Lord in the church.

2. Self-identification. Confession of the Nicene Creed is also one of the ways in which the Lutheran church seeks to make known her self understanding. The ecclesiastical and theological disputes of the sixteenth century saw labels distributed generously. In this atmosphere the Lutheran church seeks to identify herself as a church participating in the catholic tradition of the west, as standing in continuity with the one, holy, catholic and apostolic church. It did not seek to repristinate the apostolic age, but accepted the validity of all the theological, liturgical, and administrative traditions which in its judgment did not stand in opposition to the gospel.

3. Interpretation of the gospel. While the primary thrust of confession is doxological, the development of misunderstanding and perversion of the gospel thrust upon the church the necessity of using confession also as a mark of sound teaching. Inasmuch as the Scriptures present formidable problems of interpretation, and can be misunderstood even by men of good will, the confession serves as a guide to the understanding of Scripture by affirming what is sound in the teaching of a given period and rejecting what is skewed. The church of our time thus receives the help of the church of earlier days to aid her to find her way to a true understanding of the Scriptures. We do not find this merely by repeating the theological language of the creeds, but by penetrating to an historically informed understanding of what they affirmed and rejected in their own time. To overlook the historical situation and its conditioning effect puts one in peril of missing the point of the doctrinal statement or of absolutizing the language of the affirmation. In the Lutheran tradition, as in some others, the necessity of this process of historical interpretation has not always been sufficiently recognized, with the result that confession has sometimes been understood to mean only the acceptance of theological propositions about God and Christ rather than confession of faith in Christ.

D. *The creed is not an end in itself but an instrument.* It points beyond itself to the Triune God who has revealed Himself to His creatures. To confess the creed is therefore to commit oneself to God, a commitment which affords a new perspective on every aspect of human life. But because it has this instrumental function, and also because it participates fully in the historical relativity of the time in which it was written, it lays no other absolute requirement on the church. Confession of the Nicene Creed does not commit the church to the cosmology, epistemology, metaphysics, geography or church politics of the men who framed it. The task of proclaiming the gospel in our time requires that we use the language of our day and address ourselves to contemporary situations. If the language or ideas of the fourth century can help us, we are free to use them. Where they are opaque to contemporary men, their use produces more confusion than clarity. Our confession of the Nicene Creed is our recognition that given the fourth century situation we stand with Athanasius against Arius on Trinitarian and Christological issues.

Our task is not to parrot theological expressions but to find ways to proclaim that God is with us today. In Jesus Christ we are committed to the ultimate fact of the universe. Therefore all things are ours, and we must relate to them properly: assigning absolute trust and commitment to God alone, but giving due respect for every created thing in its relation to Him.

Part II

by

Dr. George Lindbeck

Yale Divinity School, Yale University
New Haven, Connecticut

The types of questions which arise concern (I) the Nicene Creed itself (in its Niceano-Constantinopolitan formulation), (II) the Catholic symbols (Apostles', Nicene and Athanasian) as a special class, and (III) the status of dogma in general.

I. In order to give focus to the discussion, it might be well to raise simply two specific questions regarding the content of the *Niceanum*:

1. Granting that the "came down from heaven" need not be understood as asserting anything erroneous, can a Roman Catholic nevertheless admit that its Gnostic overtones make it an unfortunate formulation (a) for us and/or, (b) even more seriously, in its original context?

2. If the reply to "1" is to some degree affirmative, could similar doubts arise in reference to the *homoousion*? If not, why not?

Needless to say, these are questions, not regarding the personal opinions of the theologians to whom they are directed, but regarding what is possible for a Roman Catholic to hold. The import of this distinction is developed in more detail under "3" *infra*.

II. 1. Do the ancient Catholic symbols have in some sense a higher status than other dogmas of the church? If so, how can this be given effective expression in view of the fact that all dogmas are said to be equally binding?

2. To what extent does the liturgical, "doxological" character and use of these symbols give them a special status? It is often said of dogmatic formulations that they are, in principle, capable of being improved upon. This, presum-

ably, would never be said, e.g., of the Psalms. If they were mistakenly viewed as doctrinal definitions, they would obviously have to be regarded as deficient at many points in light of the N.T. revelation; but it would appear that, even apart from the question of inspiration, their place in the liturgical heritage of the church makes it nonsensical to speak of "improving" them. Could something analogous be said of the Catholic creeds?

III. What are the conditions for asserting that "agreement" (between, e.g., Catholics and Lutherans) exists on a given dogma?

This, clearly, is an enormous problem which obviously cannot be more than superficially discussed in a preliminary meeting. The following points make an effort to specify various aspects of the question:

1. It may be assumed that, from the Roman Catholic viewpoint, doubts whether full dogmatic agreement exists on a given point can be finally resolved only by the decision to enter into full ecclesiastical communion (cf. K. Rahner, *Schriften* IV, 237 ff.). Our question, therefore, deals simply with the kind of partial and putative agreement which is possible between divided churches.

2. This limitation would seem also to require that we abstract from the "how" of acceptance: i.e., from questions regarding the (a) "grounds" and (b) "modalities" of acceptance. Thus this question does not call for a treatment of the problems raised by the facts (a) that the authority of the church and the authority of Scripture play different roles for Protestant and Catholic so that apparently at least some Catholics would doubt that a Protestant can assent to a given dogma "by divine faith", and (b) that the Catholic accepts the dogma as irreformable and the Protestant as, in principle, reformable.

3. Speaking then, not of the "how" of assent, but of the "what" which is assented to, presumably there would be a general agreement that this includes *at least* (a) rejecting what the dogma clearly and unequivocally excludes, and (b) agreeing that what the dogma unequivocally

asserts lacks positive error in the sense that it can, without self-contradiction, be interpreted in an acceptable way.

Thus, for example, to accept the *Niceanum* involves *at least* (a) rejecting the Arianism to which it is directly opposed as well as other heresies, such as Sabellianism or Origenistic subordinationism, which its authors were clearly concerned to avoid, and (b) agreeing that language about which one might have reservations, such as "came down from heaven" or *homoousion*, need not be understood in the context of the creed as asserting error.

4. This, then, brings us to our question. Is this minimal description of the "what" which is assented to in accepting a dogma a sufficient description and, if not, how specify the "more" which is necessary?

The reasons for raising the question are familiar, but it may be useful to mention some of them.

It is often suggested by Roman Catholics as well as others, that the language, concepts or categories in which a dogmatic truth is defined may be *inadequate*, not only in the relatively trivial sense that divine realities can never be fully expressed in human words and thoughts, but, more radically, in the sense that

i. fundamentally different, and more or less equally adequate, ways of expressing the same truth are possible. (This would seem to be implied by those who say, e.g., that if Christianity had first developed in an Indian environment, Trinitarian truth would have received a very different formulation).

ii. Some of these alternative formulations may be intrinsically, and not simply in reference to a new historical epoch, more adequate than those actually used in a dogmatic definition.

iii. The formulations used in a dogmatic definition may become—or even, to some extent, originally have been—positively misleading. (Cf. Küng's treatment of Trent on justification.)

Can a Roman Catholic seriously grant any or all of these points? If he can, is not this equivalent to admitting that the minimal description of the "what" which is assented to given under "3" is also a sufficient description? If so, it would seem that accepting the *Niceanum* does not *a priori* involve asserting the permanent appropriateness of, e.g., the *homoousion*, and that it leaves open the possibility of finding better categories. (It should be noted, however, that what is said under II. 2 *supra* perhaps provides a way of granting this while, at the same time, repudiating the possibility, or at least the desirability, of ever replacing, for liturgical purposes, the present Nicene Creed with a new version.)

5. The question just raised is perhaps reinforced by a consideration of Scripture. Everyone presumably agrees that one need not, and should not, accept as making truth-claims the historically conditioned conceptuality which the Bible uses in making what the Catholic accepts as its infallible and inspired theological assertions. Does not this necessitate equal freedom in the treatment of dogma which, after all, though infallible according to Roman Catholic belief, is not inspired?

   Specifically, this would mean that "dogmatic literalism" can be just as heretical as the scriptural literalism of Arius. The Arian use of the N.T. subordinationist and adoptionist concepts and images was heretical because it was, so to speak, opposed to the intention of the N.T. usage which was to exalt Christ, rather than lower Him. As a result, the church found it necessary to formulate the *homoousion* as a rule of interpretation for the N.T. Christological materials. But is not the rule of interpretation just as much subject to abuse as the originals (particularly when it serves, not as a rule of interpretation, but as an additional source of information regarding the Godhead)?

Conclusion

It will be observed that these queries are intended to press on our Roman Catholic friends the question of what they think must be included in the notion of dogmatic development (at least as this applies to some dogmas—it would seem that the Marian dogmas belong in a different category). Does it involve progress in some absolute sense? Must one accept a metaphysical outlook according to which "the dogmatic categories of being and substance" have priority over "the scriptural categories of presence and function" with the result that it is possible to say that "The Christian . . . now (after Nicea) has come to understand more fully what Christ, the Lord with us, is?" This is what Father Murray asserts in some provocative pages in which he says that "the first ecumenical question is . . . what think you of the Nicene *homoousion*?" (*The Problem of God*, New Haven, Yale, 1964, pp. 49-60 esp. 58, 50 and 53). Apparently Father Lonergan agrees with him when he says that doctrinal development involves, not simply transcultural progress from one "experimental priority" to another, but also progress towards a metaphysical "objective priority" (Cf. R. L. Richard, S.J., "Contribution to a Theory of Doctrinal Development," *Spirit as Inquiry: Studies in Honor of Bernard Lonergan*, ed. F. E. Crowe, Continuum II/3 1964, pp. 205-227).

The question is a serious one. Was de Maistre expressing a view which has no right to exist within Roman Catholicism when he tells us that the church

> "weeps over these definitions which rebellion extorted from her and which always were evils, since they all suppose disbelief or attack and could only arise in the midst of the most dangerous disturbances. A state of war raised these venerable ramparts around the truth. No doubt they protect her, but they conceal her, too. They have made her unassailable, but by that very act, less accessible". (*On Church and Society*. E.T., 1960, p. 24).

THE STATUS OF THE NICENE CREED AS DOGMA OF THE CHURCH

by

JOHN COURTNEY MURRAY, S.J.

Woodstock College, Woodstock, Maryland

There is a preliminary issue of method. For my part, I do not think it useful, at the outset of ecumenical dialogue, for a Catholic to propose to a Lutheran Catholic questions that emerge from a Catholic theological problematic. The converse likewise holds. Such questions might be considered unanswerable, or possibly peripheral, or even irrelevant. The basic question concerns the problematic which gives rise to particular questions. In what follows, therefore, I shall attempt to state the major questions which the Catholic theologian puts to himself with regard to the Nicene faith (N and NC) and to indicate the lines of answer.

I. The Nicene faith and Scripture.—Historically, this was the primary question. It still is. In a context dealing, in general, with the fallacy of archaism, the primary function of the theologian was thus stated by Pius XII: "It is also true that the theologian must constantly return to the sources of divine revelation. It is his function to show how (*qua ratione*) the truths which are taught by the living magistery are contained in Sacred Scripture and in the divine tradition, be it implicitly or explicitly. Moreover, both of these sources of revealed doctrine contain treasures so varied and so rich that they are in fact inexhaustible. Consequently, the theological sciences are kept forever young by the study of their sacred sources. In contrast, as we know by experience, speculation becomes barren when it neglects an ever more profound investigation of the sacred deposit. For this very reason, however, positive theology, as it is called, may not be equated with merely historical science. The reason is that, together with these sacred sources, God has given to his Church the living magistery, in order that the truths which are contained in the deposit of faith only obscurely and in some implicit fashion may be brought to light and formulated. The divine Redeemer entrusted this deposit to the magistery of the Church alone, not to the individual Christian or even to theologians.

When therefore, as it has often happened throughout the ages, the Church exercises this function of hers, whether the exercise be ordinary or extraordinary, it is clear that a false method would be brought into play if what is clear were to be explained by what is obscure. On the contrary, the converse method is plainly imperative. Hence when our predecessor Pius IX taught that the most exalted office of theology is to show how the doctrine defined by the Church is contained in the sources, he added, with good reason, "in the very sense in which it was defined" (*Humani generis,* DB 2314).

With regard to Nicaea, the basic relationship between the dogma and the Scriptures appears in Athanasius' famous statement of the conciliar intention in his Letter, *De decretis nicaenae synodi* (350/351). The original intention had been to adhere to the credal tradition and therefore to use the "confessional words of Scripture" (*ibid.*, n. 19; MPG 25, 448). However, the scriptural words (especially "ek tou patros") were twisted by the Eusebians to their own sense. Hence "the Fathers, perceiving their craft and their impious cunning, were forced to state more distinctly what is meant by "from (the) God" and to write that the Son is "from the essence" (*ousias*) of God, in order that " 'from (the) God' might not be considered common and equal in the Son and in things originate, but that all things else might be acknowledged as creatures and the Word alone as from the Father" (*ibid.*, col. 449).

Similarly, the Fathers had wished to adopt the scriptural theme that the Son is "the true power and image of the Father, in all things like (*omoios*) and exactly like (*aparallaktos*) the Father" (*loc. cit.*). Again, however, these phrases proved inadequate as the safeguard of scriptural doctrine against the Eusebian evasions. Hence the Fathers "were again compelled to gather up the mind (*dianoian*) of the Scriptures and to state and write again more clearly what they had said before, that the Son is consubstantial (*homoousion*) with the Father, in order that they might make clear that the Son is not merely like, but is from the

Father as the same in likeness (*tauton tê homoiôsei*)" (*ibid.*, col. 451). Therefore the anti-Arian formulas of the creed state the "mind" of the Scriptures. Between Scripture and dogma there is an identity of sense. The dogma defines what is revealed in the word of God.

What then is the mind of the Scripture that is identically the mind of Nicaea? Again Athanasius makes the classic statement, in his third *Oratio contra Arianos* (356-362, during the Egyptian exile?): "Thus, given that they (Father and Son) are one, and given that the divinity itself is one, the same things are said (in the Scripture) about the Son that are also said about the Father, except that the Son is not said to be Father" (MPG 26, 329). This is the famous Athanasian rule of faith. It is a synthesis of scriptural doctrine; it is likewise a statement of the mind of Nicaea—the sense of "ek tês ousias tou Patros" and "homoousion." The Son is all that the Father is, the one God; but he is not the Father; he is from the Father.

The polemic intention of Nicaea was to outlaw the Arian "impiety" as contrary to the mind of the Scriptures. The doctrinal intention was to make a positive statement of the Christian faith by gathering up the mind of the Scriptures. The Council had to give a positive answer to the Arian question in its first form: "Is the Son Son or a creature?" Hence it affirmed the full divinity of the Son, who is God in the fullness of the sense in which the Father is God. It also affirmed the mysterious uniqueness of the origin of the Son; it is as Son that he is "begotten" (*gennetos*), and only in this sense is he originate (*genetos*). Finally, it affirmed the unity of the Godhead in Father and Son. (It did not, however, explicitly specify the nature of this unity. This specification had to wait until the Arian question was asked in its second form, in the later, Eunomian phase of the controversy.) This threefold positive affirmation was made as a statement of the mind of the Scripture.

Hitherto it has chiefly been a question of the relationship of material identity in content between the Nicene dogma and the Scripture. There is the further question of their formal relationship—the question of Scripture as the norm of the dogma defined by the Council.

It is evident that the Nicene Church considered the relationship betwen the Scriptures and the magistery to be reciprocal

The word of the God in the Scriptures was regarded as the norm of the faith of the Church. Even Arius, and later Eunomius, felt it necessary to appeal to this norm, though their doctrinal systems owed nothing to Scripture. The Arian formulas were judged by this norm and condemned as false. Judged likewise by this norm, the Nicene formulas were put forward as the true faith; this is clear from the Athanasian rule. At the same time, the Nicene Church considered it to be the magisterial function of the Church to interpret the Scriptures and to declare their sense in formulas that were to be accepted by faith on pain of exclusion from the communion of the faithful. The word of God therefore is the norm for the magistery in declaring the faith of the Church. At the same time, the magisterial interpretation of the word of God and its declaration in the word of the Church is normative of the faith of the Church.

This is substantially the theology stated by Pius XII in the citation given above. It may be doubted whether it is possible fully to conceptualize the reciprocal relation between the word of God and the word of the Church, precisely because it is a question of a polar tension. One can at best undertake to give an adequately balanced description of a relationship which, like all relationships, in the end escapes exact definition.

The essential error would be a theological idealism, so called, which would assert that either the individual consciousness of the Christian or the collective consciousness of the Church is the norm of faith; that neither consciousness is bound on the word of God as a norm which confronts it; that the content of belief therefore is derived solely from the inward teaching of the Holy Spirit. The opposite error would be a biblical positivism, which would posit the word of God as "already out there now," and assert that the content of faith is to be derived from it by the methods of rational hermeneutic. Both errors have in common the same vice; each of them in different ways separates the Word of God from the Spirit of God.

Perhaps the analogue for a true understanding of the reciprocal relationship between Scripture and magistery is, in the ultimate instance, the indivisible Trinity itself, in which, as the

Athanasian Creed states, there is "nihil prius aut posterius." Differing in their modes or origin, the Word and the Spirit are absolutely correlative (*simul sunt*). The same correlation exists between Word and Spirit in the history of salvation, amid a difference of function. The Word of God, Christ the Son, stands, as it were, over against and above the Church, seated at the Father's right hand as the Lord-of-us. In contrast, the Spirit of God, the Father's Gift to the Church through Christ Jesus, abides hiddenly in the Church (cf. Jn 14:16) as the Lord-with-us (cf. Acts *fere passim*).

The relationship between Word and Spirit is conveyed by John (cf. 16:13-15) through the image of the relationship between Yahweh and his people—a speaker-hearer relationship (the analogy is deficient but valid). The Word spoke to men from outside them, as it were, in deed and word (cf. Jn 15:26: "all that I have said to you"). The Word still speaks to the Church through the written word of God which is also somehow outside-of-us, above the Church, like the Word himself, containing a revelation that is at once definitively given to the Church and never fully to be comprehended by the Church. The Spirit in turn, indwelling in the Church, is the true hearer of the Word, as they are the true people of God who faithfuly hear his word (cf. Ezechiel; cf. Lk 11:28). He is "the Spirit who is from God," who has been "received" by the people of God, "that we might understand the gifts bestowed on us by God" (1 Cor 2:12). It is the Spirit-with-us who gives understanding of the Word-above-us, both in himself and in the written word which is itself a gift to the Church and not, in the end, a work of the Church. The forbidden thing therefore is to separate Word (or word) and Spirit (or spirit, the charism of the Church), or to confuse them by mistaking their respective functions.

II. The authority of the Nicene faith.—The authority of N and NC as the rule of faith derives formally from the authority of the magistery of the Church, "whose function it is to judge with regard to the true sense and interpretation of the sacred Scriptures" (Council of Trent, sess. 4, DB 786). This function of judgment is a function of certification. In the case, N and NC, in virtue of the assistance of the Holy Spirit, the true hearer of the word of God, certify as true the three affirmations noted above, together with the fourth in NC (the expansion of the article on the Holy Spirit in N). It is to be noted that, when the affirmations are certified as true, the understanding contained in the affirmations is not certified as adequate (cf. infra).

It is hardly necessary to add that the authority of N and NC does not depend on the fact that the material identity of sense between Scripture and dogma can or cannot be established by the methods of rational hermeneutic. To say this would be to make biblical scholarship the norm of the faith of the Church—*quod absit.* Finally, in accord with what has been said above, that fact that the status of N and NC as dogma derives formally from the act of the magistery in no wise derogates from the authority of the word of God, the Scriptures, as the source of revelation. Nicaea certified the *homoousion* as a true statement of faith because the Scriptures say of the Son whatever they say of the Father, *excepto Patris nomine.* On the other hand, the word of God, somehow "already out there now," does not certify itself as the word of God. Still less does it wait on scholarship for such certification of its sense as scholarship may provide. Judgments of certainty belong to the magistery. And such judgments are certain because it is true to say of the Church—analogously, of course, and *proportione servata*—what is said of the Spirit himself: "He will not speak on his own authority, but whatever he hears he will speak" (Jn 16:13).

III. The immutability of the Nicene dogma.—Immutability, like certainty, attaches to judgments, to affirmations, and to the sense in which the certain judgment or affirmation is made. On the other hand, the immutability of an affirmation, again like its certainty, does not preclude development—that is, fuller understanding—of the sense in which the affirmation is made.

In the first place, therefore, it will be forever immutably true to say that the Son is consubstantial with the Father, that he is all that the Father is, except for the name of Father. Moreover, it will be forever forbidden so to understand the Nicene dogma—so to "interpret" it, so to "develop" its sense—as, in the end, to affirm that the Son is not consubstantial with the Father, not all that the Father is, except for the name of Father. Finally, it will be forever forbidden to say that the Nicene dogma is mutable in the sense that it has or may become irrelevant, of no religious value or interest (cf. infra), no longer intelligible *suo modo* as a formula of faith. No such menace of irrelevancy hangs over the scriptural revelation, that the Son is all that the Father is, except for the name of Father. Similarly, no such menace threatens the *homoousion.* The pertinent citation here would be Vatican I, *Constitution on Faith,* ch. 4, "On Faith and Reason" (DB 1800).

In the second place, however, no less pertinent is the canon of Vincent of Lérins, cited in the same chapter, which urges the Christian and the Church to growth in understanding, knowledge, and wisdom, "in eodem scilicet dogmate, eodem sensu, eademque sententia." The historical fact is that the Nicene dogma underwent development.

First, the homoousion was applied to the Holy Spirit, explicitly by Gregory Nazianzen, later implicitly by Constantinople I, still later commonly. Second, what was only implicit in the original Nicene affirmation about the divine unity came to explicit statement in the latter phase of the Arian controversy. Following on this, the *homoousion* was applied to the Trinity, the "triada homoousion" of Constantinople II (canon 1). In the course of this development, the word lost the connotations of "origin from," which it had in the original Nicene text. It came to be simply a statement of the numerical identity of the Three in the one divine substance. In this sense the notion was foundational to the systematic Trinitarian formula first struck off (it seems) by Anselm and later canonized by the Council of Florence, "All things are the one thing, where no opposition of relations intervenes." Every notion acquires fuller meaning when it becomes an organic part of a systematization.

The question, however, may be asked, whether the Nicene dogma admits further development today, whether it can be stated in other categories. The answer is no. Nicaea answered the Arian question, "Is the Son Son or a creature?" The answer was necessarily cast in the categories of the question, God or creature, from the Father as begotten or from the Father as made. There are no other categories in which the answer can be cast. And the question itself, in the categories of its asking, is not time-conditioned, the product of a particular culture; it is perennial, the product of the human mind as such.

Many other questions may indeed be asked about the Son; but they would have to be answered in their own terms, not by a reinterpretation of Nicaea. The Nicene answer to the Nicene question is final and definitive. There is no going beyond it, since it brings the believer to the very edge of the abyss of the mystery of the eternal Son, who is God of God. In this sense, the *homoousion* is a "limit-concept."

Obviously, this is not the place to enter the enormous area of theological development to which Nicaea opened the way. Every mystery of faith creates a problem for the theologian. In the case, the problem inheres in the mysterious affirmation that the Son is "God of God." But if he is God, he exists *a se;* if he is God of God, he exists *ab alio.* A contradiction seems to appear. This is the problem to which Augustine addressed himself, and to which Aquinas fashioned the solution, in so far as a solution is available. The key to the solution is the psychological analogy, glimpsed by the intuitive genius of Augustine, formulated by the philosophical intelligence of Aquinas, and—it may be added—re-stated with newly profound understanding by Bernard Lonergan.

The appeal is to human interior intellectual and moral experience, that is, to the experience of the procession of the inner mental word (concept) from the act of understanding (insight), and to the experience of the procession of the act of moral choice (love) from the intellectual estimation and desire of the good. The analogy is metaphysical, because man is the image of God. It is not therefore merely a matter of metaphor. One can be admitted to a measure of analogical, imperfect, obscure understanding of the processions of the Word and the Spirit in the inner trinitarian life of God. All this, of course, is theology, not dogma. The premise of the Augustinian and Thomist theology, however, is the Nicene dogma under its ontological aspect (cf. infra). In certifying the scriptural truth, the dogma also certified that human intelligence, under the light of faith, can and should go on to an analogical understanding of what God is—the one Being who is subsistent Intelligence—and how God is Triune: God the Father, the God who speaks; God the Son, the

Word uttered by the Father, who is begotten because uttered; God the Holy Spirit, procedent from Father Son as their Love and Gift.

IV. The religious value of the Nicene dogma.—The dogma was consciously formulated as a test of orthodoxy. As someone has said, it was not a creed for catechumens but for bishops. Here is its first religious value; for orthodoxy is a religious value. This value, however, is extrinsic. The essential inherent value of the dogma lies in its certification of what God is in himself, antecedent to whatever He may be to us. The question, what is God, is not the appropriate subject for idle musing on a summer afternoon. However unanswerable it may be in the end, it is the first and last of all religious questions. Nicaea gave the certified answer—that God is the Father and that the Son is Son. Thus Nicaea also answered the other urgent religious question, whether we are redeemed or not. The premise of its asking can only be the basic OT conviction that only God can redeem us. Nicaea answered by certifying that the Son is God of God; therefore He could save us and He did and does. This is, of course, the soteriological argument, so called, that was incessantly alleged by the protagonists of the Nicene faith (about the Spirit as well as about the Son). In a word, Nicaea explained what John meant when he said, "God is love" (1 Jn 4:16).

V. The Nicene faith and human intelligence.—It is presumably too late in the scholarly day to bother discussing the question, whether Nicaea initiated the process of "die Hellenisierung des Glaubens." The categories of the Nicene argument —God or creature, begotten or made—were not Hellenic but biblical. Moreover, the *homoousion* is not a category at all. A category is an abstract classifying concept which furnishes the essential definition of a number of individual instances. The *homoousion*, however, first defined with complete concreteness what the Son is, what only the Son is. Later it defined, again concretely, what the Spirit is. Finally, it defined, still concretely, what the Trinity is—"the one nature or substance (*ousian*), the one power and authority (*exousian*), the consubstantial Trinity, the one divinity to be adored in three subsistences (*upostasesin*) or persons (*prosôpois*)" (Constantinople II).

If there was any "categorizing" here, it was simply the collocation of Father, Son, and Spirit in the order of the Godhead. And "God" is not a category. Finally, the use of the word "*homoousion*" did not involve the Church in the endless argument about the metaphysical concept of substance—the concept which contemporary philosophy is desperately struggling to thrust out with a pitchfork, what time it always returns (to paraphrase the Horatian tag). The *homoousion* is not a metaphysical concept. It is a dogmatic coinage whose content is the mind of the Scripture with regard to what the Son is.

All this, however, only clears the way for the real argument. Nicaea said the very same thing that the Scriptures had said, but it certainly did not say it in the same way. The notorious accusation that the *homoousion* was "unscriptural" did not lack foundation. The first series of post-Nicene synods, beginning with the Dedication Council at Antioch in 341, refused to use the word. The second series, beginning with the third synod of Sirmium (357) explicitly forbade its use. The real issue, however, was not simply one of words. It concerns the ontological aspect, so called, of the Nicene dogma, and the warrant for making the transition from the scriptural mode of conception and utterance to a different mode. There are three questions—historical, dogmatic, theological.

Historically, on the witness of Athanasius, the transition was made for reasons of polemic necessity. Moreover, the new usage was defended as an exception, not as an instance of a general principle. The Nicene Fathers would have been enormously astonished, had anyone told them that they were engaging in the development of doctrine. This fact, however, is itself not astonishing. In what concerns the processes of art, whereby things are made, a man must know what he is going to do before he does it. In contrast, in what concerns movements of intelligence, whereby knowledge is acquired, a man must first reach the term of the movement—the knowledge itself—before he can know what the term is, much less understand the process whereby he reached it. This is why the great issue today—in our case, the development of trinitarian doctrine—was no issue at all while the development was going on. This would be true even apart from the energizing fact of the moment, the rise of historical consciousness and the blessed decline of "classicism."

Dogmatically, the transition was certified as valid by the authority of the Church as the authentic interpreter of the mind of the Scriptures. The certification falls both on the term of the transition—the Nicene dogma as a statement of revealed truth—and on the validity of the mode of the statement.

The theological question is much more difficult. It is not an issue of certainty but of intelligibility, and it is twofold. First, is there an intelligible relationship between the scriptural and the dogmatic modes of conception and utterance, which would explain their homogeneity of sense? Second, is the historical process of movement from one to the other intelligible? Evidently, the second question is the more difficult. It raises the issue of the intelligibility of history—and indeed in its most complicated form, which concerns the history of thought.

It is obviously impossible in this paper to explore both of these questions or either of them. It may suffice briefly to suggest some considerations relevant to each in turn.

1. The ontological aspect of the Nicene dogma.—It was a providential dispensation that Christianity was born in the world of Hebraic culture and grew in the larger world of Hellenistic culture. The providential character of the dispensation is seen in the fact that in both of these cultures the mythical consciousness, characteristic of the primitive, had been transcended, at least in principle, through a differentiation of the mythical and the intellectual consciousness. The transcendence was of course, effected in different ways.

In the Hellenic world the mythical consciousness was transcended by virtue of the metaphysical impulse, resultant in the Platonic insight, whereby man was admitted into the world of theory, distinct from the world of community, and the norm and measure of man's dramatico-practical life. Contributory also were the scientific impulse, of which Aristotle may here serve as the example, and the humanistic impulse, visible chiefly in the great Greek dramatists and historians. In the Hebraic world, on the other hand, the mythical consciousness was transcended by virtue of the prophetic word of God. The "speaking God" notified himself to the people as their Lord and Creator, He who is-with the people, He who is the Holy One. In the conception of Yahweh anthropomorphisms and symbols abounded. There was, however, a true knowledge of God, a profound consciousness of the reality proclaimed in the text of Hosea: "I am God and not man" (Hos 11:9). There was, consequently, a fuller liberation from the mythical consciousness in religion than was achieved in any other ancient culture.

To be brief, implicit in the OT understanding of the word of God there was a certain dogmatic realism. That is, there was the consciousness that the word of God is true and therefore it notifies that which is: God is God and not man. This realism was dogmatic in the sense that it was unreflective, a matter of direct consciousness that went unanalyzed. God was simply believed to be God and not man, and there was an end of the matter. The realism in consequence was only implicit. It was not thematized by explicit distinction between the mythical and the intellectual consciousness. The latter was simply manifested in the act of faith itself.

To be even more brief, the same dogmatic realism was implicit in the NT word of God. Thence it carried over into the apostolic kerygma and didache; and thence further into what Origen identified as "the certain line and the manifest rule" of faith, which required that "the preaching of the Church must be adhered to, that which has been handed on (*tradita*) from the apostles through the order of succession and abides in the churches up to the present moment" (*De principiis*, praef., 1, 2). Further witness to the realism in the preaching of the Church as in the word of God was, for instance, the exclusion of heretics from communion. Even more striking witness was the witness of the "white-clad army of martyrs" who died, not for myths or ideas or religious experience, but for their adhesion to reality, for their faithful affirmation of truths endowed with ontological reference, for their love of him whom they believed to be Lord and Father, who had not spared him who is the Only-begotten but really sent him for man's redemption.

The conclusion here is that the Nicene dogma, under the aspect of its ontological reference, did not represent a leap, as it were, into an intellectual world alien to the Christian message—

a leap from religious experience to ontology. The word of God itself, which became the apostolic kerygma and then the preaching of the Church, is a matter of true affirmations to which corresponds reality as it is—the reality of God and His saving counsel in man's regard. There is no more "ontology" in the Nicene dogma than there is in the word of God itself. In both there is the same dogmatic realism. It was always implicit in the word of God; it becomes explicit in the Nicene dogma. Therefore the word of the Church is homogeneous in its sense with the word of God. In the dogma there is no new sense, alien and heterogeneous to the sense of the word of God, accruing to the dogma by reason of the transition from the scriptural consideration of the "God who acts" to the dogmatic consideration of the "God who is" (or, in technical terms, from the *prius quoad nos* to the *prius quoad se*, from what is prior in the order of experience to what is prior in the order of being).

2. The movement from didache to dogma.—There is no question that Hellenistic culture played a part in the formulation of the consubstantiality of the Son and Spirit. Had there been no Gnostics and Marcionites, no Sabellians, and especially no Arius and Eunomius, there would have been no need to draw up the "bishop's creed." And had it not been for Hellenistic culture, there would have been no Gnostics, Sabellians, Arians. Hellenistic culture, from which these errors derived, was simply the occasion and cause, under the providence of God, which enabled and obliged the Church to render explicit what had always been implicit in the word of God—its ontological aspect, its dogmatic realism.

The long process which led to the explicit realism of the Nicene dogma was dialectical. The whole of the "ante-Nicene problem," so called, consists in the exploration of this dialectic. It will have to suffice here to indicate simply the structure of the dialectic, under omission of citation from ante-Nicene authors which would illustrate its content.

The material principle was the objective set of contradictions, either explicit or implicit, evident in ante-Nicene thought (e.g., in Origen, between his firm adhesion to the affirmations of the rule of faith and the subordinationism in his trinitarian theology, owing to the influence of Middle Platonism). These contradictions were possible and inevitable because the realism of the word of God was merely dogmatic and implicit. It is quite possible for the dogmatic realist, precisely because his position is unreflective, to make true affirmations—in the case, the affirmations contained in the word of God—and then proceed so to explain his affirmations as to contradict their sense, without perceiving the contradiction (as Origen did not).

The dialectical process was the elimination of the contradictions, which required that they first be perceived and made explicit (in this respect, Arius performed the major service by his flat and altogether correct statement of the problem of the Son).

The formal principle of the dialectical process was the thinking subject—or more concretely and historically, the whole series of ante-Nicene thinkers who wrestled with the problem of the Son (now as then, no one man can be the bearer of the process of development of doctrine, which is normally dialectical).

The term of the dialectic was the Nicene dogma, a development of the doctrine in the word of God—the affirmation that the Son is Son (the affirmation long contained in the word of God and in the rule of faith) and the affirmation that the Son is Son because he is from the substance of the Father, consubstantial with the Father, begotten and not made (the development of the rule of faith). From the dogma all the previous contradictions were removed, chiefly sabellianism and subordinationism. It had been seen that they were contradictions, incompatible with the word of God which says of the Son all that it says of the Father, except for the name of Father.

This was the term of the dialectic when the process was conducted by intelligence under the light of faith. Another term, however, was possible, and in fact it was reached—the heresy of Arius and Eunomius, for whom the formal principle of the dialectic was human reason alone, and for whom therefore its term was the evacuation of the mystery announced in the word of God. It only remains to say that none of the men engaged in the dialectic understood the dialectic in which they were engaged. This, as has been said, is in the nature of an intellectual movement. Its intelligibility, as a movement, is hidden from its participants. But when the Holy Spirit is present in a movement, men build better than they know.

A final remark is necessary. It must remain only a remark, since it really starts a whole new subject. Nicaea contains no philosophy and it canonizes no philosophy—no metaphysic or epistemology. Nevertheless, it laid the foundations of a philosophy. It accomplished the definitive transcendence of the mythical consciousness in philosophy and religion. It carried Christian thought beyond a critical realism, in which imagination substitutes for intelligence, for which the final categories of understanding are space and time, and in which the real is, in the end, the experience of the real. It also carried Christian thought around, as it were, the sublimities of Platonic idealism, which does not heed the injunction made by the word of God and obeyed by the word of God itself: "Let what you say be simply 'yes' or 'no' " (Mt 5:37). Nicaea made explicit the dogmatic realism implicit in the word of God. By so doing, it laid the foundation of the philosophical movement towards a critical realism, for which that is real which can be intelligently conceived and reasonably affirmed—in which therefore the axiom obtains, "Ens per verum": I know what is when I affirm what is true.

SUMMARY STATEMENT

Following is the text of the joint statement issued in Baltimore July 7 at the close of the first official theological discussion in the United States between representatives of the Roman Catholic Church and the major Lutheran churches.

In praise to God, and in gratitude for those gifts of His Spirit whereby He steadily draws His people to unity in Christ, we rejoice in this first official theological conversation in the United States between Roman Catholic and Lutheran believers.

Those regularly appointed to arrange for and summon this meeting selected the topic for discussion: The Status of the Nicene Creed as Dogma of the Church.

The main points of the conversation are summarized in the following paragraphs:

1) We confess in common the Nicene Faith and therefore hold that the Son, Our Lord Jesus Christ, who was made man, suffered, died, and rose again for our salvation, is true God; that He is from God the Father as Son, and therefore other than the Father; that the Godhead is one and undivided; and that the Holy Spirit, together with the Father and the Son, is to be worshipped and glorified.

2) The Nicene Faith gathers up and articulates the biblical testimony concerning the Son and His relationship to the Father.

3) The Nicene Faith, formulated by the Council at Nicaea in 325 and developed in the Nicene-Constantinopolitan Creed, was a response to contemporary errors. The Church was obliged

to state her faith in the Son in non-biblical terms to answer the Arian question.

4) The confession that Our Lord Jesus Christ is the Son, God of God, continues to assure us that we are in fact redeemed, for only He who is God can redeem us.

5) The Nicene Faith, grounded in the biblical proclamation about Christ and the trinitarian baptismal formulas used in the Church, is both doxology to God the Father and dogma about God the Son.

6) As we reflect upon the role of dogma in our separated communities, we are aware of the following:

(a) The Nicene Faith possesses a unique status in the hierarchy of dogmas by reason of its testimony to and celebration of the mystery of the Trinity as revealed in Christ Our Savior, and by reason of its definitive reply to an ever-recurring question. This does not imply that the Nicene Faith exhausted the richness of Scripture regarding the person of Christ. For example, the Council of Chalcedon in 451 confessed that He was "in every respect like us, except without sin."

(b) We are agreed that authoritative teaching in the Church serves the people of God by protecting and nurturing the Faith. Dogma has a positive and a negative function. It authoritatively repudiates erroneous teaching, and asserts the truth as revealed in the saving deeds of God and in His gifts to His Church and to His world.

(c) The way in which doctrine is certified as dogma is not identical in the two communities, for there is a difference in the way in which mutually acknowledged doctrine receives ecclesiastical sanction.

(d) Different understandings of the movement from kerygma to dogma obtain in the two communities. Full inquiry must therefore be made into two topics: first, the nature and structure of the teaching authority of the Church; and, secondly, the role of Scripture in relation to the teaching office of the Church.

7) We together acknowledge that the problem of the development of doctrine is crucial today and is in the forefront of our common concern.

SPONSORING ORGANIZATIONS

U.S.A. National Committee, Lutheran World Federation:

The Rev. Dr. Franklin Clark Fry, President, Lutheran Church in America, New York, N. Y.

The Rev. Dr. George F. Harkins, Assistant to the President, Lutheran Church in America, New York, N. Y.

The Rev. Dr. Bernhard H. P. Hillila, Dean, California Lutheran College, Thousand Oaks, California

Dr. Erling Jensen, President, Muhlenberg College, Allentown, Pennsylvania

The Rev. Dr. William Larsen, Secretary, the American Lutheran Church, Minneapolis, Minnesota

Mr. Harold LeVander, Attorney, South St. Paul, Minnesota

The Rev. Dr. Malvin H. Lundeen, Secretary, Lutheran Church in America, New York, N. Y.

The Rev. Dr. Norman A. Menter, Vice President, The American Lutheran Church, Detroit, Michigan

Mr. Cyrus Rachie, Attorney, Appleton, Wisconsin

The Honorable Hilbert Schauer, Justice of the Supreme Court of Colorado, Fort Morgan, Colorado

The Rev. Dr. Fredrik A. Schiotz, President, The American Lutheran Church, Minneapolis, Minnesota

The Rev. Dr. John M. Stensvaag, Professor of Old Testament, Luther Seminary, St. Paul, Minnesota

Bishops' Commission for Ecumenical Affairs:

His Eminence, Lawrence Cardinal Shehan, Archbishop of Baltimore, Baltimore, Maryland, chairman

The Most Reverend Joseph B. Brunini, Auxiliary Bishop of Natchez-Jackson, Jackson, Mississippi.

The Most Reverend John J. Carberry, Bishop of Columbus, Columbus, Ohio

The Most Reverend Bernard J. Flanagan, Bishop of Worcester, Worcester, Massachusetts

The Most Reverend Charles H. Helmsing, Bishop of Kansas City-St. Joseph, Kansas City, Missouri

The Most Reverend Francis P. Leipzig, Bishop of Baker, Baker, Oregon

The Most Reverend Ernest L. Unterkoefler, Bishop of Charleston, Charleston, South Carolina

PARTICIPANTS IN THE LUTHERAN CATHOLIC DIALOGUE

Lutheran Participants

The Rev. Dr. Paul C. Empie, Executive Director, National Lutheran Council (U.S.A. National Committee, Lutheran World Federation), New York, N. Y.

The Rev. Dr. Kent Knutson, Professor of Systematic Theology, Luther Seminary, St. Paul, Minnesota

The Rev. Dr. Fred Kramer, Professor of Dogmatic Theology, Concordia Seminary, Springfield, Illinois

The Rev. Dr. Arthur Piepkorn, Professor of Systematic Theology, Concordia Seminary, St. Louis, Missouri

The Rev. Dr. Warren A. Quanbeck, Professor of Systematic Theology, Luther Theological Seminary, St. Paul, Minnesota

The Rev. Dr. John Reumann, Professor of New Testament, Lutheran Theological Seminary, Philadelphia, Penna. (alternate)

The Rev. Dr. Joseph A. Sittler, Professor of Theology, Chicago Divinity School, University of Chicago, Chicago, Illinois

The Rev. Dr. Virgil R. Westlund, Secretary, Department of Theological Cooperation, National Lutheran Council, New York, N. Y.

Lutheran Participants who were unable to be present at the July sessions:

Dr. George Lindbeck, Professor of Historical Theology, Yale Divinity School, Yale University, New Haven, Connecticut

The Rev. Dr. Krister Stendahl, Frothingham Professor of Biblical Studies, Harvard Divinity School, Cambridge, Massachusetts (Dr. Reumann served as his alternate)

Catholic Participants

The Most Reverend T. Austin Murphy, Auxiliary Bishop of Baltimore, Chairman

The Very Rev. Msgr. Joseph W. Baker, Vice-Chairman of the Ecumenical Commission of the Archdiocese of St. Louis, Missouri

The Very Rev. Msgr. William W. Baum, Executive Director, Bishops' Commission for Ecumenical Affairs, Washington, D. C.

The Rev. Raymond Brown, S.S., Professor of Sacred Scripture, St. Mary Seminary, Baltimore, Maryland

The Rev. Walter Burghardt, S.J., Professor of Patristics, Woodstock College, Woodstock, Maryland

The Rev. Godfrey Diekmann, O.S.B., Professor of Patristics, St. John Abbey, Collegeville, Minnesota

Professor James F. McCue, School of Religion, University of Iowa, Iowa City, Iowa

The Rev. John Courtney Murray, S.J., Professor of Theology, Woodstock College, Woodstock, Maryland

The Rev. George H. Tavard, A.A., Chairman, Theology Department, Mount Mercy College, Pittsburgh, Pennsylvania

II

ONE BAPTISM FOR THE REMISSION OF SINS

FOREWORD

The second in a series of ongoing theological discussions between Lutheran and Roman Catholic theologians took place February 10-13, 1966 at the Center for Continuing Education on the campus of the University of Chicago, Chicago, Illinois. Like the earlier one, it was sponsored jointly by the Bishops' Commission for Ecumenical Affairs and the U. S. A. National Committee of the Lutheran World Federation.

The group decided not to issue a summary statement at the conclusion of its meeting, but rather to request a participant from each group to record for inclusion in this booklet his interpretation of what took place. Such commentaries, written by Dr. Warren A. Quanbeck and Monsignor Joseph W. Baker, appear immediately following the texts of the papers prepared as a basis for the discussion of the subject "One Baptism for the Remission of Sins."

In lieu of a summary statement from the group, a joint statement by Bishop T. Austin-Murphy and Dr. Paul C. Empie was released to the press. The text of this statement is given at the end of this booklet.

These documents speak for themselves and require no special comment. Perhaps the only additional word needed has to do with the increasing measure of communication and understanding which could be observed from session to session as representatives of these two traditions engaged in frank and penetrating discussion. An added dimension of the conversations resulted from the desire of the participants to spend more time together in worship.

The third meeting in this series is scheduled for September 23-25, 1966 at Washington, D.C. at which the subject for discussion will be "The Eucharist as Sacrifice." Although it is anticipated that the cleavage in theological positions with respect to this subject will be somewhat sharper than was the case when discussing the implications of the doctrine of baptism, past experience leads us to anticipate with confidence that even when faced with such differences the dialogue will be illuminating and constructive as Christian brethren place themselves under the guidance of the Holy Spirit.

William W. Baum
Paul C. Empie

ABBREVIATIONS

AC	Augsburg Confession
Ap	Apology of the Augsburg Confession
DB	H. Denzinger—C. Bannwort, *Enchiridion symbolarum definitionum et declarationum de rebus fidei et morum,* ed. I. B. Umberg (33rd ed.; Barcione-Friburgi Br., 1965)
Ep	Epitome (Formula of Concord)
FC	Formula of Concord
LC	Luther's Large Catechism
SA	Smalcald Articles
SC	Luther's Small Catechism
SD	Solid Declaration (Formula of Concord)
Treatise	Treatise on the Authority and Primacy of the Pope

CONTENTS

The Biblical Perspective

Baptismal Doctrine in the Churches

Reports and Evaluations

ONE BAPTISM FOR THE REMISSION OF SINS -- NEW TESTAMENT ROOTS

RAYMOND E. BROWN, S.S.

Prolegomenon

The author has been asked by the Catholic participants in the Lutheran-Catholic dialogue to investigate this credal statement in its NT roots. He hastens to caution the readers against assuming that what follows is *the* Catholic position, as if all Catholic exegetes would interpret the NT evidence in the same way, or as if necessarily there would be a difference between the Catholic and Protestant (or Lutheran) interpretations of NT evidence. Perhaps by the general and almost unconscious orientation of their backgrounds, Catholics and Protestants may tend to stress different features in NT thought; but by the common agreement of modern exegetes the aim of an investigation such as that undertaken here is descriptive, i.e. it seeks to interpret NT thought in NT categories and in the light of NT problems, not in the light of later Catholic-Protestant problems.

From the start a sense of history will suggest that there is almost certainly a difference between the understandings of baptism found in a first century document like the NT and that found in the fourth century creed, especially since the latter was the product not only of another time but also of another civilization. *A fortiori* the NT understanding of baptism will differ from that professed by the Roman Catholic Church in the 20th century. It is the work of scholarship to see how great this difference is and how important, and whether it concerns essentials or incidentals. The Catholic will tend to see such differences in terms of organic growth natural and necessary in a "living tradition whose wealth is poured into the practice and life of the believing and praying Church."[1] At times, perhaps, the Protestant will regard a particular development as a malformation. The discussion of such attitudes toward developments is the work of our dialogue. But the task of this paper is to *distinguish* between the NT thought and the developments that are a part of the living tradition of his church. As a Catholic he believes that often where the NT is silent on a particular point about baptism, the living tradition of the church may fill in the lacuna in helping to determine the fullness of apostolic thought, but it is still his duty to point out that the NT *is* silent on this particular point. As a Catholic he believes that the NT cannot teach a doctrine that is in formal and direct contradiction with the dogmatic formulations of the later church; for since the same Spirit is at work in the NT and the church, the NT and the church in treating of revelation cannot give contradictory answers to the same problem formulated in the same way. Yet it is his duty to point out that on some of the questions (or indeed on virtually all of the questions) pertaining to baptism in which there is a Catholic-Protestant difference of view, we are dealing with problems and/or formulations which were not directly envisaged in NT writings.

A particular difficulty occurs for the Catholic exegete when the documents of his church insist that a baptismal practice or doctrine of the church in the 4th, the 16th, or the 20th century has apostolic roots. It is dangerous to take such an affirmation too simply and to judge that therefore the Catholic exegete has to find such a practice in the NT descriptions of baptism. As a general principle such church affirmations are more theological than historical in their import; often they mean that the doctrines or practices of the later church bring out the potentialities of NT thought, and thus cannot be judged to be contradictory to apostolic practice and thought.[2]

---

[1] "*De Revelatione*," Ch. 2. Cf. Walter M. Abbott, S. J., ed., *The Documents of Vatican II* (New York: Guild Press, America Press, Association Press, 1966), pp. 114-118.

[2] A particular problem for our treatment is raised by the statements in *Lamentabili* (1907) against the Modernists. It is not clear what precise theological value should be attached to the condemnation of *Lamentabili,* and it must be remembered that the condemned propositions are condemned in the sense in which they were held by the Modernists and in the whole context of Modernist thought. In particular the following two condemnations create difficulty (not insuperable) for an exegetical investigation of the NT: (It is wrong to say that) the custom of conferring baptism on infants was a disciplinary evolution.

(It is wrong to say that) there is no proof that the rite of the sacrament of

We may now proceed to our treatment. The author acknowledges dependence on the standard works treating baptism in the NT: O. Cullman,[1] G. W. Lampe,[2] W. F. Flemington,[3] G. R. Beasley-Murray,[4] and the work on baptism in Paul by R. Schnackenburg,[5] The collected articles from *Lumière et Vie* (1956) have been translated as *Baptism in the New Testament.*[6] There are also the statement of the commission of the Church of Scotland,[7] and the Anglican discussion of one baptism for the remission of sins.[8] There will be three steps in the treatment: (1) The nature, necessity and manner of NT *baptism;* (2) the *oneness* of NT baptism; (3) the relation of baptism to the *remission of sins* in the NT. The brevity of treatment will inevitably lead to a certain inadequacy.

Baptism

We shall treat here the kind of baptism advocated in the NT, the problem of who were baptized, the necessity of baptism, and the formula employed.

Kind of Baptism. The NT speaks frequently of a baptism in water as part of the Christian life. To a certain extent, however, it is unexpected that baptism appears in Christian circles as a baptism *in water,* for a close reading of the NT suggests that there were indications that might have led Christians to reject a baptism in water for a less material baptism which would have been understood as a baptism in the Spirit.

In what seems to be a valid historical reminiscence, Jn 3:22 describes the early days of Jesus' career as a baptizing ministry of the same type as John the Baptist's, so that in the eyes of some

---

confirmation was used by the apostles: the formal distinction of the two sacraments, baptism and confirmation, does not belong to the history of primitive Christianity. Cf. DB 2043-2044.

[1] *Baptism in the New Testament,* trans. J. K. S. Reid (Studies in Biblical Theology, No. 1; London: S.C.M. Press, 1950).

[2] *The Seal of the Spirit; A Study in the Doctrine of Baptism and Confirmation in the New Testament and the Fathers* (London: Longmans, Green and Co., 1951).

[3] *The New Testament Doctrine of Baptism* (London: S.P.C.K. Press, 1953).

[4] *Baptism in the New Testament* (London: Macmillan, 1962).

[5] *Baptism in the Thought of St. Paul, A Study in Pauline Theology,* trans. G. R. Beasley-Murray (Oxford: B. Blackwell, 1964).

[6] (Baltimore: Helicon, 1964).

[7] *The Biblical Doctrine of Baptism; A Study Document issued by the Special Commission on Baptism of the Church of Scotland* (Edinburg: Saint Andrew Press, 1958).

[8] H. Benedict Green, "One Baptism for the Remission of Sins," *Theology,* LXVIII (1965), pp. 457-479.

Jesus and John the Baptist were rival baptizers. Nevertheless, when John the Baptist was arrested, Jesus abandoned this ministry of baptizing and turned to a ministry of preaching. The fact that he once baptized seems to have been an embarrassment for Christian tradition (perhaps when the question was raised later about the relative greatness of Jesus and John the Baptist); thus the Synoptics omit any mention of Jesus' days as baptizer, and the Johannine editor in 4:2 qualifies what was said in 3:22. Indeed Christian tradition built up a principle for contrasting the ministry of John the Baptist and the ministry of Jesus, namely, that John the Baptist baptized in water, but Jesus *would* baptize in a Holy Spirit. The reader tends to jump to the conclusion that the latter phrase means in water and a Holy Spirit, but that is not what is said. In fact, Acts 1:5 makes a clear contrast between John the Baptist's baptism in water with the baptism in a Holy Spirit that the disciples will receive at Pentecost which was obviously a baptism without water.

Of course, there is the fact that Jesus himself was baptized in water and the Holy Spirit which came upon him. Yet there are other texts that seem to indicate that Jesus' real baptism was his death (Mk 10:38; Lk 12:50). I Jn 5:6-8 seems to contrast the two baptisms of Jesus when it insists that Jesus did not come by water alone but by water and blood.

What then did determine the Christian community to baptize with water? The custom they knew of may have had some effect on them: Jewish proselyte baptism in water; the washing with water that seemingly marked entrance into the convenantal community at Qumran. The example of Jesus' own baptism in the Jordan was certainly a factor. Jn 3:5 reports a dominical saying on the necessity of being begotten of water *and* Spirit before being able to enter the kingdom of God. The exegete would find it difficult to decide whether this saying comes from Jesus and to what extent it has undergone the refraction of Johannine theology.[1] That "water"

[1]The Council of Trent (DB 858) spoke in reference to Jn 3:5 against Calvin: "If anyone says that true and natural water is not necessary in baptism, and therefore interprets metaphorically the words of our Lord Jesus Christ, 'Unless a man be born again of water and the Holy Spirit,' *A.S.*" From unbiased exegesis, it would be difficult to maintain that John was not talking about ordinary water; in fact, the Bultmannian exegetes maintain that "water" is an editorial insertion into the more original text precisely to give justification for baptism in water. Besides the problem of whether or not "water" is an editorial addition (which in Catholic thought would be an inspired editorial addition), modern exegetes would tend to make

and "spirit" could have been joined in a primitive saying of Jesus is not at all implausible, for there are excellent OT parallels employing water imagery in describing the communication of God's spirit (Isa 32:15; Joel 2:28-29; Ezek 36:25-26; also Jubilees 1:23-25; 1QS 4:19-21). In any case, the church came to believe that baptism in water *and* Spirit was the fulfillment of the promise that Jesus would baptize with a Holy Spirit.

We have gone into the above problem precisely because there remain indications in the NT, especially in Acts, that the Spirit could be given independently of baptisms in water. The Twelve were given the Spirit directly (on Easter evening according to Jn 20:22; at Pentecost according to Acts) and not through baptism in water—in fact there is no evidence that *all* of the Twelve ever were baptized in water. Acts 10:44 shows the Spirit coming upon Cornelius and company before they were baptized in water. Acts 8:15-17 and 19:2-6 distinguishes between baptism in water and a gift of the Holy Spirit which came with the laying on of hands. Some have maintained that there were separate ceremonies in the primitive church (a) baptism in water; (b) a laying on of hands or an anointing with oil which conferred the Spirit. The latter is seen as confirmation or its forerunner.[1] This author does not see that the evidence in Acts justifies the positing of a regular ceremony whereby the Spirit was conferred by the laying on of hands; it simply reflects an early stage of development where "baptism in a Holy Spirit" was not always or necessarily seen as identical with baptism in water. Nor does he find any evidence for an anointing with oil as a ceremony to confer the Spirit. The sealing with the Spirit (II Cor 1:22; Eph 1:13; 4:30) is, as far as he can see,

these observations relevant to the Tridentine statement—observations which need in no way represent disloyalty to that statement, but only a clarification: (a) the "born again" or renatus of the Tridentine citation stems from the Latin tradition of translating John; the Greek has no "again" and may well mean "begotten" instead of "born [again]." (b) In attributing the words to Jesus Christ, Trent simply follows the surface indications of scripture. Usually such attributions are not thought of as solving the scientific problem of the *ipsissima verba* of Jesus. (c) The evangelist was not concerned with the problem that divided Calvin and Trent, i.e., a baptism in water vs. a spiritual baptism. The evangelist was contrasting natural birth and a begetting from above by God.

[1]The Council of Florence (DB 697) commented on Acts 8:14 ff., especially on the verse: "They laid their hands on them and they received the Holy Spirit." The Council said: "In place of that imposition of hands, confirmation is given in the church." This would make confirmation a development from such apostolic practices, but not necessarily make such scenes instances of confirmation.

simply a figurative way of describing the effects of baptism. He agrees with Schnackenburg, "that one will seek in vain in the Pauline letters to discover a peculiar sacrament of the Spirit alongside baptism."[1] Despite the claims of some exegetes, there is no such distinction intended in Tit 3:5 when it mentions "the washing of regeneration and renewal in the Holy Spirit." Likewise, I Cor 12-13 is not distinguishing between baptism and confirmation when it says: By one Spirit we were all baptized into one body . . . and all were made to drink of one Spirit." He cannot agree with Monsignor Coppens of Louvain that Gal 4:4-6 refers to baptism and confirmation when it mentions separately our adoption as sons and the sending of the Spirit into our hearts. When it is a question of *regular ceremonies,* he thinks that Schnackenburg is correct: "The primitive church knew only baptism as a decisive means of deliverance."[2] *Salvo meliori judicio,* the problem of confirmation as a separate sacrament seems to be a post-NT problem intimately but not exclusively associated with the baptism of infants.

Who were baptized? Even though the Spirit could be given outside baptism, it seems that all Christians except the Twelve received a baptism in water. Even those who had already received the Spirit were baptized (Acts 10:47-48); even Paul was baptized after he had seen the Lord Jesus on the road to Damascus. Were children and infants baptized? There has been a long dispute on this question between M. Barth and K. Aland on the negative side and O. Cullmann and J. Jeremias on the positive side.[3] The present writer can add nothing to what has been already said. He thinks that passages like Mk 10:14 and Mt 18:3 make it plausible that sometimes, and perhaps often, children were baptized as part of a household (Acts 16:15; 16:33). He is less sure that new-born infants were baptized in NT times. However, the most that can

---

[1]Schnackenburg, *op. cit.,* p. 91.

[2]*Ibid.,* p. 10.

[3]Cf. Markus Barth, *Die Taufe—ein Sakrament? Ein exegetischer Beitrag zum Gespräch über die kirchliche Taufe.* (Zollikon-Zürich: Evangelischer Verlag, 1951). Kurt Aland, *Did the Early Church Baptize Infants?* trans. G. R. Beasley-Murray (The Library of History and Doctrine; London: SCM Press, 1963). Joachim Jeremias, *Hat die Urkirche die Kindertaufe geliebt?* (Gottingen: Vandenhoeck & Ruprecht, 1949). *Id., Infant Baptism in the First Four Centuries,* trans. David Cairns (London: S.C.M. Press, 1960). *Id., The Origins of Infant Baptism; A Further Study in Reply to Kurt Aland,* trans. Dorothea M. Barton. (Studies in Historical Theology, No. 1; Naperville, Illinois: A. R. Allenson, 1963). Oscar Cullmann, *op. cit.,* and *Le bapteme des enfants et la doctrine biblique du bapteme* (Neuchatel, Paris: Niestle, 1948).

be asserted is that such baptism of children was acceptable; there is no real evidence that the baptism of children and infants was thought necessary. The indication in I Cor 7:14 that children could be made holy through their parents suggests a way in which sanctification *might* have taken place extra-sacramentally.

Where children were baptized (if the exegesis of Cullmann and Jeremias is correct), the apparent reason is to bring a whole family into the church—a sense of solidarity. There is no clear evidence that infants were baptized to remove original sin. Indeed, the whole problem of original sin in the Augustinian sense does not seem to enter into NT baptismal thought. Some would call upon Rom 5-6. In Rom 5:12,19 Paul voices the thesis that "sin came into the world through one man" and "by one man's disobedience many were made sinners;" Rom 6 discusses baptism. The relationship between the two chapters is not clear; but perhaps by juxtaposing them one can come to the thesis that unless one is baptized, one is not free from the sin that affects all Adam's descendants. However, such a thesis seems to go beyond the focus of Paul's thought. Paul maintains that the sin that came into the world through Adam was acquitted through Jesus' act of righteousness and his obedience in death (Rom 5:18-19). Are men still born in the sin of Adam even after Jesus' death? This is not clear in Paul. Quite clearly in Rom 6 Paul is thinking of baptism as uniting Christians with the death of Jesus and taking away actual sin. The sinful state of unbaptized infants is not directly in Paul's discussion (although some Catholic scholars would see an indirect reference to it).

Was baptism considered necessary for salvation? The fact that in the post-Pentecostal period all adults were baptized in water, as far as we know, suggests that baptism was considered as necessary for Christian initiation. In one form of NT theological thought a necessity is explicitly attributed to baptism, namely Jn 3:5: "Unless one is begotten of water and spirit, he cannot enter the kingdom of God." The fact that this is a negative universal has been emphasized, and perhaps over-emphasized, in Catholic theology and has been used to prove the necessity of infant baptism. However, the exegesis of the negative universal requires us to ask what the author himself was negating. There is no evidence that the author was concerned with denying the kingdom of God to those who through no fault of their own are unbaptized. His immediate concern was one of contrasting flesh and Spirit, and of insisting that life from above is not the same as ordinary life and cannot be received without the work of the Spirit. His "unless" refers to the general incapacity of the purely natural. Therefore we should be careful to avoid interpreting NT thought on the necessity of baptism in the light of the later (Augustinian) problematic, for the NT does not speculate on the fate of the unbaptized. What the NT does stress is that in order for an adult to pass from the kingdom of death, darkness, falsehood and Satan into the kingdom of life, light, truth—in short, into the kingdom of God—he must be baptized.

Manner of Baptism. Christian baptism, unlike self-administered Jewish proselyte baptism, was administered by another. Since the NT is primarily concerned with the baptism of adult converts, this baptism was preceded or accompanied by a confession of faith. "Jesus is Lord" seems to have been the convert's usual confession, although alternates were possible, e.g., "Jesus is the Son of God" (gloss in Acts 8:37); perhaps even "Jesus is the Son of Man" (implied in Jn 9:35-38).

The "Trinitarian (or better 'triadic') formula" of Mt 28:19 is a difficult problem. Some Catholic scholars maintain that it was truly a saying of Jesus. They suggest that baptism in Jesus' name was an exception, or that the convert confessed Jesus' name while the baptizer recited the Trinitarian formula. Other Catholics think that Mt 28:19 is the end-product of a development within the church. If the Trinitarian formula was recited *by the baptizer*, it most likely came into common use as a by-product of infant baptism. If it was recited by the convert, then the confession of of Father, Son, and Holy Spirit seems to be a more evolved formula than a confession of Jesus' name. It is not at all unlikely that there was a development from the association of the Father and the Holy Spirit with Jesus' own baptism to the stage of the more primitive triadic formulae expressive of baptismal thought in I Cor 12:4-6 and Eph 4:4-6 to the further stage of the fully developed confession of Mt 28:19. If one accepts this thesis, Mt 28:19 is giving a formula in use in the Matthean (Syrean?) church of the 80's and assuring us that it is a genuine development of Jesus' own teaching.[1] In any case there seems to be no clear evidence that a

[1]We have assumed that the Trinitarian formula was part of the original text of the Matthean gospel. However, more attention should be paid to the minority opinion that it was not. F. C. Cnybeare, *Zeitschrift fur die neutestamentliche Wissenschaft,* II (1901), pp. 275-288 showed evidence in Eusebius and Justin for a shorter read-

Trinitarian formula or indeed any fixed formula was absolutely necessary in NT times. Faith in Jesus was necessary.

One Baptism

The insistence on not rebaptizing heretics seems to have influenced the credal confession of one baptism at Nicaea. That baptism can be given only once may be in mind in Heb 6:4: "It is impossible to restore again to repentance those who have been once enlightened." One can see that the frequently repeated Essene lustrations may have created confusion about the uniqueness of Christian baptism even in NT times.

Nevertheless, when one considers "one Baptism" in the NT, one thinks of the only occurrence of the phrase, namely Eph 4:4, and there the focus is *not* on the "only once" aspect of baptism. Some think that "one baptism" in Eph 4:4 means that baptism makes us one community, on the analogy of the unifying effect of the Eucharist (I Cor 10:17). Certainly Paul did consider baptism to be a unifying factor. I Cor 12:12-13 stresses that the individual Christians are one body, "for by one Spirit we were all baptized into one body."[1] Yet this undeniable effect of baptism does not seem to be the direct focus of Eph 4:4.

"One baptism" in Eph seems to mean the same baptism, i.e., just as all Christians have the same faith, namely faith in Jesus as the Lord, so there is only one Christian baptism, namely baptism into the one Lord. Thus, the oneness of baptism comes from the oneness of the Lord into whom all are baptized. In particular, this oneness is brought out by the fact that the Christian is baptized into the death and resurrection of Jesus (Rom 6:3-5)—a historic action that is *eph hapax,* "once for all." That baptism into the death of Jesus is in mind in Eph 4:4 is suggested by Eph 5:25-26 where

ing "in my name" instead of "in the name of the Father," etc. At the 1965 Oxford NT Congress H. C. B. Green gave an impressive paper arguing from structural/poetic criteria that the Trinitarian formula was an interpolation. If it was an interpolation, then the Catholic exegete, following the criterion of inspiration given by Trent (constant use in the church as attested by the Vulgate) might have to say that it was an inspired gloss or interpolation, just as he does for the adulteress story in John. The presence of the Trinitarian formula in the Didache suggests that the interpolation, if posited, would be early second century.

[1]This writer follows the thesis that is becoming more common (Cerfaux, John A. T. Robinson) that the body, at least in the earlier Pauline epistles, is not a community but the physical body of Christ to which all Christians are (mystically) united.

we hear that Christ gave himself up to sanctify the church by baptism. Thus through "one baptism" all Christians have the same radical initiation into the once-for-all Christ event.

Cullmann and John A. T. Robinson have introduced a special modality into the Pauline idea of one baptism, as an offshoot of the idea that we are baptized into Jesus' salvific action.[1] They remind us that this salvific action (Cullmann stresses the death; Robinson stresses the whole life) itself was Jesus' baptism for the whole world; and therefore the Christian's baptism is one, for he is being baptized into the one baptism of Jesus wherein the whole world was baptized. Some of Robinson's arguments for this concept are overdone, as pointed out by W. E. Moore, although there does seem to be some merit to the whole idea.[2] A thorough discussion would lead us too far afield. All that we would say is that while such a concept of world baptism may enter into the general NT concept, it does not seem to be a dominant note in the mention of "one baptism" in Eph 4:4.

For the remission of sins

We should enunciate two preliminary cautions: (a) In general the NT is describing adult baptism and the remission of actual sins. As we have insisted, the remission of original sin does not seem to be in focus. (b) We cannot expect in the NT a precise discussion of the causality of the sacraments nor a precise solution to the problem whether the sacraments have their effect *ex opere operato* (*non ponentibus obicem*). Infant baptism served as a catalyst in the latter problem, for with infants there could be nothing expected by way of cooperation on the part of the recipient. In adult baptism in the NT faith and penitence were necessary (Acts 8:37).

Remission of sins was related to baptism from the beginning. Mk 1:4 says that John the Baptist preached a baptism of repentance for the forgiveness of sins. Acts 19:4 attributes to Paul the words: "John baptized with the baptism of repentance." Mt 3:6 pictures the people "being baptized in the Jordan river confessing their sins." We are not certain how John the Baptist or those who followed

---

[1] J. A. T. Robinson, "The One Baptism as a Category of New Testament Soteriology," *Scotish Journal of Theology*, VI (1953), pp. 257-274. This article has been reprinted in J. A. T. Robinson, *Twelve New Testament Studies* (London: S.C.M. Press, 1962).

[2] "One Baptism," *New Testament Studies*, X (1964), pp. 504-16.

him interpreted the relation of this baptism and the forgiveness of sins, i.e., whether the baptism was a sign that sins had been forgiven or whether it had something to contribute to the forgiveness itself.

We must ask the same question of Christian baptism in the NT. In the book, *Die Taufe—ein Sakrament?* M. Barth seems to put John the Baptist's baptism and Christ's baptism very much on a plane.[1] He insists that in NT thought the Holy Spirit and not baptism sanctifies. Baptism is not a sacrament with the natural or magical healing power of a bath; it is not a mystery but an act of obedience, having only the role of a sign. Most NT commentators have found Barth's thesis too absolute. Perhaps the very fact that baptism is administered to the Christian by another and the verb "to baptize" is so frequently in the passive suggests that in baptism something is done to the Christian by God and that it is not simply a question of his confessing his faith. Nevertheless, there is nothing of crude magic about NT baptism. What is effective in baptism is not the physical washing with water taken alone, but the fact that God acts through this washing. And we should not neglect the passages that indicate that not only baptism but also acts of the Christian empowered by God bring salvation.

In a number of passages, especially in Acts (10:43, 48; 16:31-32), it is stated that faith brings salvation and the forgiveness of sins, and baptism follows this forgiveness. The post-resurrectional command of Jesus in Lk 24:47 is important: "Repentance and the forgiveness of sins should be *preached* in his name to all nations." This is the Lucan equivalent of the post-resurrection command to baptize found in Mt 28:19 and the Marcan appendix, and the different emphases on preaching and baptism should warn us against imagining that the concept of "baptism for the remission of sins" was fixed to the point of exclusiveness in NT times. However, there are other passages in the Lucan writings (Acts 2:38; 22:16) where the forgiveness of sins is related to baptism.

There are passages in the Pauline writings that relate baptism to the forgiveness of sins, and Rom 6:1-11 and Col 2:12 explain that in baptism we die in sin because baptism unites us with the death and resurrection of Jesus. (Whether this is an original Pauline insight or not is not clear; Rom 6:3 seems to imply earlier preaching on the subject by other apostles.) We note that in Paul's mind

[1]See Trent to the contrary, D.B. 857.

baptism has its power over sin because it brings us in relation to Christ—scarcely a mechanistic approach. Schnackenburg phrases it well: "He (Paul) does not teach a miraculous effectiveness of holy signs and rites, isolated from the one great saving event on Golgatha."[1]

The Pauline passages that speak of baptism as "washing" attribute real power to baptism but again because of the relation of baptism to Jesus. I Cor 6:11: "You (who were sinners) were washed; you were sanctified; you were baptized in the name of the Lord Jesus Christ and in the Spirit of our God." This text speaks of both a negative (washing from sinful life) and positive (sanctification and justification) effect produced by the Spirit of God given to Christians baptized into Jesus. Eph 5:26 says that Christ gave himself in death for the church that he might sanctify her, having cleansed her by the washing of water with the word. Thus in baptism Christ washes the church and this is related to his death. But notice that preaching (the word?) is closely associated with the baptismal washing in producing this sanctification.

NT passages which speak of baptism as regeneration or rebirth seem clearly to attribute to baptism real power and to make of it something more than a sign of what has already been accomplished. In Tit 3:5 baptism is the washing of regeneration and renewal in the Holy Spirit. Yet even here this is not mechanistic, for it is in Jesus that God our Savior has saved us by the washing of regeneration. In the "early Catholicism" of the Pastorals there is recognition that Jesus is acting in the sacrament. Another passage is Jn 3:5 which speaks of divine begetting by water and Spirit, and thus makes baptism the means of begetting. Yet to balance this in Johannine thought we should note that I Jn 5:1 says that everyone who believes that Jesus is the Christ is begotten of God, and this passage makes faith the principle of begetting (also Jn 1:12). I Pet 1:3, a passage related to baptism, speaks of the Christian's being born anew. Yet lest one draw the conclusion that only baptism in water has this power, it is well to note 1:23: "You have been born anew, not of perishable seed but of imperishable, through the living and abiding *word of God*" (also Jas 1:18 for the word as a principle of regeneration). Thus, even in the more developed works of NT

---

[1]Schnackenburg, *op. cit.*, p. 112.

theology baptism must share with faith and preaching the role of regeneration.

I Pet 3:21 says that baptism saves, not as a removal of dirt from the body, but as an appeal (or pledge) to God for (or of) a clear conscience. This seems to put the primary emphasis in cleansing on personal disposition. Yet Heb 10:22 uses the very imagery I Pet rejects: "Our hearts sprinkled clean from an evil conscience and our bodies washed with water."

It would seem then that NT thought is not rigorously consistent on the action that brings about the remission or cleansing of sin and Christian renewal. Many passages attribute such power to baptism, but many (without doing away with baptism) attribute it to other factors like faith and preaching. Perhaps we may say that preaching, repentance, faith, and baptism were all involved in the NT concept of the remission of sins, and that the question of precisely how much of that remission should be attributed to baptism taken in isolation is a question of post-NT theology. Gal 3:26-27 illustrates this thesis: "You are all sons of God *through faith,* for as many of you as were *baptized* into Christ have put on Christ." Also Col 2:12: "You were buried with him *in baptism* in which you were also raised with him *through faith* in the working of God."

Since we have concerned ourselves with the credal formula about baptism for the remission of sins, we should note that there are other effects and aspects of baptism in NT thought that we have not discussed but which should enter the total picture: the earnest of the Spirit, adoption as sons, participation in the Christian covenant, membership in the church, union with other Christians, etc.

THE FOCAL POINT OF THE NEW TESTAMENT BAPTISMAL TEACHINGS

KRISTER STENDAHL

In a Roman Catholic/Lutheran dialogue, this part of the creed contains less points of controversy than—perhaps—any other element in the faith. This is particularly so since at this point Luther and the Lutheran Confessions are upholding the tradition against the Anabaptists. The questions raised by a renewed study of the scriptures are rather questions equally directed to both, Roman Catholics and Lutherans. And the differences may well fall back on different ways of reacting to such questions. But in such a case it should be noted that on the Lutheran side—as presumably on the Roman Catholic—there are substantial variations in the response within the communion. A helpful example is found in the debate between Joachim Jeremias and Kurt Aland.[1] While Jeremias attempts to defend the view that infant baptism was practiced from the beginning, Aland undermines—I think, successfully—this argumentation and shows how the practice of infant baptism emerged ca. 200. In his final chapter, he argues nevertheless for the practice of infant baptism: "For the practice of infant baptism today can claim that it fulfills in a new time and in a new way what took place in early times in a different manner."[2] Aland sees the breakdown of temporal eschatology and the emerging reflection on original sin as the two main factors in this development.

I have had the opportunity to see Father Brown's paper. It would be meaningless to repeat the general presentation of "Baptism

---

[1]Joachim Jeremias, *Infant Baptism in the First Centuries* (London: SCM Press, 1960), and Kurt Aland, *Did the Early Church Baptize Infants?* (London: SCM Press, 1963).
[2]Aland, *op. cit.*, p. 113 f.

in the NT" which he gives and which well represents much of the consensus in contemporary biblical studies. I have, therefore, chosen to make a few pertinent comments and case them more in the form of a memorandum. Since his approach is mainly topical, my comments will be more oriented toward the genetic problems involved.

1) I would take my point of departure in the fact that baptism in the NT and in the early church is always an act of *initiation,* and that this fact should be the point of departure. Such an act is capable of many interpretations, but the force of initiation is primary. One cannot understand baptism by combining the elements of purification with the elements of death/resurrection, with the elements of regeneration, with the elements of receiving the Spirit, with the incorporation in the Body of Christ, etc. One must begin with the fact that in all cases the practice of baptism is the rite by which initiation takes place.

2) The Christian use of baptism has its roots in the activities of John the Baptist. And his baptism may well be a radicalized form of the initiatory baptisms or lustrations now known from the Qumran community,[1] which, in turn, can be understood as growing out of the priestly lustrations at the Temple.[2] But in both cases, and in possible similar cases in contemporary Judaism, the point of the practice has become the act by which man passes from this age to the age to come. It is a *rite de passage.*

3) This eschatological dimension is the decisive one, and it has become increasingly precarious to see the Jewish proselyte baptism as the proper background for the understanding of Christian baptism, since such a common practice is highly questionable in the first Christian century.[3]

4) The difference between Christian baptism and that of John (or of Qumran) is described in the NT as a difference in degree of anticipation. Also Christian baptism retains the element of anticipation. Hence the Pauline "arrobōn—down-payment" (2 Cor 1:22, 5:5, and Eph 1:14; cf. also the *"aparchē"* Rom 8:23). The decisive

[1] 1QS iii-iv.

[2] See N. A. Dahl, "The Origin of Baptism," *Interpretationes Ad Vetus Testamentu Pertinentes Sigmundo Mowinckel; Septuagenario Missae* (Oslo: Forlaget Land Og Kirke, 1955.), pp. 36-51.

[3] T. M. Taylor, "The Beginnings of Jewish Proselyte Baptism," *New Testament Studies,* II (1955/56), pp. 193-198, criticizing T. Torrance's article on Proselyte Baptism, *ibid.,* I (1954/55), pp. 150-154.

difference is no doubt the Spirit. This is clear both from the synoptic gospels as they distinguish between John and Jesus (Mk 1:8 par.), and from Acts 18:1-8. Thus the church claims a more definite anticipation of the age to come and its powers, and it sees baptism as the rite by which man becomes a participant in the new age.

5) I think that all other references to baptism can be understood from its function of initiation. Paul's interpretation of baptism as death with Christ toward a future (sic) resurrection (Rom 6) may well be his own constructive interpretation. It is interesting to note that the common meaning of the Greek *baptizesthai* is "to be drowned." In any case, this powerful interpretation cannot be the starting point for our interpretation of baptism. I would guess that the similar use of *baptisma* in relation to Jesus' death and the martyrdom of disciples (Mk 10:38 f. without parallels in Mt and Lk) is secondary and must be understood in the light of reflection upon the meaning of baptism in a martyrological setting. These observations make me highly critical of Oscar Cullmann's interpretation of Jesus' death as *Generaltaufe*.[1]

6) It seems that Western Creeds spoke about "remission of sins" while the Eastern mentioned baptism explicitly. Kelly is probably correct in saying that the West also understood its reference to remission of sins as a reference to baptism.[2] In any case, also here the accent on initiation comes into focus. The forgiveness here spoken of is the one which is given once and once for all. Thus it should be noticed that further discussion at this point would lead into the problem of penance and church discipline.

7) An exegete would also draw attention to the fact that the text which plays a great role in Luther's discussion of baptism (Mk 16:16 "He who believes and is baptized will be saved.") belongs to the longer ending of Mark, and is commonly considered secondary by contemporary biblical scholars. The evidence from Acts 2, 8 and 10 clearly indicates that the points about the relation between

---

[1]*Baptism in the New Testament* (London: SCM Press, 1950). This also applies to his interpretation of the baptism of Jesus. Here he takes the quotation from Is 42 (Mk 1:11 with par.) as a pointer toward "the Suffering Servant." But there is no "suffering" in Is 42, and it is only after Diehm's studies in the end of the last century that we have made the Songs of the Servant a unit. Thus we have no right to hear Is 53 when we read Is 42.

[2]J. N. D. Kelly, *Early Christian Creeds* (2nd ed.; New York: David McKay Co., 1960), p. 160 f. The lack of specific reference to baptism may be due to the fact that the Western creeds retain more of their character of baptismal creeds.

faith and baptism were not a conscious theological problem in NT times.

These observations would suggest that all discussion about baptism in the NT (and now?) must begin with the element of initiation. The "meaning of baptism" cannot be found by exploiting any one specific interpretation of this rite, be it the element of "free gift" manifested in infant baptism, or the relation to death/resurrection, or any of the other motifs which condition and enrich, but never overshadow the rite of initiation.

THE LUTHERAN UNDERSTANDING OF BAPTISM— A SYSTEMATIC SUMMARY

ARTHUR CARL PIEPKORN

Introductory Considerations

This essay proposes to answer the questions with which Roman Catholic teaching on baptism confronts Lutherans. As far as possible it will give these answers out of the Lutheran symbolical books, as representing the common conviction of all Lutherans. Where these are silent, any answer that is not clearly given by the sacred scriptures commands acceptance among Lutherans only on the basis of its plausibility and inherent persuasiveness. The answers of classic Lutheran orthodoxy—the era of the great Lutheran systematicians from about 1580 to 1713—in such cases may serve as a guide to the direction that Lutheran thinking took. The essay also attempts to take account of current Lutheran theological reflection on its subject.

The "Baptismal Booklet" Appended to the Small Catechism

On the principle *lex orandi lex credendi* the "Baptismal Booklet" (*Taufbüchlein*) appended to the Small Catechism from 1529 on (and a part of every complete edition of the Book of Concord) provides important insights into the Lutheran position on holy baptism. The "Baptismal Booklet"—an order for infant baptism—as we have it dates back to 1526. It is a simplification and abbreviation of an earlier reworking (1523) by Martin Luther of the medieval Western baptismal rite.

The 1526 rite begins with the same introduction to the Christian reader that the 1523 rite had had. Among its emphases are the following:

(1) Luther laments the carelessness with which the holy and comforting sacrament of baptism had been administered, partly because the participants did not understand the Latin rite. He has begun to baptize in German so that the sponsors and bystanders would be excited to greater faith and serious devotion and the priests compelled to proceed with greater diligence.

(2) The traditional ceremonies are not the aspects of baptism that repel the devil. To conquer him the sponsors and bystanders must attend in confident faith. They must listen to the word of God. At the priest's "Let us pray," they must pray with him. Hence the priest must say the prayer plainly and slowly, and the sponsors must really interpose themselves in prayer against the devil on the child's behalf.

(3) God himself calls baptism a new birth, which frees us from all the tyranny of the devil, from sin, and from death and hell, and turns us into children of life, heirs of all of God's goods, sons of God himself, and brothers of Christ.

A subsequent rubric implies that the rite—identical for both sexes—will begin at the entrance to the church. The priest adjures the devil with a shortened form of the *Exi et recede*. He makes the sign of the holy cross on the infant's forehead and breast. Then he offers a prayer which combines the address of the old petition *Omnipotens sempiterne Deus* with the body of the prayer *Deus immortale praesidium*. This prayer refers to the unbaptized child as "God's servant." Then follows a 169-word prayer for which there is apparently no immediate precedent in the medieval baptismal rite. It recalls the flood and the crossing of the Red Sea as Old Testament types of baptism; it sees in our Lord's baptism the hallowing of Jordan and of all waters to be a blessed flood and an abundant washing away of sin; it calls on God to look graciously on the candidate and to bless him with the gift of right faith in the Spirit, so that this saving flood may drown and destroy in him everything that he has inherited from Adam and what he himself has added to it, to the end that, severed from the number of the unbelievers, he may be preserved dry and safe in the holy ark of Christendom and, aglow with the Spirit and rejoicing in hope, may serve God's name, so that with all believers he may become worthy of God's promise and come to everlasting life.

The priest again adjures the devil in a formula abbreviated from the medieval *Exorciso te* and reads as the holy gospel St. Mark

10:13-16 (a parallel to the medieval gospel, Mt 19:13-15). Then the priest lays his hand on the child and prays the Our Father with the kneeling sponsors.

While saying Psalm 121:8, the priest conducts the child into the church and to the font. The candidate's threefold renunciation of the devil through the lips of the sponsors and the threefold creedal interrogation reproduce the Latin. The priest asks: "Do you want to be baptized?" The response is "Yes." The priest takes the child and immerses it as he says, "And I baptize you in the name of the Father and of the Son and of the Holy Spirit." The sponsors take the child and the priest vests the child in the white chrisom, saying meanwhile an adaptation of the suffrage formerly associated with the chrismation, *Deus omnipotens, pater domini nostri,* with *ipse te linit chrismate salutis in Christo Jesu domino nostro* replaced by "confirm you with his grace." The formula is of importance both for the use of the verb "confirm" and because it is one of the two passages in the rite which explicitly link baptism with the forgiveness of sins. (The other is the "Flood" prayer, referred to above.)

It will be noted that the rite of 1526 adheres closely enough to the medieval rite to demonstrate its ancestry but varies sufficiently to suggest that what has been retained reproduces the Latin deliberately.

The retention of the exorcism, the subject of a great deal of interdenominational polemics and of intra-Lutheran debate during the next two centuries, was justified by its Lutheran defenders on the ground that it characterized the spiritual condition of newly-born children, underlined the power of baptism, stressed the splendid powers by which God has destroyed the reign of Satan, and served as an anti-Pelagian witness and a demonstration of Christian liberty in indifferent matters.

The Conception of Baptism in the Lutheran Systematic Tradition

The Lutheran discussions of baptism through the last four centuries reflect the philosophical fashions of the time. The era of the Reformation itself tends to be strongly biblical, but with the revival of scholastic patterns in the age of classic orthodoxy, the vocabulary in which the theologians treat baptism is reminiscent of the high middle ages. Recent discussions in turn are likely to avail themselves of more existential and personalist concepts to describe baptism as an encounter with the God of grace himself as he works through the sacramental masks of water and people to incorporate men and women and children into his holy community.

1. *Baptism as a Sacrament*

Fundamental to the Lutheran understanding of baptism is the sacramental character. As one of the Dominically instituted sacraments, it is held, baptism participates in the characteristics of sacraments generally. But it does so without losing its particularity. Against the Swiss Reformed view, Lutherans maintain that God did not institute the sacraments "merely to be marks of profession among men, but especially to be signs and testimonies of the will of God toward us, intended to awaken and confirm faith in those who use them."[1] Sacraments moreover are "signs of the forgiveness of sins."[2] The words of Bishop Aulén are apposite here: "If we speak of baptism as a sign, it is a sign in the same sense as the works of Christ during his earthly ministry were 'signs.' Baptism is in other words really a divine 'act of power.' "[3]

The Lutheran symbolical books define sacraments as "rites which have the command of God and to which the promise of grace has been added,"[4] or as ceremonies or acts "in which God offers us the content of the promise joined to the ceremony."[5] Specifically, the Holy Spirit offers us the righteousness of the "entire obedience which, by doing and suffering, in life and in death, Christ rendered for us to his heavenly Father . . . through the Gospel and in the sacraments."[6]

The purpose of the sacraments is to constitute and identify the church, to establish the church's oneness, to offer the remission of sins, to impart the Holy Spirit, to beget and confirm faith, and to make Christians.[7]

As a sacrament, baptism is an enacted form of the word of God, *verbum actuale*. We must here think of the word of God

[1]AC XIII 1-2. See also Ap XIII 1; XXIV 69.
[2]Ap XII 42.
[3]*The Faith of the Christian Church*, trans. Eric H. Wahlstrom (2nd ed.; Philadelphia: Fortress Press, 1960), p. 337.
[4]Ap XIII 3.
[5]Ap XXIV 18.
[6]FC, SD III, 15-17.
[7]Ap VII 3; 10; 30-31; also SA Two IV 9.

chiefly as "gospel." That is, baptism is a demonstration of what God has done and still does for our salvation in and through Christ, and God's application to the individual in the church of the objective reconciliation and atonement that he accomplished in Christ. At the same time, baptism is also "law," in that it increases the condemnation of those who receive it with contempt. Similarly, as a sacrament, baptism is part of the manward initiative of a gracious God. A classic passage in the Lutheran symbolical books in this connection reads:

> The gospel . . . offers counsel and help against sin in more than one way, for God is surprisingly rich in his grace: First, through the spoken word, by which the forgiveness of sins (the peculiar office of the gospel) is preached to the whole world; second, through baptism; third, through the holy sacrament of the altar; fourth, through the power of the keys; and finally, through the mutual conversation and consultation of brethren.[1]

But baptism also involves sacrifice, our human Godward response to the divine initiative.

As an enacted form of the word of God, the sacraments are coordinated with the oral proclamation of the word of God. The fundamental difference between the communication of the divine grace in the word (*sacramentum audibile*) and in a sacrament (*verbum visibile*) is the concrete character of the sacramental action and the individualized nature of the divine address to one particular person.

> To obtain (justifying) faith God instituted the office of the ministry, provided the gospel and the sacraments. Through these, as through means, he gives the Holy Spirit.[2]
>
> When we are baptized, when we eat the Lord's Body, when we are absolved, our hearts should firmly believe that God really forgives us for Christ's sake. Through the word and the rite God simultaneously moves the heart to believe and to conceive faith, as Paul says: 'Faith comes from what is heard.' As the word enters through the ears to strike the heart, so the rite itself enters through the eyes to move the heart. The word and the rite have the same effect, as St. Augustine said so well when he called a sacrament 'a visible word,' for the rite is received by the eyes and is a sort

[1]SA Three IV.
[2]AC V 1; see also Ap XXIV 70.

of picture of the word, signifying the same thing as the word. Therefore both have the same effect.[1]

The Göttingen theologian Eduard Lohse has recently summarized the coordination of the proclaimed word and the sacraments in this way:

> Word and sacrament stand in a real mutual relationship. The sacrament secures the right understanding of the proclamation of the word and preserves it from an impermissible spiritualization. Conversely the preaching of the word protects the sacrament against a materialistic or enthusiastic misunderstanding and precludes in this way a magical conception. . . . The sacrament demonstrates in a way which cannot be overlooked that God's saving act in Christ strikes us in an historical fashion, that we are being dealt with in a bodily way, that the body that is subjected to sin is put to death and that our body from now on has been committed to the Kyrios to obey him. Just as the event of the cross and the resurrection of Jesus Christ contains reconciliation and salvation for the whole world, so at the point where a man begins to be a Christian there is the event of baptism, in which the old man is crucified with Christ, the new man is subjected to the dominion of the risen Lord, and the person baptized in being made a member of the body of Christ is incorporated into God's holy people of the end-time. As Christ died and rose again once and therewith once and for all, so baptism is administered to a human being only once. But the proclamation of justification—needing constant repetition as it does—reminds the baptized Christian again and again of the foundation for his being-a-Christian that God has laid, and it calls upon him to let himself be determined by this foundation that has been laid in baptism and constantly to appropriate it anew in confident faith and in a life of obedience.[2]

Thus in contrast to the classic Reformed doctrine of the sacraments, Lutheran theology stresses their effective, rather than a primarily cognitive, character. An intellectualistic tendency to let the proclaimed word (plus, at most, the written word) exhaust the idea of the word of God has strongly marked Lutheran theology

---

[1] Ap XIII 4-5. Cf. FC, Ep. II 2, "The grace of God [is] offered in the Word and the Holy Sacraments." See also 13; 18; SD II 18; 50; III 16; XI 72; 76.

[2] Taufe und Rechtfertigung bei Paulus," *Kerygma und Dogma*, II (1965), p. 325.

and practice for over 250 years. Notably in Europe this tendency has been reinforced by the twentieth century neo-orthodox "theology of the word" with its strongly cognitive emphasis and its basically anti-sacramental thrust. It is difficult to evaluate the final effect of this impact. That it has jeopardized the role of baptism is obvious. At the same time strong reactions that stress the importance of the sacraments in general and baptism in particular have made themselves felt in the European Lutheran community.

2. *Baptism as Water-and-Word-of-God* (*or word-of-God-with-water*)

The fact that both formulations, "baptism is water-and-word-of-God" and "baptism is word-of-God-and-water," occur illustrates the inseparable conjunction of the two. "Both, water and the word, are one baptism."[1] "Baptism is nothing else than the word of God in water commanded by the institution of Christ."[2] On the other hand, the Large Catechism declares: "Baptism is simply water and God's word in and with each other."[3]

A contemporary commentator on the Lutheran symbolical books, Edmund Schlink, warns:

> The definition of baptism which begins with water must not be weakened . . . Rather, beginning with water in defining the essence of baptism must be regarded as a highly pregnant theological antithesis against the Enthusiasts. Nor is the reversing of terms in the definition of baptism an accidental way of speaking, but it presents a kind of analogy to the relation of the divine and human natures in Christ.[4]

The Lutheran Reformation perpetuated the inherited distinction of matter and form in the analysis of the sacraments, although the Lutheran symbolical books do not explicitly use these terms. Instead they operate with the Augustinian equivalents "element" and "word." This substitution is not unprecedented. We have an interesting medieval example of the substitution of "elementum" for "materia" in connection with baptism (together with a citation

[1]LC Baptism 45.
[2]SC Three V 1.
[3]Baptism 53.
[4]*Theology of the Lutheran Confessions*, trans. Paul F. Kohneke and Herbert J. A. Bouman (Philadelphia: Muhlenberg Press, 1961), p. 145, n. 2.

of Mk 16:15 as the "word") in the letter *Non ut apponeres* o Innocent III to Archbishop Thorias of Nidaros, dated March 1 1206.[1] The epigrammatic assertion of St. Augustine *"Tolle aquam non est baptismus; tolle verbum, non est sacramentum,"* accord exactly with the position of the Lutheran symbolical books.

The Lutheran symbolical books reject both the theory tha "forgets the word, God's institution, and says that God has joine to the water a spiritual power which through the water washes awa sin" and the theory that "baptism washes away sin through the assist ance of the divine will, as if the washing takes place only throug God's will and not at all through the word or the water."[2] Th former theory the Smalcald Articles ascribe to St. Thomas an the Dominicans, the latter to Duns Scotus and the Franciscan The debatable justice of these ascriptions is not the question. Th important thing is that the Lutherans are concerned about keepin the water and the word of command and promise inseparably to gether. Schlink notes on this point:

> In the definition of the sacrament either the word or the water can be the predicate-noun. Faith can cling both to the word and to the water. Whoever does not receive the water of baptism does not receive the promise of the word of baptism. God effects salvation not only through the word but through word and water, through the word in the water and the water in the word. Water and word are now in one another. The word is visible in the water of baptism. Therefore one may and should believe that he may 'receive in the water the promised salvation'.[3]

By virtue of its combination with the divine word, the symbolic books variously describe the water applied in holy baptism as divir water, heavenly water, holy water, blessed water, fruitful wate and gracious water, and as the laver of rebirth, even though it is coarse external mask.[4]

3. *The "Matter" of Baptism*

The "sign" or the "element" in holy baptism is the washin with water. The "sign" is also called the water, but with the impl

---

[1]DB 787.
[2]SA Three V 2-3.
[3]Schlink, *op. cit.*, p. 148.
[4]LC Baptism 14; 17; 19; 27.

cation of the water in its actual application, even when the symbolical books do not so specifically state. Of and by itself and to all appearances, the water is not worth a straw.[1] In an analogous sense, it is a *larva* or mask for the divine gift, as we see the shell of a nut.[2] "Because the word embraces the water, the water embraces the word; because the word is in the water, the water is in the word," says Schlink. "The word is monergistically the agent in creating the sacrament."[3] There is no "natural theology" here, no dependence on the symbolic qualities or possibilities of water as such, nor on the symbolic-indicative significance which immersion as such could have by itself.

Such symbolism as the early Lutherans recognize thinks in terms of the water as an agent that washes, cleanses, surrounds, covers on all sides, preserves, delivers, or even kills the old man. They do not maintain any of these points of comparison with any degree of consistency. The symbolism of water as slaking thirst and of being life giving in this sense is absent. Contemporary Lutheran theology finds it necessary to antagonize a tendency to overstress the "spiritual" aspects of baptism to the point where the fact is forgotten that God is working through a material element which he has created and over which he still retains a Pantocrator's authority and power.

Because of their conception of baptism as a dynamic action and of the "matter" of baptism as being primarily a washing with water, the Lutherans criticized the use of water specially prepared and blessed on Easter Eve and Whitsuneve for use in baptism throughout the year.[4] This possibly too great fear of superstition resulted in the abolition of the services of Easter Eve and Whitsuneve among the Lutheran churches and the ultimate elimination of the blessing of the font from the Lutheran baptismal rites. But the fear of superstition was not altogether ill-founded. As late as 1580 the Church Order of Duke August of Saxony had to stipulate that pastors must warn their sacristans not to sell the baptismal water for magical purposes and must assure them that future violations of this injunction would meet with dire punishment.[5]

[1]LC Baptism 8; see also 22.
[2]LC Baptism 19.
[3]Schlink, *op. cit.*, p. 147.
[4]Cf. John Gerhard, *Loci theologici*, locus de baptismo, 74.
[5]Emil Sehling et al., ed., *Die evangelische Kirchenordnungen des 16. Jahrhunderts*

The mode of baptism may be either immersion or pouring.[1] The Large Catechism refers both to "a handful of water" and "allowing the water to be poured over you."[2] At the beginning of the Reformation immersion was normal; by the end of the sixteenth century affusion had generally replaced it. The Lutheran symbolical books nowhere countenance aspersion. As late as 1708 a Lutheran pastor's failure to use a sufficient quantity of water was punishable with suspension or ecclesiastical censure.

Early Lutheran practice reveals differences of opinion and procedure as far as baptizing in the public service is concerned, but the insistence upon the church as the normal place for the administration of baptism is unanimous. When at a later date the practice of baptism in the parents' home becomes frequent in many places, this is due largely to the concern of the lesser nobility and the bourgeoisie for social position.

4. *The "Formale" of Baptism*

The "formale" of baptism is the word of God. On this the Lutheran Reformers were agreed. The content of this word they differentiated into the baptismal command to baptize in the triune name and the baptismal promise, with the promise in a sense already implied in the fact that candidates are baptized into the divine name.

Since the word of God in baptism is the baptismal command and promise,[3] the Small Catechism has two initial sections: "What is baptism?" which appeals to Mt 28:19, and "What does baptism give or profit?" which appeals to the textually dubious passage Mk 16:16. For the same reason the Large Catechism cites both texts in its opening section of the discussion of baptism. In the analysis of baptism the reader is reminded that we need to be careful not to think of the water alone or to tamper "with God's ordinance and tear from it the precious jeweled clasp with which God has fastened and enclosed it and from which he does not wish his ordinance to be separated."[4]

The Lutheran Reformers demanded a clear Dominical institu-

(Leipzig: Reisland, 1902-1913; Tübingen: J. C. B. Mohr, [Paul Siebeck] 1955-), I, 426.

[1] LC Baptism 65.

[2] LC Baptism 15; 36.

[3] SC Baptism 4.

[4] LC Baptism 16.

tion for a sacrament strictly so called to guarantee the sacramental promise. Because more is involved than obedience to an ordinance, the divine institution of baptism receives a considerable amount of explicit stress. Replying, for example, to the spiritualizers' charge that "baptism is an external thing and that external things are of no use," the Large Catechism counters: "No matter how external it may be, here stand God's word and command which have instituted, established, and confirmed baptism."[1]

The possibility that the Trinitarian formula of St. Matthew 28:19 does not exactly reproduce the expressed command of our Lord, but that it is either the baptismal formula of the particular community within which the First Gospel emerged or a theological specification and interpretation of the baptismal act is, of course, a relative novelty. Lutheran theological opinion, as far as it is ascertainable, is divided on the issue.

The charge is sometimes made that Lutheran theology operates with the doctrine of justification through faith as a material principle. But in spite of the intimate and obvious link between baptism and the forgiveness of sins (of which "justification" in the Lutheran understanding of the term, is a synonym), the Lutheran doctrine of baptism is derived not by inference from and explication of justification as a principle, but directly from the divine institution that the sacred scriptures record.

5. *"Materia Coelestis"*

The idea of a *materia coelestis* in baptism is generally absent in the oldest Lutheran theologians. In the early 17th century Leonhard Hütter in his *Loci* makes the Holy Spirit or the blood of Christ or both the heavenly *pars substantialis*. Later in the century Abraham Calovius says:

> Correctly defined, the *materia coelestis* of baptism is the most Holy Trinity, God the Father, God's Son Christ the God-Man, to whose entirety there pertains not only his divine nature, but also his human nature, whereto his blood, of which he became a partaker of our account, also belongs, and the Holy Spirit. This *res coelestis* in one word is called the word and name of God, that is the Triune God himself, Father, Son and Holy Spirit.[2]

---

[1]LC Baptism 8; see also *Ibid.*, 4; 6 and 29.
[2]Systema, X, p. 166.

At the end of the era of orthodoxy David Hollaz defines the *materia coelestis baptismi analogice dicta* as "the entire most Holy Trinity, *peculialiter et terminative* the Holy Spirit."[1]

6. *The Effect of Baptism*

The primary and basic effect of this purifying and sanctifying sacrament is the forgiveness of sins in the broadest and most comprehensive sense, as the Nicaenoconstantinopolitanum affirms.

> The power, effect, benefit, fruit and purpose of baptism is to save . . . To be saved, we know, is nothing else than to be delivered from sin, death and the devil and to enter into the kingdom of God and live with him forever.[2]

Baptism "works forgiveness of sins, delivers from death and the devil, and gives everlasting bliss to all those who believe that it does this."[3] Baptism applies to the individual the reconciliation and pardon that God in Christ achieved for the whole world of mankind. This forgiveness includes the remission of original sin, understood as the removal of the guilt, but not of the "matter" of original sin.[4]

While Lutherans hold that the effect of baptism is not so to be understood as if it took away sin the sense that no vestiges of sin remain in the person baptized, they do assert that it takes away the culpability and liability of sin by forgiveness. Beyond that they stipulate that baptism initiates a renewal that lasts through the individual's whole lifetime as he continually puts to death the actions of the flesh through the might of the Holy Spirit and that this renewal will find its consummation in the life of the world to come. They insist that the viciousness, the disorderliness, and the lawlessness of sin is broken, diminished, and restrained by the Holy Spirit, and that he helps the baptized Christian to resist and conquer its dominion. "Sins are not only covered and remitted in baptism, but they are put to death (*mortificari*)," Gerhard declares.[5] While there is no chronological separation between the forgiveness of sins and the beginning of the new life of holiness, in the order of causality the renewal is consequent upon the pardon. "As soon as the Holy

[1] *Examen theologicum acroamaticum*, II, p. 554.
[2] LC Baptism 24.
[3] SC Baptism 6; see also LC Baptism 41.
[4] Ap II 35-36.
[5] *Confessio catholica*, p. 1128.

pirit has initiated his work of regeneration and renewal in us hrough the word and the holy sacraments, it is certain that we an and must cooperate by the power of the Holy Spirit, even hough we do so in great weakness."[1]

Intimately and inseparably associated with the effect of forgiveness are the gifts of new life through rebirth and salvation.[2] Where there is forgiveness of sins, there is also life and salvation."[3] Baptism is the sacrament of regeneration, recreation, and renewal. The rebirth of baptism involves no change in identity but a transformation of the person. The rejection of baptismal regeneration y Samuel Simon Schmucker in the "American recension" of the Augsburg Confession in the mid-19th century—never very widely ndorsed—has been universally transcended in the Lutheran community in America.

Another way of saying that baptism bestows life is the affirmaon that baptism liberates the candidate from and gives him victory ver death.[4] Thus baptism has eschatological implications for the erson baptized. "One is baptized in order . . . to be saved. To be aved, we know, is nothing else than to be delivered from sin, death nd the devil, and to enter into the kingdom of Christ and live with im for ever."[5] As the sacrament of *palingennesia* baptism points orward to the great cosmic *palingennesia to come* (Mt 19:28).[6]

In this spirit Schlink can call baptism "already the eschatological vent of the resurrection from the dead which it promises. For this eason alone the invitation to a daily return to baptism makes sense. Baptism as *promissio salutis* is not only a promise but also the beowal of what is promised, just as the gospel a *promissio* is both romise and assurance."[7]

Baptism bestows the grace of God,[8] and it imparts illuminaon and a perfecting of the knowledge of God and of his gracious isposition toward us.[9] In addition it confers on the person baptized

C SD II 65.
C Baptism 27; AC II 2; LC Sacrament of the Altar 23.
C Sacrament of the Altar 6.
C Baptism 6; LC Baptism 41; 43-46.
C Baptism 24-25.
Cf. Titus 3:5; SC Baptism 10; LC Baptism 26-27; LC Creed 54-58.
chlink, *op. cit.*, p. 151.
C IX 2; LC Baptism 41.
C, SD II 15-16. The "enlightened me with his gifts" of the Small Catechism xplanation of the Creed may also echo the old designation of baptism as *photismos.*

a "liberated will" (*arbitrium liberatum*). His relation to the law has been changed from one of servile subjugation to willing obedience in freedom, an authentic *imitatio Christi.*[1]

Since baptism is an indication of God's providential predestination to life, the baptized person is to invoke its comfort when the author of all evil tempts him even as a believer to despair of the divine mercy and to embrace the ensuing great shame and vice. "To appreciate and use baptism aright, we must draw strength and comfort from it when our sins or conscience oppress us, and we must retort, 'But I am baptized! And if I am baptized, I have the promise that I shall be saved and have eternal life, both in soul and body.' "[2]

Baptism imparts to the candidate the entire Christ in his entire life and death and rising again.[3] It is not a mere symbol of the death and resurrection of Christ; it is the mystical and sacramental participation of the candidate in those events. The link of baptism specifically with the death of Christ is underlined by the parallel language of the Second Article of the Creed and secondly of Baptism. The early versions of the Small Catechism (prior to 1540) read "im Tode" rather than, by accommodation to the vernacular bible translation, "in den Tod." Johannes Meyer sees the original form as implying not the death of the old man, but the death of Our Lord, in which we experience the burial of our sins.[4] The candidate's sharing of the death and resurrection of Christ is not to be thought of as if these events had some kind of transtemporal existence so that they can be communicated in baptism under a sacramental mask. Rather the process is to be conceived in such a way as to make Christ's death and resurrection virtually present, or, even more precisely, as an incorporation into Christ who in his incarnation has died and risen and will come again. The Nicaeno-constantinopolitanum itself suggests this with its accusative participles: *"kai eis hena kyrion Iēsoun Christon . . . staurothenta te hyper hēmōn . . . kai pathonta kai taphenta kai anastanta."* This incorporation implies that we become God's children by adoption and grace, like the Christ into whom we have been incorporated,

[1]FC, SD II 67; FC, SD IV-V.
[2]LC Baptism 44.
[3]LC Baptism 41.
[4]*Historischer Kommentar zu Luthers Kleinem Katechismus* (Gütersloh: C. Bertelsmann, 1929), p. 457.

not *kata physin* but *kata thesin*. Today the Lutheran conception of baptism as incorporation into the whole saving act of God in Christ is being enriched as Lutheran systematic theology in general increasingly stresses the significance of Our Lord's exaltation for the salvation of the world, in contrast to its previous sometimes one-sided overemphasis upon His death.

Baptism also imparts Christ's victory over the tyrannical evil powers and delivers the candidate from the jaws of the devil.[1] The vocabulary of the sixteenth century is less sophisticated than that of our own day when it comes to talk about the demonic. Where we tend to use the neuter gender, the Catechisms exhibit no reluctance to talk in the terms of a personal masculine. "Baptism effects forgiveness of sins, delivers from death and the devil and grants eternal salvation to all who believe."[2] Baptism thus becomes a means of applying subjectively the objective reconciliation which Our Lord achieved by his incarnation, his life, his death, and his exaltation. The explicit citation of Romans 6 in this connection reinforces this point.[3]

Baptism imparts to the candidate the Holy Spirit with his gifts.[4] This effect is one that endures throughout the lifetime of the person baptized, even if he falls into grievous sin. Lutheran theology would concur with St. Basil's assertion that the Holy Spirit remains present to the soul of the baptized person who lapses after baptism, if necessary awaiting his conversion from sin.[5] "The power and effect of baptism . . . is simply the slaying of the old and the resurrection of the new man, both of which actions must continue in us our whole life long. Thus a Christian life is nothing else than a daily baptism, once begun and ever continued."[6]

On this basis, the symbolical books from Luther's pen subsume the *sacramentum poenitentiae* under baptism. "Baptism, both by its power and by its signification, comprehends also the third sacrament, formerly called penance."[7] In explicating this position Luther declares:

---

[1]SC Baptism 6. Cf. LC Baptism 41; 83.
[2]*Ibid.* Cf. LC Baptism 41; 43.
[3]SC Baptism 13-14.
[4]Ap IX 9; LC Baptism 41.
[5]*On the Holy Spirit*, 40.
[6]LC Baptism 65.
[7]LC Baptism 74.

Baptism remains continually. Even though we fall from it and sin, nevertheless we always have access to it so that we may again subdue the old man. But we need not again have the water poured over us. Even if we were immersed in water a hundred times, it would nevertheless be but one baptism, and the effect and signification of baptism would continue and remain. Penance, therefore, is nothing else than a return to baptism, to resume and practice what had earlier been begun but abandoned. I say this to correct the opinion, which has long prevailed among us, that our baptism is something past which we can no longer use after falling again into sin. Indeed, St. Jerome is responsible for this view, for he wrote, 'Repentance is the second plank on which we must swim ashore after the ship founders,' in which we embarked when we entered the Christian church. This interpretation deprives baptism of its value, making it of no further use to us. Therefore the statement is incorrect. The ship does not founder since, as we said it is God's ordinance and not a work of ours. But it does happen that we slip and fall out of the ship. If anybody does fall out, he should immediately head for the ship and cling to it until he can climb aboard again and sail on it as he had done before . . . [Baptism] tears us out of the very gorge of the devil, makes us God's own, suppresses and takes away sin, and thereafter continually strengthens the new man, remains constantly efficacious and abides as long as we are in our present misery until we finally come to everlasting glory. For that reason everyone ought to regard baptism as his everyday garb, in which he is continually to walk around, that he may always let himself be found in the faith and in its fruits, that he may suppress the old man and grow up in the new man. If we want to be Christians, we have to engage in the activity from which our being Christians derives. If anybody falls away from [his baptism], let him return to it. As Christ, the mercy-seat [Romans 3, 25; Heb. 4, 16] does not recede from us or forbid us to return to him even though we sin, so all his treasures and gifts remain. As we have once obtained forgiveness of sins in baptism, so forgiveness remains day by day as long as we live, that is, as long as we carry the old Adam about our necks.[1]

As an instrument of the Holy Spirit, baptism aids the Christian

[1] LC Baptism 77-86.

in the conquest of the cardinal sins that disfigure his life—anger, hatred, envy, impurity, greed, sloth, pride, and infidelity (gluttony is the only one omitted)—and in the development of the contrary virtues, like gentleness, patience and meekness.[1] Since through baptism the Holy Spirit imparts forgiveness of sins, through it he must also foster the fruits of the Spirit. In this sense, *theopoiēsis* (divinization) is an effect of baptism.[2]

Lutherans do not feel themselves hit by Trent's Canon 10 on baptism: *"Si quis dixerit, peccata omnia, quae post baptismum fiunt sola recordatione et fide susepti baptismi vel dimitti vel venalia fieri, an. s."*[3] They do not hold that persons who fall into grave sins after baptism and persevere in them without true and earnest repentance receive forgiveness of sins merely by recalling in a perfunctory and purely historical way that they were once baptized, so that they have no need of genuine repentance and the ministry of the keys. They do hold that the power, efficacy and operation of the cleansing and hallowing that takes place through baptism perdures and avails throughout the whole life of the Christian. When he falls into grave sin after baptism, they hold that in serious and earnest repentance he can and ought to renew and reestablish the cleansed and hallowed condition by means of the recollection of the covenant into which he entered with God in his baptism. To insist that the efficacy of baptism does not extend to future but only to past sins, they hold, is unduly limiting the scope of the sacrament. "Baptism," Bishop Aulén observes, "must not be understood simply as an act of initiation. Baptism does not look toward the past but to the future, both in regard to life in the church of Christ and in regard to the eschatological consummation."[4]

What has been said about the effect of baptism on the individual needs to be complemented by indicating the ecclesiastical dimension of baptism. In the prefatory summary of his discussion of baptism Bishop Aulén writes:

> Baptism is the act of the prevenient grace of God through which man is received into fellowship with the body of Christ, the church. Herein lie both the gift and the obligation of baptism.

[1]LC Baptism 66.
[2]FC, SD II 16.
[3]DB 1623.
[4]Aulén, *op. cit.*, p. 337.

The validity of infant baptism rests on the fact that the grace of God is a prevenient grace. Infant baptism imposes upon the church an obligation and a responsibility toward baptized children. The Christian view of baptism must be distinguished from a mechanizing interpretation which nullify the primacy of grace.[1]

In baptism God makes the candidate a member of the church.[2] But from a human standpoint the church, as the body and the bride of Christ on earth, applies in baptism the universal and objective reconciliation of the whole world of mankind to the individual in such a way that he is, in and through the church, united with Christ. Through baptism the church as the nation and the people of God perpetuates herself in time. It is precisely because the church baptizes that she is our mother and the font is her womb. The Holy Spirit "has a special community in the world, the mother that conceives and bears every Christian through the word of God which the Spirit reveals and makes use of and which enlightens and sets on fire the hearts of men so that they may embrace it, receive it, cling to it and remain with it."[3] In this way baptism is not merely a means of salvation for the individual, but the church's own act of creating spiritual offspring. Baptism is the act of the whole church, even when the church is represented only by priest and sponsors. Baptism lays stress on the fact that God calls us into the church. It is a line of demarcation between Christian and non-Christian, but also in the case of each individual a line of demarcation between the pre-Christian and the Christian segments of his life. By being incorporated into the holy community the person baptized participates in the circulation of Christ's own life that flows through all of the body of Christ. This involves more than a juridical reception into membership in a denomination or church-body; it is a sacred incorporation into the church as Christ's body.

In the era between the decline of orthodoxy and the 19th century confessional revival Rationalist and Pietist influences on the Lutheran Church tended to be more concerned with the subjective aspects of baptism than about its objective significance. Even the confessional revival did not wholly redress the balance and the influence of Pietism is still strong in many sectors of the Lutheran

---

[1] *Ibid.*, pp. 335-36.
[2] LC Baptism 2.
[3] LC Creed 42.

Church. Contemporary Lutheran systematic theology has been exploring more extensively the implications of baptism as a basis for ecumenical effort and therewith as a basis for the Christian's moral and ethical activity in both the church and the world.

Because baptism is the first and fundamental sacrament, "the first door to grace, the sacrament of initiation" and incorporation into the church,[1] it is a kind of *janua sacramentorum,* a necessary prerequisite for the reception of the other sacraments.[2] The sacrament of the altar, for example, is in a sense the complement of baptism and Lutherans hold that "only those who have been baptized in the name of the Lord" may receive it.[3] Similarly holy absolution in the sacrament of penance is the restoration into baptismal grace and status,[4] and only a baptized person can be ordained.

Even though marriage is a sacrament of the old covenant,[5] holy matrimony is a sign of the mysterious relation between Christ and His bride the church,[6] but only where the contracting parties are themselves parts of the heavenly bride. Lutheran theology does not understand the Pauline privilege (1 Cor 7:15) as permitting a convert to the Christian faith to leave a pagan spouse and to marry another Christian, an interpretation that has played an official role in Roman Catholic pastoral practice since the response of the Holy Office to the Bishop of Kochchiband (Episcopus Coccinensis) in 1759.[7] Lutherans would instead concur with the statement of Innocent III to the Bishop of Tiberias in *Gaudemus in Domino* (1201): *"Per sacramentum baptismi non solvantur conjugia, sed crimina dimittantur."*[8]

7. The Role of Faith in Baptism

The requirement of faith as a condition for an effective reception of baptism is as old as the first written reflection of the church on baptism. This requirement underlies both the demand for catechetical instruction before baptism and the practice of reciting a declaratory creed before the actual rite. Similarly, repentance has

[1]Gerhard, *Loci theologici,* IX, 67.
[2]LC Our Father 37. Cf. LC Sacrament of the Altar 23-24.
[3]LC Sacrament of the Altar 87.
[4]AC XII 1-2.
[5]Ap. XIII. 14-15.
[6]SC Marriage Booklet 16.
[7]DB 2580-2585.
[8]DB 777.

been the classic pre-condition of baptism. But repentance in the Lutheran analysis is contrition and a special faith in the redemption achieved by our Lord, with amendment of life following as the fruit of repentance.[1]

Two general Lutheran sacramental principles create a problem if they are too literally applied to baptism. The first principle is that the sacraments create faith. That in a given case an adult candidate for baptism may possess faith in the sense of *fiducia* prior to baptism is probable. But there is no explicit statement in the sacred scriptures which affirms that baptism creates faith. And it is not experimentally demonstrable that in the case of an infant holy baptism creates anything that can be called faith in any of the usual senses of that word. The second principle that creates a problem if applied too literally is the principle that for their fruitful use sacraments require faith. Again, in the case of the infant candidate, Lutherans affirm the *saving value* of baptism, even though the presence of faith in the ordinary sense of the term is not demonstrable. Part of the difficulty arises from a too rigid synonymity of conversion, rebirth, creation of faith, and incorporation into the church in the conventional Lutheran theological vocabulary.

Nevertheless the stress of the Lutheran symbolical books is on faith as a prerequisite for the *profitable and fruitful use* of baptism. "Faith alone makes the person worthy to receive the salutary, divine water profitably. . . Just by allowing the water to be poured over you, you do not receive baptism in such a manner that it does you any good."[2]

We have a clue to the way in which the Lutheran symbolical books conceive of the faith that baptism creates in infants in the parenthesis interpolated into the declaration of the Large Catechism: "Even if infants did not believe—which, however, is not the case, as we have proved—still their baptism would be valid and no one should rebaptize them."[3] There is no explicit cross-reference for the "as we have proved," but the only passage that can come into consideration is this statement: "That the baptism of infants is pleasing to Christ is proved from his own work. God has sanctified many who have been thus baptized and given them the Holy Spirit.

[1]AC XII 3-6.
[2]LC Baptism 33; 36.
[3]LC Baptism 55.

Even today there are not a few whose doctrine and life attest that they have the Holy Spirit. Similarly by God's grace we have been given the power to interpret the scriptures and to know Christ, which is impossible without the Holy Spirit."[1] "To have faith" in the context of infant baptism thus means to have become a person in whom God has initiated his work of sanctification and to whom he has given the Holy Spirit. As the individual matures, the Holy Spirit enables him so to see in the divine word God's revelation of his gracious self and of his saving purpose in Christ that the individual comes to know, trust in, and worship Christ in the sense of *beneficia Christi cognoscere*.[2]

From this point of view, at least some Lutherans hold that in the case of infants baptism effects its ends of adoption into sonship, the forgiveness of sins, and participation in the life of God not immediately but through faith, although they are reluctant to pronounce on the nature of that faith or on its mode. They do not affirm that infants understand the movements of faith, but they do assert that the Holy Spirit is imparted in baptism and that the Holy Spirit is actively at work in them so that they can enter the kingdom of heaven, that is, receive the divine grace and the forgiveness of sins. They regard as unbiblical the view that baptized infants do not have actual faith or any new interior movements and inclinations similar to the acts of faith and love. They further hold that to concede that they have saving and justifying faith is to grant that this faith is living and efficacious. Heinrich Schmidt summarizes the reflections of classic Lutheran theology on this point:

> Since both the word and baptism are intended to confer saving grace, baptism is intended to produce this result only in those cases in which it is applied at an earlier period than the word; this is the case with infants who are not yet capable of understanding the preaching of the gospel. In adults who have a developed reason and can understand the preaching of the gospel, the word has precedence and produces its results before baptism. In such cases, baptism serves to seal and establish the gracious result already accomplished by the word.[3]

[1] LC Baptism 50.
[2] Cf. Ap. IV 46; 154; 228; 310.
[3] *The Doctrinal Theology of the Evangelical Lutheran Church,* trans. Charles A. Hay and Henry E. Jacobs (Minneapolis: Augsburg Publishing House, 1961), p. 537.

A modern Lutheran theologian, Ernst Sommerlath, puts it this way:

> Baptism cannot be withheld from children, since the believing church acts vicariously on the child's behalf and since baptism derives its objective validity and power from its divine institution, even though the faith of the child may lay hold on baptism only at a later date.[1]

On the other hand, some contemporary Lutherans like Bishop Aulén minimize the role of faith in the baptized infants.[2] Even in the case of the adult, however, his faith is not the prerequisite for baptism but the organ that lays hold on that which God offers objectively in the sacrament.

In essence the problem of faith in the candidate for baptism is part of the larger polarity which asserts the monergism of divine grace in the entire process of salvation on the one hand and on the other the completeness of the individual's involvement in the process. In the beginning of his conversion he is a *subjectum patiens;* after his conversion has been begun the Lutheran symbolical books call for a synergy between the Holy Spirit and the human being acting by means of the powers that the Holy Spirit has communicated to him. It is essential to recognize that in any case the faith which for the Lutheran is a prerequisite of a fruitful use of the sacrament of holy baptism is in no sense to be thought of as an intrinsically meritorious work. Beyond these considerations any attempted resolution of the problem must be regarded as a theory of a theologian rather than as a clear teaching of the symbols. Likewise, the *fiducia* that faith must exhibit to be saving faith cannot in the New Testament be merely a kind of faith in faith, as extremer types of existentialist theology seem to suggest, or a general faith of the *credere Deum* type, but a special faith that clings to the Savior as the sacred scriptures describe him and his work and that regards his saving work as including the believer personally within its scope. It must be faith in a Christ who acted and acts *pro me.*

Ultimately the problem is linked with the Lutheran rejection of the idea that the sacraments—notably the holy Eucharist offered

---

[1]*Die Religion in Geschichte und Gegenwart,* Vol. VI (6 vols.; 3rd ed.; Tübingen: J. C. B. Mohr [Paul Siebeck], 1962), p. 647.
[2]Aulén, *op. cit.,* p. 341.

as an expiatory sacrifice for the sins of the living; and the dead—are effective *ex opere operato sine bono motu utentis.* This vulgar misunderstanding of the *opus operatum* principle was apparently widespread enough in the 16th century to justify the vehement polemics of the Reformers against it.[1] The Lutheran symbolical books are not denying the objective validity of the sacraments. A properly administered sacrament is always and unfailingly a divinely valid offer of grace. This fact is utterly independent of the faith of the recipient. But the offer becomes effective, the communication of grace actually takes place, the sacrament is used fruitfully, only when there is a right *motus,* that is faith in the proffer of grace, in the user's heart. The Lutheran Reformers felt that they could appeal to St. Augustin's opinion on this point: *"Ait Augustinus ut fides sacramenti non sacramentum justificet."*[2] The cited words are an epigrammatical reformulation of St. Augustine's words with specific reference to baptism: *"Unde ista tanta virtus aquae, ut corpus tangat et cor abluat, nisi faciente verbo, non quia dicitur, sed quia creditur?"*[3]

At the same time, with specific reference to infant baptism, a Lutheran can hardly refuse to deny what appears to be the theological intent of the scholastic assertion that the sacraments achieve their purpose *ex opere operato sine bono motu utentis* as long as the recipient does not interpose an obstacle (*obicem non ponet*). It is noteworthy that the Lutheran symbolical books do not discuss the scholastic principle in question with specific reference to baptism, but only in connection with its application to Eucharist as an expiatory sacrifice for the sins of the living and dead. Strictly speaking, the technical terms *ex opere operato, sine bono motu utentis, and obicem non ponere* had acquired a vulgar meaning that their original authors did not intend them to have. In essence, the declarations of the Large Catechism that baptism is not our work but God's and that this sacrament is not a work of ours, but a treasure which God gives and which faith only appropriates, assert implicitly what the medieval schoolmen sought to affirm by their teaching on the *opus operatum.*[4]

Two factors are directing Lutheran systematic theology to a new consideration of faith in connection with baptism. One factor

[1] Ap XIII 2-3; 18-19.
[2] Ap XIII 23.
[3] *in Joannis evangelium* 15, 3, Tract 80. Migne's *Patrologia Latina,* vol. 35.
[4] LC Baptism 36.

is the size of the gainsaying community before which the Lutheran Church must defend its practice of infant baptism. In the European homelands of the Lutheran Church the groups that insist on "believer's baptism" constitute in the main relatively small sectarian minorities. On this continent the bodies that insist on believer's baptism constitute an impressive fraction of organized Christianity and one denominational family of this group—the Baptist community—is the second largest denomination in the United States. The second factor is the increasing number of adult converts who enter the Lutheran Church through baptism. These factors are demanding a view of faith that takes into account not only the effect of baptism upon an infant recipient of the sacrament, but also the nature of faith as a mature commitment to Christ created by the Holy Spirit through the witness of the corporate church to the gospel prior to the reception of baptism.

8. *Stress on Certainty*

The basic question of the Lutheran Reformation, as conventionally formulated, is "How can I find a gracious God?" This question underlies the concern for the "thoroughly terrified conscience" in the Augsburg Confession and the Apology and the concern for deliverance from the demonic tyrants of sin, death, hell, flesh, world, and devil. The calculated theological stress of the late middle ages lay on these elements of the Christian revelation that contribute to the individual's subjective uncertainty of salvation. The unabashed emphasis of the Lutheran symbolical books is on those elements in Christianity that establish the objective certainty of salvation for all who lay hold on the divine promise of pardon through faith. Both emphases involve elements of authentic truth that must be held in tension. When the paradox is relieved either by an exclusive nomistic stress on the divine wrath and the divine judgment or by an antinomian stress on a purely cognitive and intellectual conception of faith, spiritual tragedy results. The concern of the Lutheran symbolical books is advanced by their stress on baptism as evidence of the divine concern for the individual. The fact of baptism serves the person who stands in a state of faith and of grace as evidence that God will provide him with all the means necessary to assure him a happy death and a resurrection to everlasting life.

Nevertheless, it is possible to receive baptism, but not the benefit of baptism, without faith. From this follows not only that the fruit of baptism may be received later than the baptism itself but also that the benefit received in baptism can be lost if the person baptized rejects his faith and no longer makes use of his baptism.

9. *Necessity of Baptism*

The Lutheran symbolical books categorically affirm that "baptism is necessary for salvation."[1] Put negatively, original sin, understood as the condition in which human beings are natively full of evil desires and inclinations and are by themselves unable to have genuine reverence for and faith in God, "is truly sin, which even now damns and brings eternal death on those who are not born again through baptism and the Holy Spirit."[2] This necessity of baptism, however, as the theologians have always stressed, is not absolute but ordinate.

10. *Infant Baptism*

An inference both from the divine command to baptize and from the conviction of the necessity of baptism for salvation is the baptism of infants. "Children are to be baptized."[3] The Lutherans aver that they cannot tolerate in the church the article "that in the sight of God unbaptized children are not sinners but are righteous and innocent, and that as long as they have not achieved the use of reason they will be saved in this innocence without baptism (which according to this view they do not need),"[4] or the article "that without and prior to baptism the children of Christian parents are holy and the children of God by virtue of their birth from Christian and pious parents."[5]

In infant baptism we see the monergism of divine grace operating most explicitly and most dramatically. Here God, on the basis of his predestination and vocation, makes a child of wrath, who has been able to do nothing toward his own salvation, his own child and imparts to him by sheer grace the sonship that the eternally begotten Son possesses by nature. As the child is carried to the

[1] AC IX 1.
[2] AC II 3.
[3] AC IX 2. Cf. Ap IX 2, "The promise of baptism applies also to little children . . . ," and LC Baptism 49-50.
[4] FC Ep XII 6.
[5] *Ibid.*, para. 8.

font, it is incapable of meeting any precondition. It does not have contrition; it does not have faith; it does not have the intention of receiving a sacrament; it cannot comprehend or respond to a proclamation of the gospel. What is more, the minister of the sacrament may be immoral and unrepentant. The sponsors that represent the church may be members of the holy community *nomine tantum non re*. Whatever happens in baptism must be God's work. Thus infant baptism becomes a paradigm of God's dealing with man.

The Lutheran symbolical books explicitly reject the logic that concludes from the absence of faith in the infant candidate to the invalidity of infant baptism. On the contrary, they argue *ad hominem* that "precisely because baptism has [in some cases] been wrongly received it has existence and value."[1] The baptism of infants is regarded as a prime example of the proper use of tradition in early Lutheran theology.[2]

The Lutheran apologetic for infant baptism has always conceded the absence of a direct Dominical (or even apostolic) command to baptize infants in the sacred scriptures. But it is now taking into account increasingly the fact that the patristic evidence is not as absolutely decisive as it had once appeared to be, and is making its appeal to the biblical theology of baptism a stronger component in its defense of infant baptism.

The necessity for baptism is a witness to the role of the institutional necessity of the church and her ministry for the salvation of those whom God calls into fellowship with himself. It is through the witness of the church and the activity of the sacred ministry that the Holy Spirit confers the new birth on men and women and preserves them in the faith. Outside the regular ministrations of religion within the holy community of the church the new life would die very soon. Since infants are *extra ecclesiam* as they come into the world, they can enter the family of God only through baptism. Infant baptism is essential to apply to small children the promise of salvation according to Christ's command, and the nurture of the church is no less necessary to preserve them in the faith.[3]

The Lutheran community has not remained wholly unaffected by contemporary controversies about infant baptism. The awareness

---

[1] LC Baptism 59.

[2] Cf. Martin Chemnitz, *Examen concilii tridentini, locus de traditionibus*, sec. V, paras. 2-3.

[3] Cf. Aulén, *op. cit.*, pp. 339-40.

of living in a "post-Constantinian" era has caused some Lutheran clergymen in Germany to revolt against the idea of an "automatic baptism." They have proposed that even their religiously committed parishioners postpone the baptism of their children until the latter can make a decision for themselves. (In a few cases they have reportedly set their parishioners an example.) This line of thought, although nowhere very influential, seems to be more seriously pursued in the German Democratic Republic, where the possibility of apostasy is a clear and present peril.

Because baptism is a divine gift of which man stands in dire need, it is not something which the church has in her competence to administer or withhold but which she must administer and to which the Christian has a right for himself and for his children. However, pastoral prudence normally requires baptism to be withheld from the minor children of non-Christians, unless one of the parents is a Christian, and of heretics, unless one parent is orthodox. Exceptions are to be made in the case of children in imminent danger of death and in such cases where there is reasonable hope that the other part of the baptismal commission, "to teach them to observe everything that I have commended," will be carried out.

In view of the ordinate necessity of baptism, Lutheran theology traditionally teaches that, while "baptism is the ordinary sacrament of initiation and means rebirth for all men, necessary for the rebirth and salvation even of the children of believing parents, at the same time, we say that in a case of deprivation or of impossibility, the children of Christians can be saved through an extraordinary and special divine dispensation. . . . We are bound to baptism; an extraordinary action of God is not, however, to be denied."[1]

Also in the case of the death of unbaptized children, born or unborn, of Christian parents the theologians argued from the ordinate necessity of baptism and from the thesis that "we are bound to baptism, God is not." They invoked St. Bernard's principle *"Contemtus sacramenti damnat, non privatio."* In the case of the unbaptized children of non-Christians they generally refuse to pronounce and commit such children to the mercy of God.

11. *Surrogates for Water Baptism*

The Lutheran symbolical books have nothing to say explicitly

[1]John Gerhard, *Loci theologici,* locus XX, 236.

about "baptism of desire" or "baptism of blood," tacitly recognizing the metaphorical use of "baptism" in these designations. "Baptism" in their vocabulary is always water baptism.

12. *Adult Baptism*

Adult baptisms were so rare that most of the 16th century Lutheran church orders make no formal provision at all for them. Where they did take place, they usually involved Jewish or Moslem converts among prisoners of war. In such cases pastors invariably instructed the candidates in the Christian faith and the significance of Trinitarian baptism and adapted the rite for the baptism of infants.

The Smalcald Articles contemplate a delayed action of the preaching of the gospel in the case of previously unbaptized adults. "Adults who have attained the age of reason must first have heard, 'He who believes and is baptized will be saved' (Mk 16:16), even if they did not at once believe and did not receive the Spirit and Baptism until ten years later."[1] Noteworthy is the implication that they will receive baptism, indeed that they must receive baptism.

Adult baptisms underline the fact that baptism has more than an exclusively cognitive significance, although this aspect must not be depreciated. Again they stress that baptism is more than an act of confession, although it has this too as a secondary aspect.

In reflecting on the date of Christian history, contemporary Lutheran theology is impressed by the fact that it is precisely in the era of the New Testament and of the primitive church, when the bulk of the church's new accessions came through adult baptisms, that baptism is credited with saving power, with communicating the Holy Spirit, with imparting forgiveness of sins, with banishing demons from the heart, with equipping Christians with weapons for spiritual warfare, with effecting rebirth, with bestowing illumination and the knowledge of God, with making men "no longer the sons of mortal men only, but also the children of the immortal and indefectible God," and with supplying them with an earnest of the resurrection.

13. *Who Baptizes?*

The first answer is: God. "To be baptized in God's name is to be baptized not by men but by God himself."[2] "Baptism is pri-

[1] SA Three VIII 7.
[2] LC Baptism 10.

marily an *action* of God," Bishop Aulén declares, "with respect to which the church's act is a *re-actio*."[1]

From another point of view, the Church baptizes.[2] Immediately, the ordinary minister of the baptism is the priest, to whom God has given the authority of orders (*potestas ordinis*) through the vocation of the church.[3] While it is desirable that the ordained ministers of baptism be believers and personally pious, this is not a condition of a valid or an efficacious baptism. "It is allowable to use the sacraments even when they are administered by evil men. . . . Both the sacraments and the word are effectual by reason of the institution and commandment of Christ even if they are administered by evil men."[4]

Because baptism is necessary for salvation, the Lutheran Church approves and enjoins emergency baptism. The Lutheran symbolical books hark back to medieval canon law to exemplify the principle that a layman may baptize validly in a life-and-death emergency.[5]

It is nowhere specifically asserted that a baptized laywoman can be the extraordinary minister of the sacrament of baptism, but it is not stated that she cannot be. In the polemics against the Reformed rejection of emergency lay baptism the competence of a midwife or other laywoman is specifically emphasized as a Lutheran practice.

The Lutheran symbolical books do not speak of the question of the validity of baptism administered by a heretic or an unbaptized person. The dogmatic tradition reflects the divided opinion of the pre-Reformation church and is not without inconsistencies. Baptism in a Trinitarian Christian denomination like the Roman Church or the Reformed community is presumed to be valid, but baptism administered by a "Photinian," or a "Sabellian," that is to say, by a Socinian, was held invalid by the classic orthodox theologians. Baptism by an unbaptized person was held valid by Gerhard, on the analogy of the effective proclamation of the word by an unreborn and not truly converted preacher. But he notes that St. Gregory II regarded such a baptism as invalid, that St. Augustine was undecided, and that St. Nicholas I and St. Thomas regarded it as valid.

---

[1] Aulén, *op. cit.*, p. 336.
[2] SA Three V 4.
[3] Ap XXVIII 13 and AC XIV.
[4] AC VIII 1-3. cf. Ap VII 28; 47.
[5] Treatise 67.

Sponsors, as representatives of the church, are to be communicants.[1] The number of sponsors was fixed at one, for the divine unity, or two, for the duality of parenthood, or three, for the divine Trinity. Where there were three sponsors, custom directed that two be of the candidate's sex. No spiritual affinity is created by sponsorship, and the traditions that it does so are branded as unjust.[2]

14. *Symbolism and Ceremonies*

The catechisms try to steer a course between a reduction of baptism to a merely symbolical action and a rejection of the obvious symbolism of baptism. Its concern is with God's word and activity. Baptism is not "an empty sign,"[3] it saves. Yet the symbolism is undeniably there in the sacred scriptures themselves. "What does such baptizing with water signify?" asks the Small Catechism. "It signifies that the old Adam in us is to be drowned through continual contrition and repentance and die with all sins and evil desires and again a new man who lives everlastingly in God's presence in righteousness and purity is continually to emerge and rise."[4]

In the view of the Large Catechism the immersion in or the generous affusion with water and the candidate's emergence from the font similarly symbolize the continuing slaying of the Old Adam and the resurrection of the new man.[5]

Subsequent Lutheran liturgiology distinguishes between the *ceremoniae essentiales* in baptism and the *ceremoniae accidentales.* The latter are the prayers, reading of the sacred scripture, the admonitions and warnings, the use of sponsors, the abrenunciation, the giving of a name, the exorcism, the signing with the Holy cross, and the use of the chrisom.

One of the most prominent of these ceremonies is the renunciation of the devil and all his works and all his pomps. As Hans Kirsten sees it, this is not merely one more ceremony but a key to the understanding of the whole rite, possibly *the* key to such an understanding. Historically a part of the most primitive level of surviving customs and antecedent both to the exorcisms and to the blessing of the water, it is closely linked with the idea of putting

[1]SC Preface 11.
[2]Treatise 78.
[3]LC Baptism 63.
[4]SC Baptism 11-12.
[5]LC Baptism 64-65.

off the old man and being clothed with Christ, and it is the negative human side of the baptismal compact, as the confession of faith is the positive human side of it.

15. *Baptismal "Character" and the Unrepeatability of Baptism*

The Lutheran symbolical books nowhere explicitly reject the idea of an indelible sacramental character. They do not, however, operate with this construct, in part because of its late origin in Western theology, in part because of the lack of a biblical basis, in part because of the obviously metaphorical nature of the term, and in part probably because of a vague uneasiness about the Hellenistic rather than biblical doctrine *de anima* which underlay it. Their insistence on the unrepeatability of baptism, which is all that the teaching of an indelible character seems to have intended to say, in a sense makes this construct unnecessary. The repetition of a valid baptism "would be to blaspheme and desecrate the sacrament in the worst way."[1] Thus, when we lapse after baptism and repent "we need not again have the water poured over us."[2] These passages accord with the convictions that the grace of baptism is amissable, but not the baptism itself; that the unrepeatability of baptism is implied by the once-and-for-all act of Our Lord; and that precisely because baptism is a new birth it is unrepeatable.

Pastoral practice in the Lutheran Church in cases where the baptismal status of a prospective member of the church is uncertain generally reflects the pastor's theological presuppositions. The obligation devolving on him to exercise due diligence to establish the facts surrounding the reported baptism is universally recognized, and he ought to have credible documentary evidence of the prospective member's baptism. When he holds that it is sufficient that the baptizer understood his act as the administration of Christian baptism and that he applied a sufficient quantity of water that it ran while saying "I baptize you in the name of the Father and of the Son and of the Holy Spirit," the pastor will accept a credible previous baptism regardless of the baptizer's affiliation with the Christian community. Where he holds that only a baptized Christian may validly baptize, he will not accept the administration of the sacrament by an unbap-

[1] LC Baptism 55.
[2] LC Baptism 78.

tized person. Where he has not been able to establish decisively the fact of a previous baptism he will normally baptize absolutely. The number of pastoral theologians who have endorsed baptism *sub conditione* in dubious cases is small, and the tradition of the Lutheran Church which discountenances conditional baptism goes back to Luther himself.

A problem is presented by baptisms administered in the liberal churches, where the form and matter may technically be acceptable but where the understanding of the nature of the Godhead is so defective as to be sub-Christian at best. Conventionally in the cases of Uniterian-Universalist baptisms a Lutheran pastor baptizes a convert. The case of baptisms administered in denominations without a specific and universally asserted Trinitarian confession—such as the United Church of Christ and the Disciples of Christ—creates particular casuistic problems.

16. *Vulgar Misconceptions Related to Baptism*

Lutherans objected to the "baptism" of inanimate objects, such as altar-stones and bells, coupled as they were with characteristic features of authentic baptism, such as a name-giving and the presence of sponsors who were expected to make contributions.[1] The belief that the bells thereby received special power to repel diabolical attacks, to ward off thunder and lightning, and to help the poor souls was looked upon as a compounded superstition.

The Lutheran symbolical books energetically reprehend the notion that the monastic profession has the same saving effect that baptism confers.[2] It must be conceded that the proofs which the symbolical books submit as evidence that the followers of the pope held this view are too general for examination or they are inaccurate in their specification. That the view was held, not only at the vulgar level, but that it enjoyed rather respectable traditional and official support among influential theologians is also true.

In the 16th century both popular piety and liturgical practice linked baptism and holy water. The Reformers regarded holy water —despite its 1000-year-long history in the church—in the form and understanding of this sacramental that the 16th century had inherited as inextricably bound up with vulgar superstition and mis-

[1]SA Three XV 4; cf. FC SD VII 87.
[2]AC XXVII 11; Ap XXVII 9, 20.

leading opinions to a point where, along with some other traditional ceremonies that had suffered a similar fate, it could no longer be rescued and rehabilitated.[1]

17. *Some Questions for Roman Catholic Theologians to Answer*

The impression that a Lutheran is likely to take from Roman Catholic discussions of grace in connection with baptism is that grace is conceived of as something quantifiable. If this impression is correct, does this adequately communicate the idea that this kind of language must be understood metaphorically and that the grace which the sacraments really convey is primarily the divine love and pardon?

May not the insistence on water ritually prepared on Easter Eve and Whitsuneve be conducive to superstition?

On the basis of the word of God, is the designation of implicit desire for baptism or of death by martyrdom as species of baptism defensible as anything more than a figure of speech? Can one conclude with theological certainty that these "baptisms" meet the requirement of the absolute necessity of baptism for salvation? Is it the "baptism" of desire that saves or the "perfect contrition" that is demanded in conjunction with it?

Does a limbus of unbaptized infants have any basis in the word of God?

Does the common opinion which denies the beatific vision to children who die without baptism take full account of God's universal love and Christ's universal redemption?

Does the Roman Catholic attitude toward the sacrament of penance take adequate account of the perduring effect of baptism and its efficacy with reference to sins committed after baptism?

How can the existence of an internal intention (as distinguished, say, from a merely external or a habitual intention) in the minister of baptism be adequately certified to the recipient of baptism?

How can one determine the existence of the habitual desire requisite for a valid reception of baptism by an adult with a sufficient degree of certainty to satisfy the doubt that baptism was actually received?

Is the idea of an indelible character imparted in baptism in

[1] Ap IV 282; XV 44 (Sermon).

actuality anything more than a metaphorical assertion of the unrepeatability of baptism? Is the character as *signum distinctivum* certainly known to anyone except God?

What basis in the word of God is there for the doctrine that baptism needs completion by means of an anointing of the forehead with chrism?

SOME OBSERVATIONS ON THE TEACHING OF TRENT CONCERNING BAPTISM

GODFREY DIEKMAN

At the Council of Trent the question of baptism necessarily received considerable attention both in Session V, dealing with original sin, and in Session VI which was concerned with justification. The problem of justification was recognized as central to the Council's task. In their report to Rome on June 21, 1546, the leaders of the Council had stated: "The significance of this Council in the theological sphere lies chiefly in the article on justification. In fact, this is the most important item the Council has to deal with." (So heated did the discussion become that during it occurred the famous incident of one Council Father grasping another by the beard, and calling him knave and fool.) For this reason, the Council did not limit itself to extracting propositions from the Reformers' writings in order to anathematize them, but determined to present the Catholic doctrine as fully and objectively as possible. The six questions proposed to the Council as the basis of the discussion reveal how essential was the problem of the relative role of faith and sacraments:

1) What is meant by justification both as regards the name and the thing itself? 2) What are the causes of justification? What is God's part in the process and what man's? 3) How are we to understand the assertion that man is saved by faith? 4) Do works play a role in the process of justification—both before and after—and in what way? What is the role of the sacraments in that process? 5) How describe the process of justification—what precedes, accompanies and follows it? 6) By what proofs from scripture, the Fathers, the Councils and the apostolic traditions is the Catholic doctrine supported?

Although the Council had repeatedly expressed its determination not to employ scholastic terminology, but to restrict itself whenever possible to modes of expression derived from scripture, early apostolic tradition and the Fathers, (according to the Bishop of Fiesole, "In theology, scholasticism must be directed by the teaching *magisterium,* and not vice versa.") it failed to carry out its good intentions in describing the "causes" of justification in Chapter 7.[1] It there speaks of the sacrament of baptism as the "instrumental cause" of justification; it is "the sacrament of faith," without which no man was ever justified. There had been considerable discussion on the respective roles of faith and baptism, a discussion obviously complicated by the problem of infant baptism. All agreed that, in the case of the adult, a personal faith was necessary. But wherein that required faith consisted was a matter of dispute: whether it was faith as a preliminary condition to baptism (this was urged especially by members of the Franciscan school), whether it coincided with the scholastically developed term *habitus fidei* (the virtue of faith infused at baptism), or whether it was "the faith of the church" as mother, of which the baptismal rite itself was an expression. Cardinal Cervini, the papal legate who played the leading role at these sessions of the Council, in presenting the text made it clear that this last-mentioned, more ancient, understanding was intended by the expression "sacrament of faith." Baptism itself is of its nature a *professio fidei,* a profession of that faith of the church which finds essential utterance in the traditional baptismal rite itself. This interpretation is underscored by the reference to Augustine. If "faith" had been interpreted primarily as the *"habitus fidei,"* this would of course have helped to clarify the problem of infant baptism. But it would also have contributed to a further neglect of the "sign" nature of the sacrament, by placing such one-sided emphasis on the sacraments as *causes,* inclusive of causing the virtue of faith.

Of critical importance, furthermore, in the Decree on Justification is the declaration in Chapter 8 that "we are said to be justified by faith, because faith is the *beginning* of human salvation, the foundation and root of all justification, 'without which it is impossible to please God' (Heb 11:6)."

[1]Cf., "Decree Concerning Justification," H. J. Schroeder, ed., *Canons and Decrees of the Council of Trent* (St. Louis: B. Herder, 1941), pp. 24-46; especially pp. 33-34.

The Decree on Sacraments

Three items would seem to be of special significance in the Foreword of the Tridentine report: 1) The decree on the sacraments was viewed as "the completion" of the teaching on justification. (Fortunately, the personnel of the session dealing with justification and that treating of the sacraments, remained substantially identical, thus assuring continuity of outlook.) 2) Nevertheless, while in Chapter 8 "On Justification" it was stated that "faith is the beginning of salvation, the foundation and root of all justification," it is here said of the sacraments that "through them all true justice either *begins,* or being begun is increased, or being lost is restored." 3) The decree's purpose is "to destroy the errors and extripate the heresies that in our stormy times are directed against the most holy sacraments."

Perhaps the concern expressed in number three above, especially the pressing need of furnishing immediate and clear answers to the pastorally all-important matter of administering the sacraments, motivated the fateful decision, contrary to traditional procedure, merely to condemn false doctrines, and not to attempt a positive exposition of the Catholic doctrine on the sacraments. But perhaps equally decisive was the simple fact that such a variety of theological opinions was represented among the Council Fathers and theologians, that a consensus on a full and positive presentation was regarded as impossible—or at least very difficult; and by now, after the strenuous previous six months of discussion on justification, a certain general weariness had begun to make itself felt. For there were Thomists, followers of the Augustinian and Scotist traditions, and disciples of the schools of Gabriel Biel and Okham, not to speak of a few who were in some circles suspicioned of being soft on Lutheranism (e.g., the influential Seripando, general of the Augustinians).

We have no certain knowledge as to who was ultimately responsible for the decision. All we know is that Cardinal Cervini had, in preparation for the discussion on the sacraments, ordered several theologians to draw up a list of propositions, extracted from the Reformers' writings and professions of faith, which conflicted with Catholic sacramental teaching. This list, consisting of 14 errors about sacraments in general, 17 about baptism, and 4 about confirmation (35 theses in all), were extracted for the most part, though not always verbatim, from Luther's *Babylonian Captivity,* and from his *Disputations,* as well as from several other of his writings, chiefly from his earlier period; from the *Augsburg Confession;* and from Melanchthon's *Loci Communes.* Six of the propositions carried no indication of their sources, and three were simply labeled as Anabaptist doctrine. In any event, this was the first time in the conciliar proceedings that textual extracts from the writings of the Reformers were presented as the basis of the discussions. (Later, the theologians presented 16 further theses; these 51 theses were then reduced to the 30 present canons, and presented for debate in the 12 general congregations, February 8-21, 1547, with the explanation that they constituted the contents of Protestant teaching, even if the texts were not always to be found verbatim in their writings.)

Several comments suggest themselves. Ehses, in editing the Goerres Gesellschaft's Volume V of the acts of the *Concilium Tridentinum* tried to verify the citations of the 36 original theses from the Wittenberg and Jena editions of Luther's writings, but much further work needs to be done in this matter with the help of the Weimar edition and other means of research. In at least one case, in which Luther is quoted as denying that there is true baptism in the Catholic Church, Ehses admits that he was unable to verify the quotation. And Jedin dryly adds: "Nor has any one studied the extent to which Catholic controversial theology should be regarded as a transmitter of the theses."[1]

But even if the citations were textually exact, it is seriously questionable whether they sufficed to serve as a reasonably adequate presentation of Luther's views on the sacraments in general, and on baptism in particular, to the bishops and theologians of the Council. Even abstracting from the fact that the list of these bishops and theologians (approximately 60 prelates and 50 theologians) reveals only an occasional name from north of the Alps, who might be expected to be personally acquainted with the controversy, such individual texts, removed from their context, cannot do justice to such a delicately nuanced problem as that of Word-Sacrament-Faith. "Luther's view of sacraments can be understood only if one lifts it out of the isolated position into which it has too often been forced and places it in the totality of his theology."[2] One would have

[1]*History of the Council of Trent* (2 vols.; London: Nelson, 1957-61), II, p. 371, n. 1.
[2]Heinrich Bornkamm, *Luther's World of Thought,* trans. Martin H. Bertram (St. Louis: Concordia Publishing House, 1958), p. 94.

to conclude, therefore, that it is not in these anathematizing Canons on sacraments in general and on baptism in particular that one may expect to find anything like a fair and balanced synthesis of Luther's sacramental theology. This is all the more true in that the condemnations are based for the most part on Luther's earlier writings, and do not take into account his later matured reflections, particularly after his struggle with the Anabaptists. These canons, rather, are above all a solemn declaration of the church's *magisterium* on certain carefully delimited areas of the church's own doctrine on the sacraments, a declaration occasioned by the Reformation, and intended to safeguard Catholic faith from current heretical attacks. Tragically, however, these inherent limitations of the canons were not appreciated in the polemical heat of succeeding generations and centuries, and the Catholic view of Lutheran sacramental theology was all too largely derived from them.[1]

But equally deplorable has been the inevitable narrowing and impoverishment of their teaching and understanding of the sacraments on the part of Catholics themselves, as a result of the Council's decision, not to present a positive over-all declaration, but to restrict itself to such points of sacramental doctrine which were judged to be under attack. Sacramental theology in our Catholic textbooks until a very recent date reflected clearly (and too exclusively) the Tridentine concerns: the septenary number of the sacraments, their institution by Christ, the principle of their causality *ex opere operatoto non ponentibus obicem,* etc. Failure of the Council to situate all these doctrines positively into their fuller context, namely, Christ and his redemptive mysteries now operative in the church, permitted if it did not actually encourage a spiritual pragmatism, concerned predominantly with the sacraments as channels of grace profiting the individual. It was not until the liturgical movement of our own century, supported in recent years by the biblical revival, that the ecclesial dimension of the sacraments has been, as it were, rediscovered (in the case of penance, this is only now rather gingerly opening to discussion), and that their nature as a personal faith encounter with Christ within the ecclesial community is again being stressed.

[1]Speaking personally, such a book as Jaroslav Pelikan's *Luther the Expositor* (St. Louis: Concordia Publishing House, 1959), in which Luther's exegetical writings on word and sacrament are synthesized, altered drastically my own views of his teaching in this matter, views too largely—I must confess—still conditioned by my seminary training.

A striking instance of how polemical preoccupations affected the Council's declarations had occurred earlier in the debate on original sin. In number 3, the original text had read: "or if he denies that the merit of Jesus Christ is applied both to adults and to infants by *faith and the sacrament of baptism*." This was criticized as being liable to misunderstanding, because it was too similar to Article 2 of the Augsburg Confession, and hence the "faith" was dropped, and there was substituted "rightly administered in the form of the Church."[1] While it is clear from the discussion that the Council intended by this latter phrase, not merely the *forma* of the sacrament of baptism, but the entire traditional rite in which the *professio fidei* plays an integral role, this interpretation is not immediately evident from the revised text, and the impression has remained that the Council here says nothing about the remission of original sin by faith joined to the sacrament.[2]

It was however in the decree on sacraments, by its merely negative statement of the Catholic faith through condemnatory canons, that apologetic stress tended to obscure the role of faith. Against the *sola fides* principle of the Reformers, the Council contented itself with declaring a *non sola* principle,[3] which, while leaving open many possibilities of the requisite "more," also *includes* the positive aspects of the Reformers' teaching. "Not faith *alone*" implies "faith plus something else." The Council Fathers were agreed on the necessity of faith. Yet their merely negative formulations inexorably led to a further neglect of requisite stress on faith (and sign) in subsequent Catholic theology, and a continued weighting of the "causality" emphasis.

As in the earlier debates on original sin and justification, the Council in discussing sacraments had likewise determined to take advantage of the insights furnished by the scholastics, where these proved helpful, but not to take sides in the controversies of the schools, nor to use scholastic terminology where it could be avoided in favor of biblical and patristic language. However, in a last minute intervention, the Archbishop of Palermo, supported by two other

---

[1]Cf. "Decree Concerning Original Sin," Schroeder, *op. cit.*, p. 22.

[2]By way of contrast, cf. St. Thomas' statement: "After the coming of Christ, men are incorporated into Christ by faith . . . and therefore, while the sacrament of baptism was not always necessary for salvation, faith, of which baptism is the sacrament, has always been necessary" *Suma III*, 68, I ad.

[3]Cf. Canons 5 and 8, "On the Sacraments in General," Schroeder, *op. cit.*, p. 52.

bishops, suggested that in Canon 6 the clause, "the sacraments confer grace on those who receive them worthily" (*rite et digne suscipientibus*) be replaced by "on those who place no obstacle" (*non ponentibus obicem*). This latter scholastic formulation had been in the original draft, it is true, but was subsequently suppressed; now it was reinstated. I think there would be quite general agreement today that this hurried decision was regrettable. *Rite et digne suscipientibus* (borrowed from the *Decretum pro Armenis,* promulgated by the Council of Florence in 1439) suggests positive dispositions on the part of the recipient (which would include faith in the case of baptism); whereas *non ponentibus obicem* has in fact been understood all too widely in post-Tridentine Catholic theology in the merely negative sense of absence of mortal sin.

Another decision of the last moment was the addition in Canon 8 (On Sacraments in General) of the phrase *"ex opere operato"* to the statement that sacraments of the new law confer grace. This scholastic term too (first encountered in Peter of Poitiers in the 13th century), had been eliminated from the original draft, but was now reinserted for the sake of clarification. Again one can only express regret that, if clarification was needed, the greatest scholastic of them all was not called upon: for St. Thomas in his *Summa* had already eschewed *ex opere operato* and had substituted *ex actione Christi,* or *ex virtute Christi.* This would not only have benefited Catholics by relating the sacraments more expressly with Christ and his redemptive action in the present, but would have served better to answer the Reformers' violent attacks on Catholic sacramental practice as "magic." But ecumenical motivation was scarcely the order of that day. As a matter of fact, it seems certain that very few of the Council Fathers had any awareness that Protestant objection to contemporary sacramental *practices* (and abuses) played such a decisive part in their opposition to traditional Catholic teaching.[1] It was only at a later period of the Council that a bishop demanded "greater care and reverence" in the administration of the sacraments. The reinstatement of the *ex opere operato* phrase, without positive explanation of its true significance in terms of Christ's ministry in the present, could only contribute to a hardening of the polemical

[1]Jedin, *op. cit.,* II, p. 385, remarks appositely: "It is evident that an overwhelming majority of the members of the Council did not pay adequate attention to the connection between the ignorance of the faithful about the sacraments and the abuses in their administration."

status quo, and to the continuing very real danger of attributing a quasi-magical causality to the sacraments in general Catholic teaching.

A final instance of scholastic influence on the Council may be cited. The medieval *Summas,* by a process of induction from scriptural and patristic sources, had arrived at a summary tract on "Sacraments in General." But this soon led to a reversal of procedure: The tract on sacraments in general was placed at the beginning, and the treatment of the individual sacraments was all too largely derived from it deductively. Trent simply followed a current practice, and thereby, of course, served to perpetuate it in Catholic theology manuals. Whatever its pedagogical advantages may be, such a *modus procedendi* tends to weaken the immediacy of the scriptural witness for the individual sacraments. It was therefore hardly calculated to win a hearing from the Reformers, for whom the word of scripture was all-decisive.

A few concluding remarks that may prove relevant to our understanding of the Tridentine canons. The septenary number of the sacraments was excluded from debate: it had already been authoritatively declared by the *Decretum pro Armenia* (1439). That the sacraments were instituted by Christ was also taken for granted, and was not subjected to any thorough discussion. Only a last minute intervention by the Bishop of Porto secured the declaration now in Canon 1 "On Sacraments in General." Because there were such divergent opinions as to how the baptism of John differed from Christian baptism (it was one of the matters most warmly discussed), Canon 1 on baptism leaves the matter vague, and merely declares the fact of difference. Canons 6-10 on baptism were directed against the Lutheran teaching on the efficacy of baptism as a *perpetuum sacramentum.* (Question: did they reflect authentic Lutheran teaching?) Canons 11-13 were aimed at the Anabaptists, and Canon 14, against Erasmus. Canons 2, 4 and 5 embody traditional doctrine, which it was thought necessary to shore up.

A Brief Appendix on Vatican II

Here a purposeful abstention from anathematizing canons, and only a positive exposition with special reference to the Constitution on the Sacred Liturgy.[1] At the very outset, the Council "sees particularly cogent reasons for undertaking the reform and promotion of

[1]Liturgy means sacraments in action.

the liturgy" in order also "to foster whatever can promote union among all who believe in Christ."[1] For this same reason, the exposition itself, of sacraments and of sacramental life, is consciously ecumenical. The attempt to avoid "school" language is successful. Of particular interest is the fact that the term *ex opere operato* was deliberately avoided.[2] More important, the urgent plea of Professor Skydsgaard, spokesman for observers at the audience with Paul VI in 1963, for a consistent biblical theology, has been met.[3] Source and continuing root of sacramental efficacy are "the Paschal Mysteries." (Revealing is the fact that the term—and even the concept—is still missing in Pius XII's encyclical on the liturgy, *Mediator Dei,* 1947).

All centers in Christ the Highpriest, active in the here and now. Of cardinal importance is Article 7, dealing with "the presence" of Christ: in the sacrificial action of the Mass; in the action of the sacraments, "so that when a man baptizes, it is really Christ himself who baptizes;" in the "Word," since it is he himself who speaks when the holy scriptures are read in the church; in the worshiping assembly. In the sacraments, and above all the Eucharist, "the victory and triumph of His death are again made present."

Hence sacraments are our personal faith-encounter with Christ, in the priestly assembly. The document repeatedly and insistently underscores the role of faith. Thus: "Since the sacraments are signs, they also instruct. They not only presuppose faith, but by words and objects, they also nourish, strengthen, and express it. That is why they are called 'sacraments of faith'. They do indeed impart grace, but, in addition, the very fact of celebrating them most effectively disposes the faithful to receive this grace in a fruitful manner, to worship God duly, and to practice charity. It is therefore of the highest importance that the faithful should easily understand the sacramental signs, and should frequent with great eagerness those sacraments which were instituted to nourish the Christian life."[4]

---

[1]"Constitution on the Sacred Liturgy," Art 1, *The Teaching of the Second Vatican Council; Complete Texts of the Constitutions, Decrees, and Declarations* (Newman Press: Westminster, Maryland, 1966), p. 13.

[2]This was revealed by Cyprian Vaggagini in his commentary on the Constitution. He personally, however, is unhappy about the "loss". *Constitutio de sacra liturgia cum commentario* (Rome: Edigioni Liturgiche, 1964), p. 59.

[3]Kristen-Ejnar Skydsgaard, "A Word to the Pope," *The National Lutheran,* XXXII (January, 1964), pp. 12-13.

[4]"Constitution on the Sacred Liturgy," Art. 59, *op. cit.,* p 37.

Hence, among other reforms, the introduction of the vernacular, and the plan of introducing scripture readings into the reformed rites of baptism and other sacraments besides the Eucharist.

The Constitution reflects contemporary Catholic sacramental thought, which speaks of Christ as the *Ur-Sakrament,* the primal Sacrament; consequently, the church, too, is the primal sacrament;[1] and finally, the Eucharist, as the making present again of the covenant, of the total work of redemption, is also *Ur-Sakrament.*[2] It is understood to consist of 1) *the service of the word,* and 2) *the service of the sacrifice-meal.* The celebration of the Eucharist is the "most important self-manifestation," the epiphany, of the church.[3]

Baptism and the other sacraments are subsidiary, complementary to the Eucharist. "All who are made sons of God by faith (!) and baptism should come together to praise God in the midst of His Church, to take part in the Sacrifice, and to eat of the Lord's Supper." [4] "Participation (in the liturgical, and especially the Eucharistic action) by the Christian people 'as a chosen race, a royal priesthood, a holy nation, a redeemed people,' is their right and duty by reason of their baptism."[5] The ecclesial nature of baptism is stressed. (Subsequent documents explain further that baptism is the bond that unites all Christians.) And baptism as a *professio fidei* is given greater prominence by the functional restoration of the catechumenate for adults.[6] Baptism is not only a transient act, but is the always-alive wellspring of Christian action. Finally, though all seven sacraments are mentioned, and their personal and communal role explained, a more biblical perspective is restored by relative concentration on baptism and Eucharist.

---

[1]Article 26 calls the Church "the sacrament of unity."

[2]Cf. Article 10, *op. cit.,* pp. 19-20, on the Eucharist as not merely, one even if most important of the sacraments, but as the "source and fountain."

[3]*Ibid.*

[4]Art. 10, *op. cit.,* p. 19.

[5]Art. 14, *op. cit.,* p. 22. This text from I Peter is one of the most frequently cited scriptural passages in the conciliar declarations.

[6]Art. 64, *op. cit.,* p. 39.

THE SECOND THEOLOGICAL CONSULTATION BETWEEN LUTHERANS AND CATHOLICS

WARREN A. QUANBECK

At the first meeting between the Roman Catholic and Lutheran groups in Baltimore in July 1965 the discussion centered upon the topic "What does it mean to confess the Nicene Creed?" The topic was chosen because both churches regard the creed as authoritative and because it was hoped that the understanding of its authority in each tradition might illuminate the function of dogma and the place of theology in the churches.

The discussion showed that Roman Catholics and Lutherans have much in common in their attitude toward christological dogma, agreeing both in what the Nicene Creed affirms and in their reflection of misunderstandings of the person and work of Christ. Not entirely unexpectedly, differences were also apparent, and much time was given during the discussion to the examination of them. Both sides were anxious to penetrate beyond the customary text-book knowledge of the other's position, so as to understand its theological concerns, its use of terms, its way of thinking, and its theological style. They took care not to assume either that the use of the same terms meant identity of assertion or that the use of different language indicated unbridgeable differences. During the discussion both groups gained a deeper and more detailed understanding of the other's way of theological thinking. It was thought desirable to continue the exploration of the common creed, and at the same time move on to another area of theology. Therefore it was decided that the second theological discussion between the two groups should deal with the statement of the Nicene Creed on baptism: "One baptism for the remission of sins." As preparation for the discussion two sets of papers were assigned, one dealing with the biblical teaching concerning baptism, the second expounding the doctrinal presentation of baptism in each tradition.

It is worth noting that Professors Brown and Stendahl, who were asked to prepare the biblical papers, came to substantial agreement on what the New Testament says about baptism. They agreed that it is essential to see baptism as a rite of initiation, a means of entry into the church, a passage from the old aeon to the new, and that the other biblical statements concerning baptism are to be seen in the light of this fact. Baptism thus has an eschatological and ecclesiological significance, relating to God's redeeming deeds for his people. It is also presented as union with Christ in his death and resurrection, and is connected with the gift of the Holy Spirit and with the forgiveness of sins.

It was pointed out that there are many difficulties in interpreting the NT references to baptism, inasmuch as they occur not in the context of systematic expositions of the meaning of baptism, but incidentally in relation to the discussion of other problems of the early church. For example, while it is clear that adult baptism was the customary practice of the early church, and was regarded as necessary for membership in the church, there is no way of determining whether it was considered necessary to baptize children. Tertullian makes it clear that infant baptism was common by the end of the second century, and it is possible that it grew up gradually in analogy to the Jewish practice of circumcision. Furthermore, while the need for baptism seems clearly agreed on, there is little evidence that the church agreed on a clear theological reason for its necessity. The connection of baptism with the remission of sins is not everywhere clear in the NT, and the later distinction between original sin and actual sin does not appear to be a part of the world of thought of the writers of the NT.

As the participants explored the ramifications of the doctrine of baptism many topics were examined: the problems of infant baptism and emergency baptism, the relation of baptism to original sin, the necessity of baptism, the minister of baptism, the problem of dominical institution, the relation of baptism to penance, to the gifts of the Spirit, to forgiveness, to membership in the church, the relation of the church to the kingdom of God, and the authority of the church to make changes in the mode of baptism. It became clear in the course of the discussion that a rite as fundamental as baptism inevitably impinges on almost every point of christian doctrine.

During the discussion of the historical papers the development of the doctrine of baptism in the two traditions was reviewed. It was noted that the Council of Trent and the Formula of Concord say substantially the same things about baptism, and that contemporary theology in both traditions affirms what has been asserted in the past and at the same time seeks other language for the exposition of the doctrine of baptism today. This is so both because of more adequate biblical scholarship in our day and because the questions raised in modern experience of the world are asked out of different presuppositions and from different perspectives. Thus a Lutheran finds himself in continuity with the presentation of the doctrine of sin in the Lutheran confessions and at the same time finds the categories of the 16th century theology too individualistic and too impersonal to do justice to the teachings of the scriptures. He stands with the Reformers as they face the questions asked by their century, and he also seeks new formulations to meet the questions asked today.

The problem of Dominical institution of the sacraments was discussed at some length. For theologians of the 16th century Dominical institution of baptism clearly meant that baptism had been instituted by Jesus Christ on a specific historical occasion. This conviction underlays Luther's desire to treat as sacraments only the two (or three) specifically instituted by Christ. The historical study of the NT has however raised the question whether we can speak of this problem in the same way today. Some Lutheran participants expressed themselves as being unconvinced by the critical discussion. They regard the NT texts as sufficient basis to assure them of a specific historical institution of the sacraments by Christ himself. Others agreed with the majority of the Roman Catholic participants that the question of Dominical institution must be seen in a different light, and that this new situation might well be advantageous from an ecumenical standpoint.

Because the discussion at the outset was necessarily broad in scope it was decided to focus it more precisely by having each group address questions to the other.

The Roman Catholics addressed the following questions to the Lutherans:

1. What do you understand by Dominical institution? What is required in order that Dominical institutions may be affirmed?
    a. What is the relationship between Dominical institution and the full definition of the sacrament?

   b. What are the empowerments of the church in regard to the modalities of baptism, and what is the relation of confessional statements to the church and scripture? Can they add anything to what scripture says?
2. What is the relation between the confessional statements of the church and scriptural statements on the sacrament of baptism? Can the church add something to what scripture has already said?
3. What is the basis for the efficacy of baptism? Do you assign remission of sins as the primary effect signified by the rite? Is there some order or primacy in the gifts bestowed in baptism?

The Lutheran questions were:

1. What is meant by the remission of sins?
   a. What is the significance of baptism for sins committed after baptism?
   b. What does the sacrament of penance add to baptism?
   c. Is the sacrament of penance as practiced in the Roman Catholic Church totally in accord with our understanding of the gifts and grace bestowed in baptism?
2. On what grounds are those who are baptized in non-Catholic and non-Orthodox churches excluded from the Roman Catholic sacrament?
3. What is the relationship of faith and baptism in Roman Catholic theology?

The problem of the remission of sins was discussed first because it was raised in both sets of questions. Here again it became clear that Roman Catholics and Lutherans say many of the same things about sin and forgiveness, and are also alike in their uneasiness about certain traditional formulations. The historical study of the scriptures, for example, raises questions about the traditional statement of the doctrine of original sin. At least in its popular expositions it is too individualistic and inadequately personal to do justice to the scriptural teaching. Similarly the new appreciation of the eschatological language of the scriptures has called into question many of the temporal or dogmatic sequences posited by theologians in the life of the believer.

The discussion of the sacrament of penance brought out a sharp difference in ways of theological thinking and speaking. Roman Catholics can speak of human collaboration with God as involving merit. They are careful to point out that man's collaboration is brought about under the influence of God's grace, but nevertheless does add a "plus" to the individual. Their concern is to stress that when God meets man with his grace, something really happens in the human being thus touched, and his life is changed by God's work in him. The Lutheran is concerned to keep any idea of merit out of the context of man's relationship to God, and to insist that whatever worth man has is God's work in him. The Lutheran is certainly not indifferent to the necessity of man's response to God, but does not want to designate that response by the term merit. Time did not permit further exploration of this question, but it was noted as a difference to be examined in the future. It is possible that further discussion may show that the differences may be a matter of complementary emphases and not necessarily mutually exclusive thrusts.

The second Lutheran question concerning the exclusion of baptized non-Roman Catholics from the Roman Catholic sacraments opened up a complex of theological problems. Answers emerged at several different levels, theological, canonical and pastoral. Theological questions involved the meaning of membership in the church, the eucharist as sign and means of unity, the relationship of baptism and confirmation, and the question of episcopal orders. It was pointed out that Lutherans are not agreed on one simple set of answers in this area, and also that as a result of the Second Vatican Council the Roman Catholic position is undergoing reexamination.

The Roman Catholic question 1 b raises in effect the question of development of doctrine. Prof. Lindbeck prepared a Lutheran reply in the form of a series of theses:

1. The church is empowered to develop new ways of organizing itself, administering the means of grace and formulating authoritative doctrine in view of (a) the needs of the situation in which it finds itself and (b) faithfulness to the scriptural witness. Thus, for example, infant baptism and affusin are legitimate.
2. Developments cannot be dogmatically binding, that is, used as tests of orthodoxy, unless explicitly required by the scriptural witness either (a) in itself, or (b) in confrontation with new post-biblical questions. (Nicea and Chalcedon are dogmatically binding in view of (b) but not (a). Application: (1) The practice of infant baptism cannot be made a dogmatic requirement. (2) Anabaptist dogmatic denial of the validity of infant

baptism is also an illegitimate development.

3. Developments which are not dogmatically binding may also be binding although to a lesser degree, in view of (a) the importance of not disrupting nor further injuring the unity of the church in space and time, or (b) the weight of the pastoral and theological considerations in favor of them. Application: The antiquity and generality of infant baptism means that it cannot be lightly abandoned. In addition one could argue that infant baptism best displays the sign function of baptism as an initiatory rite in those situations where entrance into the kingdom of God is usually associated with birth into a Christian family.
4. Dogmatically binding decisions cannot be formally declared to be infallible, irreformable or irreversible because:
   (a) The church is obligated to a continuous search (in reliance on the Holy Spirit and with the help of reason) for fuller understanding of what faithfulness to the scriptural witness involves. This means that developments which were at one time thought legitimate may later be discovered to be in opposition to the scriptural witness and even that some matters which were once tests of orthodoxy are not required by the scriptural witness.
   (b) This is the only way to preserve the genuine primacy of scripture over against the church and later developments (traditions) and therefore the only way to maintain unambiguously the finality of the revelation in Christ.
   (c) There is a hierarchy among dogmas so that in some cases the irreversibility becomes a matter of "moral certainty". (This does not apply equally to the time-conditioned forms in which they are expressed).

It is not clear what the nature of Roman Catholic and Lutheran disagreement on thesis 4 is. On thesis 2, however, the Lutherans would suppose that they are clearly in disagreement with Roman Catholics (e.g. this thesis excludes the dogmatization of the papal and Marian affirmations, although perhaps not necessarily their admissability as theological opinions.

In the short time remaining discussion focused on thesis 4. Roman Catholics objected that it is inadequate: the assertion made about Christ at Nicea is irreversible. The Lutheran reply pointed out that there is a hierarchy of truths and that the decision of Nicea, although not absolute, does have the effect of closing off certain lines of theological definition. If a theologian finds himself taking a line differing from his fellow believers, he is under obligation to question his own procedures and conclusions, because faith is held in community and not as a merely individual affair. Furthermore, the language used at Nicea cannot be absolutized. Each generation is compelled to face anew the issues confronted at Nicea and to formulate its answers in the language of its own time. The errors condemned at Nicea were in fact errors and must always be regarded as such, but must be handled with the conceptual apparatus and language of our time.

The participants in the discussion would not claim that the three days' meeting accomplished an exhaustive analysis of the problems of baptism. The theological encounter was, however, sufficiently open and genuine to give confidence that it would be possible to discuss at the next meeting a topic which produced great heat at the time of the Reformation, that of Eucharist as sacrifice. It is a measure of their confidence both in the mutual respect of the participating groups and in the progress of biblical studies and ecumenical theology that such a controversial issue can be approached.

A CATHOLIC VIEW OF THE CHICAGO LUTHERAN-CATHOLIC DIALOGUE

Joseph W. Baker

Interdenominational dialogue is both a result and an instrument of the present-day ecumenical movement. It would be a mistake to look upon dialogue as the totality or as the essence of the ecumenical movement. To regard dialogue as sum and substance of ecumenism would be equivalent to ignoring the operation of the Holy Spirit working reconciliation within Christendom.

Although Catholic involvement in the existing ecumenical movement is of quite recent origin, it has long been recognized that officially-established dialogue must be a process in the task of Christian unity.

While its wording may seem cautious in the light of present-day developments, an instruction of the Holy Office on the ecumenical movement issued December 20, 1949, helped to prepare the way for a new era of Catholic involvement in the dialogue of Christian unity. This document urged upon the bishops of the world a concern for the ecumenical movement as a "distinguished portion in the universal pastoral charge" and "an object of concern that the whole Catholic people take to heart and recommend to God in fervent supplications." In addition to calling upon individual bishops to exercise leadership in the work of dialogue towards unity, the instruction suggested that corporate leadership of bishops in any given region would be advantageous. In this country, despite some local initiatives, the full flowering of ecumenical involvement under the guidance of the American Catholic bishops is a result of the Vatican Council.

Urged on by the Council's Decree on Ecumenism, the Catholic bishops of the United States have approved the appointment of a body of specialists to act as a liaison with the National Council of Churches in addition to teams established to carry on conversations with those church bodies indicating an interest in such an undertaking. Early establishment of a Catholic group to converse with representatives of Lutheran bodies in the United States must be attributed in great part to the activities of the National Lutheran Council in behalf of this project.

To provide for continuity in these conversations, it was decided that they be held twice each year. The participants are in no sense to be regarded as negotiators nor the meetings as negotiating sessions. Rather, the meetings are an officially approved forum for theological exchange. There is no question that participation in a theological discussion of this caliber is an inspiring and rewarding experience. If, however, the exchange is to be beneficial for the church as a whole, it is necessary that some report be made to the churches.

The first Lutheran-Catholic exchange held in 1964 was on the subject of the Nicene Creed as Dogma of the Church. The first day of the meeting was devoted to a discussion of the papers; the second to formulation of a summary statement.

When the second round of these discussions was held in Chicago, most of the participants agreed that entirely too much time had been devoted to the preparation of the final statement, and too little to points at issue. Still, without some form of report, the papers might prove of little value to local pastors and congregations.

The subject chosen for the second round of meetings was "One Baptism for the Forgiveness of Sins." Papers outlining the biblical perspective on this topic were prepared by Father Raymond E. Brown, S.S. and Doctor Krister Stendahl; while theological observations from the Catholic and Lutheran traditions were given by Father Godfrey Diekmann and Doctor Arthur K. Piepkorn, respectively.

The first day of the three-day session was devoted to an examination and discussion of the papers. For all practical purposes, there was no disagreement on the biblical presentations. It was generally agreed that baptism is the rite of initiation into the community of faith; that it involves transition from the realm of darkness into the realm of light; that through it the believer is united to the death and resurrection of Christ; and that certain biblical passages relate it to the forgiveness of sins. The early Christian community surely had a conviction of the necessity of baptism, although there is no clearly expressed conception of the reason for this necessity. The necessity of baptism seems at least in part to be connected with the giving of the Spirit.

The question of infant Baptism, practiced by both Lutherans and Catholics, was raised inasmuch as there is no clear New Testament passage indicating approval or disapproval of this usage. This question was discussed at some length and recurred at intervals during the meeting because it involved the concepts of development of doctrine and the church's authority with respect to the sacraments. At the same time, it led to consideration of the process of justification and notions of original sin.

The attention devoted to a discussion of infant baptism should not be regarded as an excursion into ecclesiastical trivia. Whenever this practice had its origin, Tertullian makes it clear that the practice was common by the end of the second century. It had been noted in the 1965 dialogue session that full inquiry must be made into two topics: "first, the nature and structure of the teaching authority of the church; and secondly, the role of scripture in relation to the teaching office of the church." Since infant Baptism is not explicitly commanded in the New Testament Scriptures, the question was pursued to determine what clues it might offer for this inquiry.

The question of infant baptism led logically to some commentary on the subject of original sin, emergency baptism in danger of death, and the fate of infants who die without baptism. In view of current theological studies, it was considered precarious to attempt too close a definition of what is meant by "original sin." It was asked if the practice of emergency baptism did not perhaps indicate an overly mechanistic view of the sacrament. And it pointed out that the concept of a "limbo of infants" is not a doctrine of the Catholic Church, but merely a theological opinion.

The papers on the respective church traditions served to emphasize the fact that throughout the seventeenth century Lutherans and Catholics were in basic agreement about baptism and actually spoke the same language in this regard. It was noted that a comparison of the Formula of Concord and the promulgations enacted at Trent served to illustrate this point.

To narrow the field of discussion to manageable proportions, it was decided that each team of consultants should propose three questions on the subject matter to the other. In the event time did not permit full discussion of all six questions but a good beginning was made towards identifying points of divergence in the two traditions. Each set of questions was aimed at drawing out responses which would serve to clarify the role ascribed by the other tradition to church authority in the process of justification. Thus, Lutherans were led to ask about the significance of baptism for sins committed after baptism and to inquire after the Catholic understanding of what the sacrament of penance adds to baptism. In a similar vein, Catholics asked on what basis Lutherans accept the institution of baptism by Christ; what authority the Church possesses over the modalities of baptism; and if the confessional statements of the church are able to add anything to what scripture says.

This is only a partial listing of the questions posed, but it was principally on these topics that the remainder of the discussions centered.

Considerable time was devoted to a consideration of the meaning of "remission of sins." A Catholic participant observed that the primary element in baptism is the giving of the Spirit, carrying with it the infusion of grace resulting in the remission of sins. The ensuing discussion on sin in general and the state of original sin made evident the need for further study and more adequate definitions of sin. This involved a partial discussion of the Catholic penitential system and its relationship to merit and satisfaction. As might be anticipated, Lutheran participants voiced opposition to the concept of merit as suggesting that man has some claim to make upon God.

The general agreement on the nature and effect of baptism led to the Lutheran question, "On what grounds are those who are baptized in non-Catholic and non-Orthodox Churches excluded from the Roman Catholic sacraments?" Catholics responded that while this question has not been finally solved, especially in view of exceptions made in the Vatican Council's decree on the Oriental Churches with respect to the Orthodox, that the question was broader than that of recognition of the validity of Orders. In the Catholic understanding of the Eucharist, the sacrament of the Eucharist is celebrated under the authority of the local bishop and ultimately of the Bishop of Rome. Thus one who presents himself for the reception of the Sacrament of Communion is implicitly acknowledging the authority of the Bishop of Rome.

Turning to the questions asked of Lutherans by Catholics, the emphasis of the discussions was placed on the notion of a sacrament and whether or not a clear scriptural indication of institution by Christ is essential to such a notion. An excellent contribution to the discussions was made by one of the Lutheran delegates in the form of four theses responding to the Catholic question about the power of the Church in the sacrament of Baptism and the possibility of confessional statements developing further the content of Scripture. In capsule form, the theses are 1) That the church is empowered to develop new ways of organizing itself, administering the means of grace and formulating authoritative doctrine in view of the needs of the situation in which it finds itself and faithfulness to the scriptural witness; 2) Developments cannot be dogmatically binding unless explicitly required by the scriptural witness either in itself or in confrontation with new post-biblical questions; 3) Developments which are not dogmatically binding may also be binding, though in a lesser degree, in view of not disrupting or injuring the unity of the church or the weight of pastoral and theological considerations favoring them; and 4) Dogmatically binding decisions cannot be formally declared to be infallible, irreformable or irreversible.

Although these theses can only be regarded as a private theologian's attempt to crystalize the position of his tradition, they proved most helpful for the dialogue in progress and will undoubtedly be useful in the future. Although not every Lutheran theologian would subscribe to these theses completely, they have the virtue of outlining a position in which the divergencies between Catholic and Lutheran positions are more readily seen.

Noting that no serious attempt had been made to define what is actually meant by sacrament, it was decided to devote some time to this in the next dialogue round when the topic will be "The Eucharist as Sacrifice."

The reader will note that this brief summary touches only on some of the key themes which emerged during the three-day dialogue. As in the actual dialogue, no attempt is made here to suggest that areas of agreement or disagreement were clearly delineated. Instead, the need for continuing dialogue becomes quite evident when it is recognized that there are so few areas or even terms which have yet been clearly defined. It will require many such sessions before the participants will find themselves able to translate readily from one theological idiom into another.

The problem of dialogue is complicated by the state of theological flux in each tradition. Indeed, by reason of the theological rethinking now in progress, it is possible to have a wider divergence of position on a given point between two Catholic or two Lutheran theologians than between certain spokesmen for the two traditions. For this reason, I believe that the selection of members on both sides has been particularly happy. In addition to the fact that specialists in theology, scripture, liturgy, patristics and church law are included, there is a broad spectrum of personal outlook represented. It might be easier to define positions if each side spoke from a single viewpoint, but such a dialogue would be a poor representation of the church as it really is in all its diversity.

The conversations are carried out wtih the utmost good will and sincerity on each side. And if progress at this point is scarcely discernible, the very fact of these meetings and their continuation is a significant sign of the Holy Spirit working reconciliation among the people of God.

JOINT STATEMENT

by

BISHOP T. AUSTIN MURPHY and DR. PAUL C. EMPIE

The series of theological conversations in which we are engaged continue to be exceedingly fruitful. We were reasonably certain that the teachings of our respective traditions regarding baptism are in substantial agreement, and this opinion has been confirmed at this meeting.

At the same time, discussions dealing with several aspects of the subject brought to light the fact that although at times we use the same words with somewhat different meanings, we also upon occasion have quite different ways of saying the same things. It has been especially interesting to discover that we have common problems related to the development of doctrine in this and other theological areas, and a comparison of approaches to the solution of these problems has been mutually useful. Some points of misunderstanding have been clarified in the process.

We will be examining subjects in future meetings which present greater difficulties, but are encouraged to proceed in the knowledge that the conversations held thus far have deepened mutual understanding and respect while strengthening the bonds of brotherly affection.

PARTICIPANTS

Catholics:

The Most Rev. T. Austin Murphy, Auxiliary Bishop of Baltimore, Maryland

The Very Rev. Msgr. Joseph W. Baker, Vice-Chairman of the Ecumenical Commission of the Archdiocese of St. Louis, Missouri

The Very Rev. Msgr. William W. Baum, Executive Director, Bishops' Commission for Ecumenical Affairs, Washington, D.C.

The Rev. Raymond Brown, S.S., Professor of Sacred Scripture, St. Mary Seminary, Baltimore, Maryland

The Rev. Walter Burghardt, S.J., Professor of Patristics, Woodstock College, Woodstock, Maryland

The Rev. Godfrey Diekmann, O.S.B., Professor of Patristics, St. John Abbey, Collegeville, Minnesota

Professor James F. McCue, School of Religion, University of Iowa, Iowa City, Iowa

Lutherans:

Dr. Kent S. Knutson, Professor of Systematic Theology, Luther Theological Seminary, St. Paul, Minnesota

Dr. Fred Kramer, Professor of Dogmatic Theology, Concordia Seminary, Springfield, Illinois

Dr. George Lindbeck, Professor of Historical Theology, Yale Divinity School, Yale University, New Haven, Connecticut

Dr. Arthur Piepkorn, Professor of Systematic Theology, Concordia Seminary, St. Louis, Missouri

Dr. Warren A. Quanbeck, Professor of Systematic Theology, Luther Theological Seminary, St. Paul, Minnesota

Dr. Joseph A. Sittler, Professor of Theology, The Divinity School, University of Chicago, Chicago, Illinois

Dr. Krister Stendahl, Frothingham Professor of Biblical Studies, Harvard Divinity School, Cambridge, Massachusetts

Consultants:

Dr. Paul C. Empie, Executive Director, National Lutheran Council (U.S.A. National Committee, Lutheran World Federation), New York, N.Y.

Dr. Virgil R. Westlund, Secretary, Department of Theological Cooperation, National Lutheran Council, New York, N.Y.

III

THE EUCHARIST AS SACRIFICE

FOREWORD

This booklet is the third in a series published in connection with current theological dialogues between representatives of the U.S. Catholic Bishops' Committee for Ecumenical and Interreligious Affairs and the U.S.A. National Committee of the Lutheran World Federation. The first two publications dealt with the subjects "The Status of the Nicene Creed as Dogma" and "One Baptism for the Remission of Sins."

The topic considered in this volume is "Eucharist as Sacrifice." This subject has been one of the most thorny among the issues dividing the church and historically has been a major stumbling block in the road to Christian unity. Not only did Lutherans have questions to ask of their Roman Catholic brothers about the meaning of "sacrifice" in this connection but also the Roman Catholics sought clarity regarding the Lutherans' doctrine of "real presence." As was expected, much time was taken to clarify the meaning of words and concepts in the context of 20th century thought. Although some disagreements were not resolved, a surprising measure of agreement was discovered in the course of the discussion.

Three meetings were devoted to the examination of this issue: September 23-25, 1966 at Washington, D.C.; April 7-9, 1967 at New York, N.Y.; and September 29-October 1, 1967 at St. Louis, Missouri. The third meeting was utilized almost in its entirety for the drafting of the summary statement. Due to the extended discussion which surrounded each of the papers the reader may not find it easy to bridge the gap from them to the summary in which the agreements and disagreements are carefully and precisely stated. Two interpretive essays, one by a Lutheran participant and one by a Roman Catholic participant, should help at this point.

The participants judged the outcome of the dialogue on this particular subject to be especially significant. The fact that it occurred during the 450th anniversary year of the Protestant reformation may be another sign of a turning point from cleavage toward convergence. Because of the unusual import of the summary statement it must be re-emphasized that participants, although officially appointed by their sponsoring groups, speak only on their own behalf and their findings are in no way binding upon the groups they represent.

A remarkable spirit of Christian understanding and fellowship has developed during the course of these conversations. The group was deeply sensitive of the loss occasioned by the death of Father John Courtney Murray in August of this year. Father Murray had provided leadership in many ways, drawing upon his incomparable reservoir of scholarship and insights. His contributions were invaluable and the whole church is indebted to him for them.

> The following resolution was adopted by the group:
> "We, the members of the Theological Consultation between the U.S.A. National Committee of the Lutheran World Federation and the Catholic Bishops' Committee for Ecumenical and Interreligious Affairs, meeting in St. Louis September 29-October 1, wish to express communally our profound sense of loss in the death on August 16 of Father John Courtney Murray, S.J. Father Murray, our colleague in discussion from the beginning, impressed us and assisted us by his uncommon possession of precisely those qualities which make for fruitful dialogue and give us added hope that one day we shall achieve the unity we seek: broad theological knowledge, openness to the ideas of others, effective communication, personal warmth, and love for God and for man. It is our privilege to thank God together for giving us this remarkable example of Christian vision and courage."

Paul C. Empie
✠ T. Austin Murphy

December 15, 1967

Contents

Introduction

EUCHARIST AS SACRIFICE ROMAN CATHOLIC–LUTHERAN DIALOGUE

BY KENT S. KNUTSON

After conversations on the Nicene Creed as Dogma and on Baptism, the Roman Catholic-Lutheran Dialogue chose Eucharistic Sacrifice as a topic for discussion. This was done in the knowledge that it was a topic of greater controversy than the first two. The first conversation on the Nicene Creed had been satisfactory primarily because both traditions regard the creed as authoritative. The second conversation went equally well. Since both traditions regard baptism as a means of grace and accept each other's baptism as being valid, the exploration of many nuances of their common views provided no particular surprises or difficulties. These two successes then enabled the members to gain such confidence in each other and sufficient experience in conducting such dialogue that taking a more sensitive area seemed both possible and necessary.

Eucharistic Sacrifice seemed a suitable topic. Both traditions have great interest in and defined views of the Eucharist and each recognizes problems in its relationship to the other concerning this sacrament. Eucharistic sacrifice has been a controversial doctrine since the 16th century and at the same time affords an entree into many other concerns which are basic to an understanding of the Gospel.

The Roman Catholics came to this discussion armed with a substantial dogmatic history, a vocabulary extending back into the early church and theological commitments of long standing and broad in context. For Catholics Eucharistic Sacrifice is especially sensitive because it touches upon the heart of their faith as well as their personal piety and entire worship life. Further, they began the discussion at a time when the doctrine is under wide discussion in their own church. Roman Catholic language, emphasis and practice are undergoing re-interpretation and transition and causing not a little controversy. This presented them with both a handicap and an opportunity. Certainly it would have to be handled with great skill. Further it was rather natural that they should be puzzled by what they understood to be Lutheran views and suspicious of some Lutheran commitments.

The Lutherans, on the other hand, have a sparse and limited theological history on the precise topic of Eucharistic Sacrifice. The term Eucharistic Sacrifice had been virtually cut out of Lutheran theological vocabulary by the Apology of the Augsburg Confession, at least in the sense in which Roman Catholics would want to press the question. The term had by definition been limited to the sacrifice of prayer, praise and thanksgiving of the individuals participating in the Supper. Furthermore, the four and one-half centuries since the writing of the Lutheran Confessions had produced little further reflection. Only in the present and immediately past generation had the topic again come to the fore and then primarily in the context of conversations in the Faith and Order Movement and not in relation to Roman Catholics, a situation not altogether helpful in providing experience for discussion with Catholics. In addition, Lutherans have been sensitive of what they regard as abuses in the Catholic Church which are derived, they had often assumed, from a wrong theological perspective of sacrifice. Lutherans had clear theological commitments regarding the character of sacrament, the meaning of Christ's presence and the effect of the sacrament, but again these had been formed primarily in relation to the left wing of the Reformation.

Both traditions suffer from the burden of misinterpretation of the church's doctrine among their own people and from practices in their respective churches of which they would not approve. Both traditions, however, were aware of new possibilities for dialogue, ready to explore new language and eager to find ways for mutual learning and common expression.

The difficulties exposed required three sessions of conversation extending over one and a half years of time in comparison to single meetings in the first two topics. Related areas were often explored in detail. The whole history of thought came into play as well as much discussion regarding the influence of contemporary thought which both share. The papers presented and analyzed are available elsewhere in this publication and should be read against the background of the final statement and commentaries such as this. Since the conversations ranged so widely and often returned again and again to certain basic areas, it would be difficult if not impossible to present a clear line of development from the beginning of the conversations to the final conclusion. Consequently, in this paper we will comment on a number of issues discussed, although not all, which may provide the reader some additional insight into the nature of the discussion which led to the final statement. The conclusion of the discussion was to both parties most agreeable, considering the gravity of the problem. Although, as the final statement relates, certain areas need further exploration, the Lutherans generally understood the discussion to have achieved a breakthrough in understanding on basic Eucharistic issues.

The discussions focused on two areas—the meaning of Eucharist as Sacrifice and the meaning of presence. The final statement, therefore, adopted the format of comment on these areas. Midway in the conversation, each group withdrew to consider what it was hearing the other side say and what questions needed further exploration. As an example of the concerns expressed, these two papers by sub-committees are here submitted. It should be emphasized that they are statements made in the progress of the discussion and not at the end. The fact that a final statement was agreed shows that much progress was made following the delineation of the questions.

I
A ROMAN CATHOLIC UNDERSTANDING OF THE LUTHERAN POSITION ON EUCHARISTIC SACRIFICE

A. SACRIFICE

1. We hear a Lutheran affirmation that there are definite sacrificial elements in the Eucharistic celebration, especially insofar as it is the crucified and risen Lord who is really present in the species.

2. The concern lest the Eucharistic Sacrifice derogate from the absolute sufficiency of the sacrifice of Calvary is seen to be a common concern of both Roman Catholic and Lutheran theology.

3. The Lutheran tradition hesitates to use the terminology of "offering a victim to God," or of "offering the sacrifice of the Mass." Even more sensitive seems to be the Roman Catholic usage of the term "propitiatory" sacrifice, although the precise difficulty here has not been adequately discussed.

4. We find it difficult to understand why the expressions "offering to God," "propitiation," and "sacrifice" are more objectionable when applied to the Mass than when applied to Calvary, since the Mass is a re-presentation of Calvary by way of sacramental sign. This leads us to wonder whether the Roman Catholic theology of sign and sacramental re-presentation have been fully heard.

B. **REAL PRESENCE**

1. We appreciate and have full confidence in the Lutheran confession that, when the communicant receives the eucharistic bread and wine, he receives the true body and blood of Christ.

2. We have heard a strong emphasis on "real" presence *in usu* and within the context of an eschatological banquet.

3. We have heard the Lutheran affirmation that bread and wine are "signs" of the real presence. Yet, from our discussion of the Lutheran theology and practice of the permanent sacrament, we seriously wonder whether the relation between sign and signified is understood in the same way by the two confessions.

4. Our points of difference here can perhaps be clarified by discussing the precise manner in which eucharistic presence differs from presence in the word.

C. **CHANGE**

1. We have not heard sufficient discussion of the Lutheran concept of the change which takes place in the elements. Hence we feel that our original request for some positive affirmations on this question has not yet been adequately handled.

2. Perhaps a further discussion of the Lutheran theology and practice of reconsecration could focus the question of the nature of the change which takes place.

II
A LUTHERAN UNDERSTANDING OF THE ROMAN CATHOLIC POSITION ON THE EUCHARISTIC SACRIFICE

A. **SACRIFICE**

1. Sacrifice is a proper, an essential, and a principal category, but not the only or even necessarily the primary category, for understanding and explicating the Holy Eucharist.

2. The sacrifice of the church in the mass derives its sacrificial character and efficacy from the presence of the incarnate, suffering, and glorified Son of God in the sacrament of the altar.

3. The sacrifice of the church in the mass is not supplemen-

tary to the sacrifice of Christ upon the cross in objective redemptive efficacy.

4. The sacrifice of the church in the mass is adequately explained by describing it exteriorly as a cultic and ritual pleading before God of the benefits secured by the incarnation, life, passion, death, and exaltation of Christ and of the once-and-for-all sacrifice of the cross, and interiorly by the subjective affirmation of the sacrifice of the cross for me and by accepting its implications for my life.

5. Not discussed or inadequately discussed were the meaning of representation, atonement, propitiation, and immolation, and the contemporary implications of the pertinent Tridentine canons and decrees.

B. **PRESENCE**

1. The real (so called in distinction to a merely nominal) presence of Christ is not limited to the Holy Eucharist. Other equally real modes of presence include his presence in the midst of his church, in his word read and proclaimed, in the person of the ministers of the sacraments, and in the individual members of the people of God.

2. Christ's real presence in the Holy Eucharist is unique, but not qualitatively better, or quantitatively greater, than his presence according to other modes. Its uniqueness consists in this that the holy eucharist provides the point of encounter where God makes his incarnate Son as victim accessible to the members of the people of God to eat, to drink, and to offer to the Father, and that the holy eucharist produces an object for their adoration and worship during and after the liturgical action.

C. **CHANGE**

1. The change that is effected in the elements of the holy eucharist is (a) irreversible and (b) total, in that the bread and wine as substances are so completely replaced by the body and the blood of Christ that what remains is not, and is not rightly called, bread and wine.

2. Not discussed or inadequately discussed were the meaning of consecration, sacramental sign, and transubstantiation.

III
COMMENTS ON PARTICULAR ISSUES

We will explore nine points briefly from the point of view of the original Lutheran misgivings and a Lutheran interpretation of the Catholic reply.

1. Propitiatory Sacrifice

Lutherans by tradition have confined the use of this term to Christ's salvatory work. When it is used to describe the Mass it has often meant to Lutherans that the Mass became a new work which adds to Calvary and which pictures Christ's work as appeasement of an angry God. Discussion revealed that Catholics use the word sacrifice to designate the entire work of Christ, although it is not to be regarded as the exclusive way of doing so. The word sacrifice thus includes God's suffering on behalf of man, the cost of God in the work of redemption, the self-giving love of God and the offering of the Son to the Father. It is not a word wedded exclusively to an Anselmian understanding of the atonement. The word sacrifice has a much older tradition than this explication of the atonement and is meant to incorporate all the rich implications and interpretations of the atonement found in the Scriptures.

When the adjective propitiatory is added it signals the emphasis of the sacrifice as being *for you*, for men. The propitiatory sacrifice is God's act for men through his Son and at the same time Christ's work for man to the Father. The word may also designate Christ's involvement in man's sin, his obedience to the Father, his pleas to God for mercy for man, and his complete dependency upon the Father. Sacrifice is then understood not only in relation to the wrath of God but also an appeal to his mercy. With this Lutherans can have no quarrel although further discussion on nature of the atonement itself would be helpful. To Lutherans ears, propitiatory sacrifice is nearly synonymous with Christ's redemptive work or saving work of grace.

2. The Mass as Sacrifice

Roman Catholics have called the Mass a sacrifice. They mean by this that the Eucharist is a gracious act in which God makes present and communicates this propitiatory sacrifice for man. This is not a new, or different sacrifice but the same sacrifice of Calvary. The Mass is properly, and necessarily, called sacrifice because the Christ who is the sacrifice is present in the Supper. Sacrificial language, such as "given for you" and "shed for you," is used in the Words of Institution, and the whole understanding of the character of God's work for man is brought into focus in this cultic act which communicates God's grace to man. Lutherans agree when the Mass is understood in this way.

3. The Relation of the Sacrifice of the Mass to Calvary

Lutherans have often understood Roman Catholics to say that the Mass adds to Calvary, is a "re-doing" of Calvary and by this have implied that the one sacrifice of Christ is defective and incomplete. Catholics agree that some of the language used in the 16th century by Catholics could be so interpreted. Lutherans agree that it was this Catholic understanding of the Eucharist which brought about the strenuous objection by Luther and the Lutheran Confessions. Now we can agree that this is not what Roman Catholics intend to say. The sacrifice of Christ is complete and unalterable and cannot be supplemented or completed by any subsequent action. Rather, that sacrifice, complete in itself, is made present, made effective and the benefits communicated in the Eucharist.

Catholics have used the word "re-presentation," not in the sense of doing again, but in the sense of "presenting again." Lutherans can agree wholeheartedly. Lutherans have sometimes used the term "actualize" to communicate the same understanding. It was not concluded, however, that any available word was either necessary or completely definitive for a common understanding. It was agreed that the unrepeatable sacrifice which *was*, now *is* in the Eucharist. There is therefore a continuing work of Christ in the sense that he continues to plead before the Father and continues to communicate to man his work of redemption.

4. The Phrase "Offer up the victim to God"

This phrase is both familiar and meaningful to Roman Catholics. It is a foreign phrase to Lutherans and has implied for them that Christ is still suffering, has not yet been exalted and must be sacrificed again for the sins of the world. Roman Catholics do not understand the phrase in this sense. Rather they mean that the church as the body of Christ identifies itself with Christ's sacrifice and pleads to God for mercy on the basis of the one sacrifice of Christ. The Mass is then understood not only as a sacrifice of prayer, praise and thanksgiving but also as a redemptive act which offers up the completed work of Christ. This is not an offering to an angry God but a plea to God to remember his own mercy. This mercy is not based upon man's act of celebrating the Eucharist but upon God's own action in his Son. This grace, however, is effectively communicated to man only when man says yes to this mercy. Lutherans may not prefer this language and may continue to point out the dangers of misinterpretation in it but cannot disagree with this intended understanding.

5. The Centrality of the Eucharist

Lutherans have sometimes understood the Roman Catholic description of the Eucharist as the "heart of the faith" and the "central act of grace" as meaning that there are no other means of grace or that the Eucharist offers a "qualitatively better" or "quantitatively more" grace than other sacraments or the proclamation of the Word. In the conversations Lutherans understood the Catholics to agree that there are "manifold" presences of God and therefore manifold acts of grace. Lutherans could agree that the Eucharist is a central act in the life of the church and not in any way to be de-emphasized but probably will continue to be more comfortable with a broader context and assign the term "central" to the Word of God with the Eucharist understood as a full, dramatic and objective expression of the Gospel.

6. Change

The word change occasioned much discussion. Lutherans have been unhappy with this word since it raised for them suspicions regarding the meaning of the doctrine of transubstantiation. Catholics have said consistently that in appearance the bread remains bread and the wine remains wine but that at the same time they become the body and blood. They have further interpreted this in the Aristotelian categories of accidents and substance. That is, it is only the appearance or accidents of bread and wine which remains and the substance changes. Lutherans can agree that a change occurs in the sense that the bread and wine are no longer ordinary bread and wine, that is, they do not now exist for the singular purpose of sustaining the body. In the Eucharist they become signs of the presence of our Lord and effectively communicate that presence. There is a change in the sign character of the bread and wine. Lutherans have always been reluctant to use the Aristotelian categories of accidents and substance to communicate this understanding of change, although they have in the past commonly used "substantive" language to emphasize the wholeness and "realness" of the presence. Transubstantiation has meant to Lutherans an attempt to "explain" the presence, to make it rational and therefore believable. Catholics insist that the intention of this language is to emphasize the mystery of the presence and not to "explain" the presence. Lutherans have not objected to transubstantiation as a speculative suggestion but have not wanted to align themselves with a single philosophical language and its attendant dangers. Catholics are bound to this language but are presently engaged in discussions among themselves as to its usefulness and the implications of its past meaning. Both Lutherans and Catholics agree that "substantialist" language is less useful in our contemporary context than it apparently was in past history. Whatever it communicated to past generations, it no longer carries the same communicative power and is even sometimes so misleading, when not properly interpreted, as to distort the understanding of the mystery of the presence. Lutherans will admit to the use of the word "change" in the context of this discussion. The doctrine of transubstantiation needs further clarification before much more can be said.

7. Presence

Lutherans were surprised to hear that Roman Catholics were suspicious of the Lutheran commitment to the "real presence." The term "real presence" no longer has the same weight as it once did. It is not an exclusive Lutheran term, as many Lutherans once thought, and is redundant. Lutherans were able, or so it was their understanding, to communicate their full commitment to the doctrine that the crucified and risen Lord is wholly, truly and personally present in both his human and divine natures in the sacrament. He is not present only "spiritually" or "in memory" or "merely" symbolically. Lutherans see no difference of emphasis or understanding at this point.

Roman Catholics had been led to believe that the Lutheran concept of the presence was only "in usu," that is, only in the eating and drinking. Lutherans were happy to correct this misunderstanding and articulate their belief that the Lord is present in the whole Eucharistic action, both before and after the eating and drinking. No extended discussion took place concerning the moment of the beginning of this presence. Lutherans may not have complete clarity concerning this among themselves. Generally Lutherans have not specified any such moment but have emphasized the presence in the whole action.

8. Sign

It was agreed by both groups that the language of sign is a useful way to speak of the character of the sacrament. A sign or symbol is never "merely" such but a sacramental sign is always effective, it always communicates what it promises. Both agree that it is proper to speak of the bread and the wine as signs of our Lord's presence. Lutherans emphasize the communal aspect of the Supper. The whole eucharistic action which includes the coming together of the faithful, the preaching of the word, the reading of the Words of Institution, the liturgical service, and the eating and drinking are integral parts of the sign. The sign is the action of the whole service. Catholics are also eager to emphasize the meal character of the sacrament, but Lutherans understood the Catholics to favor the central importance of the elements which makes possible eucharistic celebration without a congregation and the cult of adoration of the host.

9. The Permanency of the Presence

Much discussion centered upon the "ending" of the presence and concentrated upon the Roman Catholic practice of reserving the host. Lutherans have the custom of reverently removing the unused bread from the altar and storing it for use at the next Eucharist. Catholics retain the host upon the altar and consider it an object for adoration. With their understanding of sign as involving the whole of the eucharistic action and thus not placing exclusive focus on the elements themselves, Lutherans have considered the sign to be concluded with the end of the service, although some Lutherans have extended the time of the service to include the carrying of the bread and wine to the sick.

This matter was not successfully concluded and more discussion is needed. Some progress was made when several of the Catholic representatives were willing to speak of the presence of the host on the altar as an extension of the eucharistic action. The ending of the presence comes, for them, when all the elements are consumed, and the "action" continues until that happens. Whether this is a satisfactory approach to the problem is not yet clear.

Certain questions relating to the Eucharist did not receive sufficient treatment. Such matters as other aspects of the Eucharist, the number of sacraments, the effect of the sacrament, frequency of the sacrament, and admission to the sacrament, therefore, could not receive comment in a final statement. The next discussions will consider the topic Intercommunion which will touch on these matters and in addition undoubtedly will raise the question of what constitutes a valid ministry.

Lutherans are grateful for the patience and good will of the Roman Catholics as well as their candor and skill. We look forward to further discussion together.

FROM POSITION PAPERS TO FINAL STATEMENT

By Harry J. McSorley, C.S.P.

A JOYOUS sense of accomplishment prevailed among the participants in the Lutheran-Roman Catholic Theological Consultation when they adjourned on Sunday, October 1, 1967 in St. Louis. The group realized that not all aspects of the theme had been explored. They recognized that their joint statement signified neither an advance in the realm of theoretical renewal nor an original contribution to liturgical or pastoral practice. The participants were gratefully aware, nevertheless, that at no time since the Reformation have representative Lutheran and Catholic Christians been able to speak with such unanimity on the meaning of the Lord's Supper.

The first of the three long weekends devoted to working sessions was held in Washington, D.C. from Friday morning, September 23 to Sunday afternoon, September 25, 1966. Originally entitled "The Eucharist as Sacrifice," the conversation theme was soon widened, as we shall note, to include a treatment of the presence of Christ in the sacrament.

All of Friday morning was given to discussion of Prof. Bertil Gärtner's position paper on the sacrificial aspects of the Eucharist in the New Testament. All agreed that the death of Jesus is conceived by the New Testament in sacrificial terms and that even in the words of institution of the Eucharist and in I Cor. 10 and 11 there is an element of sacrificial language. Opinions differed among both Lutherans and Catholics as to how conscious the early Christians were of the sacrificial dimension of the Lord's Supper and to what extent this dimension was central for them. The failure of the Epistle to the Hebrews explicitly to mention the Eucharist when dealing with the sacrifice of Jesus was cited as a warning against a premature conclusion that the Eucharist was conceived as a sacrifice in the New Testament.

None of the participants questioned that the sacrificial interpretation of the Eucharist became dominant in the church long before the Reformation. It was likewise agreed that this interpretation was not a development *ex nihilo*. But the question remained unanswered as to why such strong biblical emphases as the eschatological and the banquet-character of the Eucharist did not develop as clearly as the sacrificial aspect.

On Friday afternoon the discussion centered on the position papers of Father Walter Burghardt and Prof. James McCue. Much attention was given to Father Burghardt's finding that, for the Fathers (this is always understood as "some of the Fathers"), the Eucharist was not only a sacrifice of praise and thanksgiving to God for His measureless benefits but also an act of propitiation effective for the living and the dead.

In response to questioning about the meaning of propitiation, Father Burghardt explained that he used the term simply to convey the belief of the Fathers—at least from the time of Cyprian and Origen—that the Eucharist was a sacrifice that was of advantage to the living and the dead. Specifically it was regarded as advantageous with reference to forgiveness of sin and in general with reference to union with God. A Lutheran participant noted that, at least as far as the living were concerned, this would give a propitiatory dimension to both Lutheran and Catholic views of the Eucharist.

This last observation illustrated an elementary but important principle of ecumenical methodology. On so many issues Christians have emotionally reacted against slogans or characteristic phraseology of other Christians without giving evidence that they understood the meaning attached to this language by those who used it. "Faith and grace alone," "scripture alone," "the Eucharist is a propitiatory sacrifice" are examples of such traditionally divisive slogans. When one asks: What do you *mean* when you say that we are justified by faith alone or that the Mass is a propitiatory sacrifice?, one often finds a much greater possibility of agreement than existed when one operated on the pre-ecumenical level of simply opposing one emotion-laden slogan to another.

On the question under discussion, it was pointed out by some of the Catholic participants that we have no evidence for supposing that the Council of Trent, in speaking of the Mass as a propitiatory sacrifice, intended anything essentially different from what the Fathers of the Church held. A Lutheran colleague added that it would also be incorrect to interpret the Fathers' thought on propitiation against the background of the much later thinking of Anselm and Calvin on atonement as a kind of transaction in which God's honor is satisfied or in which a punishment is somehow substituted.

In the discussion, Father Burghardt noted that in the post-Nicene period it was frequently and emphatically affirmed that one who has died, who has fallen asleep in Christ, is helped by the eucharistic sacrifice. Nevertheless, he added, there is no clear patristic theology as to the precise way in which the Eucharist is advantageous to the departed faithful.

Another area where patristic theology is unclear, Father Burghardt observed, concerns the relationship between the sacrifice of Christ—which all of the Fathers regarded as once-for-all, all-sufficient, unrepeatable—and the eucharistic sacrifice which all regarded as effective and of advantage because of its connection with Christ's sacrifice. To be sure, they did not regard the Eucharist simply as a mental recollection of past saving events. For many of the Fathers *anamnesis* or memorial involved a mysterious making-present of the once-for-all event of salvation. Cyprian, Chrysostom and several of the Eastern Fathers were among those who clearly saw the problem, but they did not offer satisfactory explanations. To the present day Catholic theologians have been grappling with the problem of the one sacrifice and the many Masses.

In the discussion of Prof. McCue's paper the author pointed out that unlike the words "table" and "chair," "sacrifice" is a term which is rich and diverse in meaning and which has not been carefully defined by Christian tradition. Furthermore, there seems to have been very little attempt in the sixteenth century, even at Trent, to clarify its meaning. A Catholic participant suggested that it is impossible to get a clear definition of what sacrifice means in the Eucharist or in Christ's self-offering because we are here facing a mystery which always escapes definition. Nevertheless it could happen that by rejecting the notion of sacrifice in connection with the Eucharist one might be rejecting the real mystery that is involved.

An intra-Catholic discussion emerged when one participant, granting the possibility that Luther was reacting against the Mass because it seemed to him to be just another "human work," suggested that Trent still did not find that Luther's position represented what it understood by the Mass as sacrifice. Against this view it was urged that Trent's primary concern was not to make definitive judgments about the orthodoxy of Luther or any of the other reformers on particular points of doctrine. This would have required too much painstaking research into their numerous writings. Works of the reformers were examined, to be sure, but with an eye to ruling out erroneous doctrinal tendencies so as to give guidance to Catholic pastors and teachers.

Questioning one of the earlier affirmations about Trent's understanding of propitiation, a Lutheran theologian contended that since Anselmian theology was dominant in the sixteenth century, Trent's references to the Mass as a "propitiatory sacrifice" necessarily involved the notion of placating an angry Deity. It was claimed that this represented a real collision with Luther's thinking. A Catholic theologian would wish to make several observations here: (1) the Anselmian theory of satisfaction, which has been widely accepted by Catholic theologians, underwent significant modifications in scholastic theology; (2) the idea that redemption or propitiation necessarily involves the placating of an angry God is not essential to this theory; it can also be explained in terms of forgiveness of sins, reconciliation with God, reparation for the glory of which sin has deprived God, or satisfaction for guilt. (cf. K. Rahner, "Redemption," "Satisfaction, Theories Of" in: *Theological Dictionary* [New York, 1965], pp. 423 f.; T. G. Tappert, ed. *Cook of Concord* [Philadelphia, 1959], p. 252, *Apology*, XXIV, n. 19); (3) the magisterium of the Church has made use of the Anselmian theory but has never made it dogmatically binding; (4) the question as to whether the Mass is the re-presentation or the making contemporaneous of the once-for-all sacrifice of our redemption is related to but not dependent on one's theological explanation of the meaning of that one-for-all sacrifice.

One of the break-through moments of the discussion, in this observer's judgment, came at the end of the afternoon when the Lutheran and Catholic brethren found basically acceptable the explanation by K. Rahner of the sacrificial dimension of the Mass that was cited in Prof. McCue's paper (notes 44 and 45).

On Friday evening the papers of Prof. Knutson and Father Ambrogi were discussed. A Lutheran spokesman said in response to a question raised by Father Ambrogi's paper that Lutherans can fully agree with the Catholic understanding of the mediation of salvation through created means: through the humanity of the glorified Christ, through the Church and through the sacraments.

A Catholic participant questioned Father Ambrogi's statement that the doctrine of the real presence is at the heart of the Lutheran-Catholic controversy on eucharistic sacrifice. He pointed out that Luther never claimed that the doctrine of transubstantiation was heretical. Luther, he continued, while never questioning the true, substantial presence of the body and blood of Christ in the sacrament, did object to the idea that transubstantiation was the only conceptual vehicle for affirming the real presence. A Lutheran recalled Luther's statement that if he had to choose between Zwingli's view and transubstantiation, it would have to be transubstantiation.

The raising of the question of the real presence of Christ in the sacrament led eventually to a widening of the initial topic. This explains why the joint statement no longer bears the original title: "The Eucharist as Sacrifice," but: "The Eucharist: A Lutheran-Roman Catholic Statement." One happy result of the expansion of the theme as far as Catholics are concerned is that the statement hopefully will convey to Catholic priests and laity that Lutherans believe just as firmly as Catholics in the reality of Christ's presence in the sacrament. The general Catholic consciousness (and this is by no means confined to the laity!) has for too long imagined that "the Protestants" only believe in a symbolic presence of Christ in the eucharist, or "the Protestants" don't believe in the real presence. As far as the Lutheran tradition is concerned nothing could be farther from the truth. In the light of the Faith and Order discussions of the World Council of Churches during the past thirty years—which are happily reflected in the Principles of the Consultation on Church Union—the traditional Catholic generalizations about "the Protestant" view of the eucharist prove to be pitifully inadequate descriptions of the eucharistic belief of non-Lutheran Protestant churches as well.

With reference to Prof. Knutson's paper, a Lutheran colleague agreed that contemporary Lutherans are uncomfortable with the term "change" in connection with the bread and wine used in the liturgy. He suggested, however, that on this point Lutherans were alienated from their own tradition and illustrated this by four items of historical evidence.

In rejecting the doctrine of transubstantiation, observed one of the Catholic participants, the Lutheran Confessions thought this doctrine implied an annihilation or a destruction of the natural substance of bread and wine. Such a view was entertained by certain Scholastic theologians, he added, but is surely not implied in Trent's definition. Catholic theologians today insist that all the natural or physical properties of the bread and wine remain unaffected by the sacramental change which is, to be sure, a change that touches the deepest meaning of the bread and wine and should thus be called an ontological change.

Attention shifted to the veneration of the reserved sacrament in the Catholic tradition. A Catholic participant predicted that the current liturgical renewal would lead to the placing of devotion to Christ in the reserved sacrament on a secondary level of significance. Another Catholic colleague granted that there has perhaps been an undue emphasis on this aspect of the meaning of the sacrament at the expense of more important aspects. He added, however, that one could not simply say that the traditional devotion as such was wrong or invalid.

The Lutheran brethren were asked, in turn, if they ought not re-examine their own ambiguous tradition in regard to their understanding of and practical attitude toward the consecrated elements which remain after the service—an ambiguity that goes back to a difference between Luther and Melanchthon. As can be seen from the joint statement, the question of the abiding presence of Christ in the sacrament after the eucharistic celebration has been completed was still unresolved at the conclusion of our discussions. This was the only area of our theme where substantial agreement was not reached.

Are we at an impasse here? The writer of this essay does not think so. This is not the place to develop fully the rapprochement I have in mind. I believe however, that the following points will serve as some of the ingredients that will help prepare an acceptable solution to the problem of the reserved sacrament: (1) Eastern Orthodox Christianity, whose doctrinal and liturgical integrity concerning the eucharist has never been questioned by the Roman Church, even though it has practiced reservation of the sacrament for the sick, has not developed a cult of the reserved sacrament. (2) Ways other than reservation—immediate consumption of all consecrated elements, burning, pouring into the ground, burial, etc.—have historically served to manifest belief that the consecrated elements were no longer ordinary bread and wine and were thus to be treated reverently (cf. J. Jungmann, *The Mass of the Roman Rite*, Vol. II [New York, 1955], pp. 406-419). (3) In agreement with the Catholic and Orthodox practice, certain areas of the Lutheran tradition, such as the Church of Sweden, explicity provide in their liturgical books for a reverent reservation of the consecrated elements that remain after the service. These elements may be administered to the sick without repeating the words of institution, thus indicating belief that the body and blood of Christ remains present beneath the elements even after the service. (4) The Council of Trent defended the legitimacy of adoring Christ in the sacrament, but did not make such devotion mandatory (cf. Denzinger-Schönmetzer, *Enchiridion Symbolorum*, ed. 33 [Freiburg, 1965], nn. 1643 f. and 1656); to have done so would have been to rebuke the divergent Orthodox custom, something that was far from Trent's intention. (5) During the very lengthy discussion on the perduring presence of the Lord under the consecrated elements a distinction was made between the *necessity* of reserving the sacrament and the legitimate *possibility* of doing so. The Catholic participants agreed that it would be impossible to insist on the necessity of reservation. They nevertheless defended the possibility not only of reserving but also of legitimately and meaningfully venerating the reserved sacrament. This possibility has, of course, been actualized during a great part of the Catholic Church's history.

Christian freedom should surely play a decisive role in helping Catholics and Lutherans live in communion despite divergence of practice concerning the reservation or non-reservation of the sacrament. As the *Decree on Ecumenism* states (n. 4), following an important insight of St. Augustine: "While preserving unity in essentials, let all members of the Church . . . preserve a proper freedom in the various forms of spiritual life and discipline, in the varieties of liturgical rites, and even in the theological elaborations of revealed truth. In all things let charity prevail." This liberty is seen as resulting in an "ever richer expression to the authentic catholicity and apostolicity of the Church."

All of Saturday was given to general discussion of the papers of the previous day. Considerable time was spent on the three themes "sacrifice," "presence" and "change" (of the elements). There was no disagreement by any of the participants that it was legitimate to use these terms in referring to the Lord's Supper. Some of the Lutheran participants wished to know, however, why it was that these particular aspects of the Eucharist—which are not stressed in the New Testament accounts—should have received such stress in the later theology and life of the Church. Further, why were other aspects of the eucharist that are clearly found in the New Testament accounts—its eschatological dimension, its meal character—relatively understressed in the later tradition? Both groups agreed that over-concentration on one or more elements of the Lord's Supper detracts from the fullness of the sacrament. All likewise agreed that all aspects of the eucharist—personal as well as communal benefits; word as well as sacrament; the presence of Christ primarily in order to be received, with adoration a consequence, not the purpose of the presence; making-present of the once-for-all sacrifice of the past as well as the expectation of the coming of the Lord; service to God as well as to man—all of these must be integrated if preaching, teaching and Christian life are to be integral.

On Saturday evening members of each group met to formulate statements indicating what they had understood the other group to have been saying during the previous two days. These statements are reproduced in Prof. Knutson's interpretative paper. The technique proved to be most useful in pin-pointing areas of possible misunderstanding.

In the Sunday session the group mutually examined the statements prepared the previous evening. Each side was able to recognize that there had been some deficiencies in the way its position had been stated, and helpful clarifications were made. Due to lack of time it was agreed that the next meeting—scheduled for New York City, April 7-9, 1967—continue the task of examining certain points which had been insufficiently discussed. Five of the participants agreed to prepare papers to help clarify the notions of sacramental sign, consecration, change and propitiation, as well as to provide some historical background for the development of the concept of transubstantiation. These papers are also published in this volume.

During the New York meeting considerable progress toward agreement was made. The application of a basic but important methodological principle at several junctures helped the New York discussions to move more positively toward consensus than was the case in Washington. The principle simply involves recognition of the distinction (real though not always clear) between a Church's binding dogmatic confessional affirmations or definitions and theological reflections on, and explicitations and systematizations of those ecclesially binding affirmations.

Christians are not in full communion when they disagree on binding dogmas of faith. It is one of the tasks of the ecumenical theological dialogue to overcome such dogmatic disunity between Churches. But this is not to say that theological unity must be sought. A variety of theologies can legitimately be developed within the one confession of faith. Consequently, when the ecumenical theologian finds himself in disagreement with a theologian of another tradition, he must ask himself: is his theological affirmation clearly incompatible with my Church's confession of faith, or can it be embraced as a legitimate theological viewpoint within the catholic unity of the Church?

One of the participants mentioned some methodological observations made by Karl Rahner that proved to be helpful in the discussions. Rahner, whom no one has accused of failing to see theological differences, suggests "that a too neurotic fear of being perhaps 'really' in agreement 'in depth' could disrupt the unity which is possible." "Such fears" he adds "then give rise to those strange efforts . . . to find new sets of ever more subtle formulae and nuances so as to prove the existence of mutual dissent. . . . To have the right to live in separate Churches, one would have to be sure . . . that one is clearly in disagreement about the truth. It is not enough not to be quite sure of being really in agreement, or of what the other exactly means or of having understood him quite correctly" (Theological Investigations, vol. IV [Helicon: Baltimore, 1966], p. 196).

The outcome of the New York meeting was the appointment of Prof. Lindbeck and Father McSorley to prepare the draft of a possible joint statement which would bring together whatever consensus had been reached in the Washington and New York meetings. This two-man drafting team met in New Haven, Connecticut July 30-August 1, 1967 and prepared the draft that was discussed by the entire consultation in St. Louis on September 29-October 1, 1967.

The original draft was carefully evaluated in general discussions at St. Louis. The participants then separated into two Catholic-Lutheran committees which devoted themselves for a full day to detailed examination and modification of the respective parts of the statement: the eucharist as sacrifice and the presence of Christ in the sacrament. All modifications were explained, discussed and evaluated in final joint sessions. A rough copy of the joint statement finally emerged at the close of the meeting on Sunday, October 1.

A four-man Drafting Committee was assigned the task of putting the joint statement into final form. This committee met in New York on Saturday, October 10. The resulting statement was then submitted to all the members of the consultation for their approval or suggestions for modifications. The suggested "modi" were evaluated and incorporated—if judged acceptable—into the final version of the joint statement prepared by the Drafting Committee (Lindbeck, Quanbeck, Burghardt and McSorley) at its meeting in New York on November 3, 1967.

This sketch of the genesis of our joint statement on the Lord's Supper will hopefully assist the reader in placing the published papers in the larger context of the discussions and of the critical process which led to the joint statement.

All of the discussions were conducted in an atmosphere of prayer in the name of God the Father, Son and Holy Spirit, who enabled us to experience our brotherhood as well as the unmistakable call to deeper expression and realization of that brotherhood in one holy communion. For this we are all deeply grateful and hopeful as we move to our next dialogue: The Problem of Intercommunion.

THE EUCHARIST AS SACRIFICE IN THE NEW TESTAMENT

By Bertil E. Gartner

THERE is no doubt that the eucharist in the New Testament is closely related to the idea of the death of Christ as a sacrifice. It is Christ's once-for-all death, which the Lord's Supper commemorates. Therefore his sacrifice on the cross is one of the keys to understand the eucharist. The offering motif is indissolubly connected with the eucharist, since Christ is present in the eucharist not only as the risen and living Son of God but also as the Son put to death for the sins of men.

This contribution to the discussion is an attempt to point to some main aspects of the relation between the eucharist and the redeeming act of Christ. It is not my intention to present my own ideas of the relation, but to sum up what seems to be the opinion accepted by many exegetes. To a certain extent, of course, the selection of the points of view and the stressing of some aspects show my own way of thinking.

In this context, I do not find it necessary to discuss all the different formcritical analyses of the pericopes describing the institution of the Lord's Supper, the complicated problems concerning the date of the Last Supper, the relation between the eucharist and the *agape*-meal etc., but rather try to understand the eucharistic texts as they now exist in the New Testament as the basis of the Church's interpretation of the eucharist. It is impossible to state that there is only one fixed theology of the eucharist in the New Testament, one *doctrina*, since the different New Testament traditions reflect a number of perspectives, expressing the theological variety which characterized the New Testament church. The emphasis of this paper will be laid on the sacrificial aspect of the eucharist.

1) The words of institution in all the four versions are stamped by the relation between the eucharist as a meal and the death of Jesus as a sacrifice. The explicatory words

of Jesus at the distribution of the bread and the wine belong to the traditional cult terminology: "This is my *blood* of the covenant, which is *poured out for* many," Mk. 14:24; "which is *poured out for* many for the forgiveness of sins," Mt. 26:28; "This is my *body* which is *given for* you," Lk. 22:19, cf. 1 Cor. 11:24. The reference to the death of Jesus (the broken body, the outpoured blood) also contains a characterization of it as a substitute death, an atonement for sins (the formula "for you"). Jesus interpeted the bread and the wine as his body and blood, anticipating his death on the cross. The expression "body and blood" is a reflection of the usual separation of the body and blood of the animals offered in the temple. This shows that Jesus intended his own death to be a sacrifice to God and the eucharistic eating and drinking to be a share in the fruits of the sacrifice.

I am inclined to understand John 6 as the fourth evangelist's explanation of the eucharist. Even if in this chapter other aspects of the eucharist dominate, it is clear that the idea of Jesus' death as a sacrifice is behind the expressions. The terms "bread," "eat," "drink," "blood," manifest that in John's theology as well the eucharist is understood in relation to the atoning death of Jesus. (See particularly 6:53-58, and "the bread which I shall give for the life of the world is my flesh," 6:51.)

2) If there is a connection between the words of institution and the death of Jesus as a sacrifice, we must discuss the character of the sacrifice. This leads us to a complicated complex of ideas, which I only can hint at in this survey. The background of the sacrifice commemorated in the eucharist is formed first of all by the slaughtering of the Passover lamb in the temple as it is prescribed in the Old Testament and further explained by later Jewish teachers. Secondly, it is necessary to refer to the expiatory sacrifices, particularly the sacrifice on the Day of Atonement. Thirdly, it must be mentioned that theologians often have stressed that the death of Jesus may not be considered only as a propitiatory sacrifice, but also as a sacrifice of obedience, and it could be added that the death was only one part of this sacrifice since the whole life of Jesus—the fact of incarnation—was a sacrifice. It is difficult, (if even possible), to distinguish between these three aspects of the sacrifice of Christ, but we can

speak about emphasis, and no doubt the first two are the most important ones.

It has been discussed whether or not we should understand the institution of the Lord's Supper within the compass of the Jewish Passover liturgy. As far as I can understand, the Passover feast ideology is the only possible background of the eucharist, and it is out of this sphere of ideas, the context of the Passover celebration, that the eucharist of the Early Church grew. If we accept the Jewish Passover as the ideological background for the Last Supper, the question could be raised why the words of institution so strongly emphasize the atonement motif of Jesus' death, although in the Passover Haggada the slaughtered lamb never was interpreted in terms of a propitiatory sacrifice. As an answer to the question one has referred to the fact that the blood of the killed Passover lambs on the night of the Exodus had a redeeming character according to Jewish explanations. It protected the Israelite families against death and destruction, Ex. 12. The blood of the slaughtered Passover lambs was not sprinkled on the corner of the altar in the temple at Jesus' time, and thus did not mean a propitiation. But the words of institution did not refer to the offered lambs in the temple, but to the Exodus lambs, whose killing signified salvation and the establishing of the covenant. Jesus' death as a sacrifice was the counterpart to the death of the Exodus lambs and the Exodus covenant.

It has also been suggested that the best explanation of the expression "my blood of the covenant" in the words of institution is to refer to Ex. 24:8 "And Moses took the blood and sprinkled it on the people and said: Behold the *blood of the covenant* which the Lord has made with you in accordance with all these words." (The version of Targum Onkelos comes closer to the words of Jesus: "Behold *this is the blood* of the covenant.") Here we find all the most important elements in the eucharistic texts—the blood, the covenant, the sacrifice, the application to the people. In the Exodus passage there are two more significant moments which have bearing on the interpretation of the eucharist, namely that the blood of the peace offering was sprinkled on the people and that the people ate the sacrifice, v. 11. Both of these moments were re-interpreted or neglected by the Jewish rabbis, since it was impossible according to their understanding of the offering rules to sprinkle the blood of a peace offering on the people and to let the people eat the sacrifice. The Exodus passage is also unique in the Old Testament as to these two moments. In the words of institution the idea of the slaughtered Passover lamb has been combined with the Exodus text in order to state that the death of Jesus and the partaking of the sacrifice in the eucharist are extraordinary in that the sacrifice is the Son of God. The true Passover lamb—Jesus—was slaughtered as a redeeming sacrifice. His shed blood and his broken body were given to the people of the new covenant so that they could eat and drink and have a share in the fruits of his sacrifice. Bread and wine were the substitute for the sacrifice once for all but also a "vehicle" of the presence of the offer. According to Jewish rules such a sacrifice or sin-offering could not be eaten but had to be burnt "outside the camp." (Lev. 4:21, Hebr. 13:10-12). But "in Christ" the one sacrifice has to be eaten, giving the people of the new covenant a share in the redemption, brought about by the sacrifice, and a share in the redeemer. (1 Cor. 10:16-21). The expression "Those who eat the sacrifices are partners in the altar," 1 Cor. 10:18, does not mean in this context that they are "partners" in the redemptive action of Christ, (as if Christ could be offered again), but they are "partner" in the fruits of Christ's sacrifice.

As regards the combination of the Passover lamb and the idea of Jesus' atoning death in the words of institution, we may also remember that a number of Christological passages in the New Testament show that it was a common interpretation in the Early Church to put together the conceptions of the Suffering Servant (Deutero-Isaiah), the Righteous Servant (Ps. 34:19-20), and the slaughtered lamb (Exodus). (John 1:29; 19:36; 1 Cor. 5:7, 1 Peter 1:19, Rev. 5:6,9 etc.).

It is misleading and a one-sided interpretation if, when explaining the New Testament view of the eucharist, we pay attention only to the sacrificial death of Christ, since it could mean that we have forgotten that what once happened, now is, and shall be, are united in Christ at the celebration of the mass. It is true that the New Testament eucharistic texts speak about the Lord's Supper as primarily a commemoration of the atoning sacrifice offered by the incarnate Son of God as a redemption for the sin of men. It is this unique finished event and all its far-reaching effects that are in the focus of the sacrament. But the sacrament is more than a commemoration of Calvary. It is the now living Lord who is present in the elements and thus we find that the past and the present are united in Christ.

3) The next question that must be discussed is how the repeated eucharist in the Church is related to the sacrifice of Christ, the sacrifice once for all. Can Christ be put to death again? Is the eucharist a repetition of Calvary? Is the eucharist a commemoration of Calvary or only a commemoration of the Last Supper? If there is only one past sacrifice—Jesus' death on the cross—how can the Supper be a sacrifice? How is the command to repeat the Last Supper to be understood?

An important way of understanding the connection between now and then, present and past in the eucharist is to interpret the Last Supper by referring to the ideology of the Jewish Passover meal and its Haggada, particularly emphasizing the idea of "making present and actual," the "re-presentation." Two moments in the Haggada are in this context of special interest, namely that the eating and drinking was accompanied a) by a recitation of the Passover texts in Exodus, commemorating the deliverance out of Egypt, the creation of the peculiar people, the establishment of the covenant, and b) by an explanation of the ingredients of the meal. These two moments meant that the past salvation was actualized, re-presented. To the Israelite the Passover meal could not be separated from the salvation history, God's mighty deeds when he delivered the people out of Egypt, and it was natural to him to think of a connection between God's act of salvation in the past and the present meal, as it is said in the Haggada: "In every generation a man must regard himself as if he came forth himself out of Egypt . . . we bless him who wrought all these wonders for our fathers and for us. . . ." And there was the obligation to interpret the elements of the meal: the lamb whose blood protected against the death, the unleavened bread that is the bread of affliction that Israel ate during the flight (or: because the fathers were redeemed from Egypt), the bitter herbs that is the embittered lives of the fathers in Egypt. The recitation of the Passover texts and the explanation of the ingredients of the meal meant an actualization of God's salvation so that the past and the present were brought together.

Moreover, the eucharist cannot be separated from the salvation history, from Jesus as the sin-offering, God's final event "when the fullness of the time was come." And there is a connection between the one decisive event in the past and the present eucharist. Celebrating the mass is to re-present this event which, however, does not mean that it is repeated but is actualized. The actualization has two moments as in the Passover meal—a recitation of the words of institution and the explanation of the elements. The bread is the body of Christ and the wine is the blood of Christ. But in the eucharist there is something more than a commemoration and actualization. In a mystical way the eating and drinking is a communion of the body and blood of Christ. (1 Cor. 10:16, John 6:53). Thus the sacrifice of Christ is made contemporaneous with us. The sacrifice is present because the living Lord is present. The Lord cannot be present without an actualization of his sacrifice.

There is only one sacrifice, Jesus on the cross, which in the eucharistic context is understood as an atoning offering. The offering of Christ cannot be repeated but it is substantially and essentially made present. Its effects are operative now and always in the eucharist. Eating and drinking the elements of the eucharist means to share in the fruits of Jesus' offering and to be united with the living and glorified Christ. The offering of Christ is eternally valid and to commemorate it is to realize and experience personally its present operative significance as an event with abiding consequences.

4) The expression *eis anamnesin,* "in remembrance," should be interpreted against the background of the *lezikkaron* of the Passover Haggada, signifying the actualization of God's salvation act in Christ. It does not mean a mental recollection only but to make us contemporaneous with the cross event or to make Christ's sacrifice contemporaneous with us in the eucharist. God is not reminded in the eucharist of what Christ did, but the Supper reminds us of the redemption which Christ won by his death. In this context one could explain Paul's words that follow the words of institution, "For as often as you eat this bread and drink this cup, you pro-

claim the Lord's death until he comes." (1 Cor. 11:26). Reciting the Passion texts and explaining the significance of the elements the sacrifice of Christ is actualized—in remembrance of him.

5) The presence of Christ in the eucharist signifies among other things that Christ's sacrifice is effectively present. The eucharist therefore is a sacrifice in the sense that Christ is present as crucified, glorified and interceding, being the eternally valid offering before God. We do not offer in any way an expiatory sacrifice in the eucharist because expiation has been made once for all. But the fruits of the death of Christ are made present. To regard the Lord's Supper as our offering of Christ is contrary to the New Testament idea of the eucharist.

We find the idea of the real presence of Christ in the eucharist primarily in 1 Cor. 10:16-22, and in the words of institution "This is my body . . . ," cf. John 6:53 ff. It can be discussed how this presence is to be understood systematically or philosophically, since the New Testament passages do not present any definition. One thing, however, seems to be clear: there is in the eucharist a definite connection between the sacrifice of Christ and the real presence of Christ. The now invisible Lord who once died on the cross as a man and will return in the future as the glorified Son, is present and with him the atoning power of his sacrifice.

6) We often find in the literature the conception that Christ now is High Priest in the heavenly temple and continues to offer himself there as the only offering that can please God. References are made to the Epistle to the Hebrews and its description of Jesus as High Priest and to the Book of Revelation with its picture of Christ in heaven like a lamb that had been slain. The eucharist would therefore mean a participation in the sacrifice which our exalted High Priest continually presents at the heavenly altar before God. I find it hard to accept an interpretation of the eucharist in the light of this concept. It is stated by the author of the Hebrews that Christ "had offered for all time a single sacrifice for sins" and then "sat down at the right hand of God." (10:12). It is also written that "where there is forgiveness of sins, there is no longer any offering for sin." (10:18). It could be objected that it is also said in the same epistle that

it is necessary for the High Priest in the heavenly temple "to have something to offer," (8:3) and that this refers to Christ's eternal sacrifice. But he cannot offer a continuous sin-offering since such an offering always includes killing and destruction, things that do not exist in heaven. Therefore Christ's eternally valid sacrifice, offered once for all, can be referred to and made present in the eucharist, but this is not the same as to speak about a continually sacrificing. After his ascension and enthronement in heaven Christ has fulfilled his offering task. We may, however, not forget that in the New Testament Christ is both the High Priest who offers and the sacrifice, the consequence of which is that where Christ is present his sacrifice is also present.

It has been maintained that when Christ as High Priest in heaven offers himself as the eternal sacrifice, the Church is "in Christ" and thus participates in the continuous offering, which is of significance for the celebration of the mass. I think that this interpretation runs the risk of drawing wrong conclusions, Christ and the Church being too simply identified and thus leading to the idea that the work of the Church is Christ's own work and the sacrifice of the Church in the eucharist is Christ's own sacrifice. According to this view Christ's offering of himself in heaven continually is identified with the sacrifice which the Church on the earth continually offers in the eucharist. When speaking about Christ's continuous offering in heaven, it is in my opinion more adequate to say that it means a continuous offer of his salvation in the Church. The eucharist is an instrument of the Living Lord through which he continues his salvation act and we are able to receive the fruits of his sacrifice.

7) The New Testament speaks of the Christians as a holy priesthood, the redeemed community of God's people, that is called to offer up spiritual sacrifices, acceptable to God by Jesus Christ. (cf. 1 Peter 2:5, Hebr. 13:15-16, Rom. 12:1 etc.) This idea is often connected with the interpretation of the eucharist as a sacrifice. Man's self-oblation, his offerings of thanks and praise have always made a part of the celebration of the eucharist, but these spiritual sacrifices may not be mixed with the one sacrifice of Christ. We have to distinguish between these two kinds of sacrifice, because one has to do with our offerings to God, the other with a re-

ceiving of the fruits of Christ's offering. In the New Testament eucharistic texts we never find mentioned a combination of Christ's sacrifice and ours, his unique offering once for all and our self-oblation or spiritual sacrifices. It is correct to say that I can offer myself in and with the community as the Church offers itself to God as a living and holy sacrifice, but I do not think that it is according to the New Testament to say that this sacrifice is renewed at each celebration of the mass. A sentence like "the whole Christ offers the whole Christ" can be misleading.

PROPITIATION

By Jerome D. Quinn

THE archaic Jerusalem kergma, as theology began to emerge from the chrysalis of polemic,[1] compressed the essential faith-content (revelation) of the witnessed fact of Jesus' death into four words, *hyper ton hamartion hemon* – " . . . that Christ died *for our sins* in accordance with the scriptures" (1 Cor. 15.3b). Perhaps the two-word formula of 1 Cor. 11.24b – "for you" *hyper hymon*[2] is the most primitive Greek form of all expressions of this faith. It may represent a germinal logion from the historical ministry of Jesus, which Mk. 14.24b renders more literally into Greek as "for many" *(hyper pollon*). In this form a Semitic substratum is most evident as well as an allusion to Is. 53.10-12. We may well be catching an echo of the *ipsissima vox Jesu* in the later but more literal Greek of Mk.[3] In either wording, we are encountering in all its density the reality that lay behind the most archaic attempts to preach and to penetrate the scandal of the cross.

The OT was the primary source and control for the theological inquiry of the Jerusalem church into how the death of Jesus could be "for you (*or* us)" or "for many." If the latter phrase indeed represents the *ipsissima vox*, then the method employed is already implicit in Jesus' own allusive use of the OT. It is notable that not only the persons, things, and events described in the OT documents were pressed into service but also the words themselves of the OT became the privileged language for this theological inquiry. All previous revelation, everything connected with it, became an instrument for

---

[1] D. Stanley, *Concilium* 10[2] (Dec. 1966) 48.

[2] p[46], S/S*, A, B, C*. The variants of course should be studied in their own right for the light they shed on the exegesis and theology of the second through the fifth Christian centuries (cf K. W. Clark, "The Theological Relevance of Textural Variation . . .," *JBL* 85 (1966), 1-16).

[3] J. Jeremias, *The Eucharistic Words of Jesus* (London: SCM, 1966) 167-168, 179-182, 195-196, 225-231 (hereafter *EWJ*) and *The Central Message of the New Testament* (NY: Scribner's, 1965) 45-46 (hereafter *CMNT)*. In Mk the phrase has moved to cup-saying.

penetrating, understanding, and explicating the mystery of Jesus whose person and work both transcended and yet remained in continuity with the whole previous salvation-history (Lk. 24. 25, 27, 44). Thus not only the death of Jesus but its occurrence "for our sins" must be understood "according to the scriptures."

The apostolic church, and not least, Paul, constructed images and employed language from several different areas of the OT to explicate from as many different points of view, how Jesus had died *hyper hymon*. The terminology and images of OT criminal law, of social institutions, of ethical substitution were pressed into service.[4] Like squares inscribed within a circle, these images covered and conveyed a major portion of the reality and purpose of Jesus' work, but neither singly nor all together could they convey everything.

The heaviest levy was laid on the area of OT worship, and especially that of sacrificial cult. Within this area, the terminology as well as the persons, events and things connected with expiation-propitiation were found most useful. As the *hamartion* of 1 Cor. 15.3b makes evident, the "for you" was first of all interpreted of the "sins" of the "many."[5] Accordingly, with the death of Jesus so accepted as a *terminus a quo*, the apostolic theological inquiry began to probe its meaning in terms of the sacrificial cult of Israel, one of whose purposes was the purification of a people who had been called into relationship with a God who was holiness itself and the expiation of their sins. "The precise degree to which this idea was present depended on the particular act of worship and the stage of religious development at the time."[6]

The NT documents bear witness to the use of several different forms of OT sacrificial ritual to probe and elaborate the meaning of Jesus' death. Thus in 1 Cor. 5.7 we read, "For Christ, our paschal lamb *(to pascha)* has been sacrificed *(etythe)*."[7] The death of Jesus is

---

[4]cf J. Jeremias, *CMNT*, 36-39.

[5]cf *hamartiai* in LXX Is 53.4, 5, 6, 10, 11, 12.

[6]R. de Vaux, *Ancient Israel* (NY: McGraw-Hill, 1961) 272 (hereafter *AI*); that OT sacrifice was offered for other purposes, cf 415-456 and esp. 447 ff: on expiatory sacrifice in particular, *Studies in Old Testament Sacrifice* (Cardiff: U. of Wales, 1964) *passim* but esp. 91-112 (hereafter *SOTS*). H. Ringgren, *Sacrifice in the Bible* (N.Y.: Association, 1962) 28 (hereafter *SB*) remarks, "The only case in which the OT expressly states the purpose of a sacrifice is the sacrifice for the expiation of sins."

[7]cf Ex 12 and R. de Vaux, *SOTS*, 1-26: J. Jeremias, *CMNT*, 36: H. Ringgren, *SB*, 76-77.

explicitly set forth in terms of the Passover sacrifice and meal, and is surrounded with allusions to the unleavened bread – ". . . as you really are unleavened."[8] 1 Pt. 1.19 and Jn. 19.36[9] exploit the same OT locus and cultic action.

The fact that in later Jewish thinking the Passover sacrifice was not considered expiatory[10] perhaps exerted the pressure that turned the primitive Christian theological inquiry to the precisely expiatory sacrifices in order to elaborate the basic datum that Jesus' death had indeed been "for our *sins*." The text of Is. 53, which explains the Servant's suffering in terms of its vicarious character and specifically because it had the character of an *'asam*, gave warrant and encouragement for thus proceeding.[11]

Paul certainly utilized the language and ritual of the OT *hatta't* (sin-offering) when he said, "For our sake he (God) made him (Christ) to be sin *(hamartian)* who knew no sin *(hamartian)* . . ." We see again the primitive and basic affirmation of the *hyper hemon* – "for our sake." The former *hamartian* (sin) surely means "victim for sin," just as the Hebrew *hatta't* "means all at once the sin, the sacrifice which deletes it, and the victim of such a sacrifice."[12] Again Rom. 8.3 exploits the same locus, saying that God sent "his own Son in the likeness of sinful flesh and as a sin-offering,[13] he condemned sin in the flesh." In Eph. 5.2 Christ gave himself "for us *(hyper hemon)*, a fragrant offering *(prospheran)* and sacrifice *(thysian)* to God" (Ps. 40.6 and Ex. 29.18: cf Ez. 20.40-41). Here the ritual of burnt offering[14] – the "total" sacrifice of OT cult – is employed.[15]

In Rom. 3.25 the ritual of the Day of Atonement with the ex-

---

[8]a Passover variant on the theologoumenon of 1 Cor 10.17, "Because there is one bread, we who are many are one body . . ."

[9]*pace* C. H. Dodd, *The Interpretation of the Fourth Gospel* (Cambridge: Cambridge Univ. Press, 1953) 233-234, 424, 427-428 and *Historical Tradition in the Fourth Gospel* (Cambridge: Cambridge U. Press, 1963) 42-44, 131-132. Cf. E. Schweizer, *The Lord's Supper According to the NT* (Philadelphia: Fortress, 1967), 30n.

[10]J. Jeremias, *EWJ* 225: cf R. de Vaux, *SOTS*, 19-20: *AI*, 429, 441, 484-493.

[11]cf H. H. Rowley *Worship in Ancient Israel* (Philadelphia: Fortress, 1967) 127-128, 130 n. 1 and the bibliography there (hereafter *WAI*).

[12]R. de Vaux, *SOTS*, 91, 94 and bibliography there. W. Grundmann in *Theological Dictionary of the NT* (Grand Rapids: Eerdmans, 1964) I, 312 (hereafter *TDNT*).

[13]RSV note: *peri hamartias.*

[14]*'olah:* LXX, *holokautoma.*

[15]cf R. de Vaux, *AI*, 415-417. J. Behm's inferences from these data (*TDNT*, III, 184-185) would leave Paul writing poetically but not theologically.

piatory sacrifice of the *hatta't* which was essential to it,[16] became the lens through which the death of Christ for us and for our sins was refracted. Paul had just said (23f) "Since all have sinned and fall short of the glory of God, they are justified by his grace as a gift, through the redemption[17] which is in Christ Jesus, whom God put forward as a *hilasterion* by *(en)* his blood, to be received by faith." Though *hilasterion* could be construed as a masculine, singular accusative (RSV: "an expiation"), it is the normal LXX translation of *kapporet,* the golden plate which Ex. 25.17-22; 37. 6-9; and Lev. 16.2, 13-15 describe as the cover poised over the ark in the Holy of Holies but which was probably the successor to the lost ark (a kind of catafalque) in the post-exilic but pre-Herodian Temple.[18] It was here and only on the annual Day of Atonement that the high priest brought sacrificial blood into the Holy of Holies. It was sprinkled upon the golden *kapporet (hilasterion).* As Stanislas Lyonnet notes[19] the *kapporet* was not only the place of revelation, where God spoke to Moses and through him to the people, but it was the place where God kept forgiving the sins of his people, kept exercising his saving justice. Hence when it was a matter of the sins of the whole people, a Jew could scarcely allude to God's forgiveness coming through sacrifice without thinking of the ritual with the blood upon (or toward) the *kapporet.* As Philo[20] remarked, the *kapporet* was a "symbol of the merciful power of God." Thus Paul represents the crucified Jesus as the *kapporet* where God was present, revealing his mercy and forgiving the sins of his whole people. The sacrificial blood sprinkled once for all and in full view of all upon this *kapporet* was Jesus' own.

The OT terminology, imagery, and ritual which Rom. 3.25 used allusively, the author of Hebrews took up explicitly (cf 9.5 of the actual *hilasterion)* and at great length. Jesus the Son is where God speaks his last word to mankind (1.2); he is the high priest, exalted after "he had made purification for sins" *(katharismon ton*

---

[16]R. de Vaux, *SOTS,* 95-97: *AI,* 507-510. H. Rowley *WAI,* 92-94, 133-135 with extensive bibliography. H. J. Kraus *Worship in Israel* (Oxford: Blackwell, 1966) 68-70.

[17]*apolytroseos:* cf F. Buechsel, *TDNT,* IV 351-356.

[18]R. de Vaux, *AI,* 300-301.

[19]*De Peccato et Redemptione* (Rome: Pontifical Biblical Institute, 1960) II, 113-114 (hereafter *DPR).* The words here are a translation of Lyonnet's own summary (p. 114).

[20]ap. S. Lyonnet, *DPR,* II, 112

hamartion poiesamenos: 1.3). In Hebr. 2.17 the priestly work of the Son incarnate is explicitly introduced and propounded in terms of his having become a "merciful and faithful high priest in the service of God, to make expiation for the sins of the people" *(. . . eis to hilaskesthai tas hamartias tou laou).*

At this point one must summarize not only what the Hebrew Bible meant by *kipper* and *hillah* but also what the LXX meant by *(ex-) hilaskesthai.* The semantic fields are not fully coincident. It is even more difficult to determine precisely how much of this traditional meaning a given NT author actually intended to press into service for his own theological inquiry whose starting point, basis, and measure were the death of Jesus for our sins. Later theological development and our own usage of expiation-propitiation make it difficult to express the biblical perspective even when it has been attained.[21]

Both *kipper* – "to appease" (Gen. 32.20) and *hillah* – "to entreat" (Prv. 19.6) may have as an object a human being. The sense then is etymologically of covering or wiping clean a face black with anger, or of making a man's face sweet or pleasant in order to entreat a favor.

The application of these terms and the reality of personal relationships which they signified to the personal relationship of a believer with Yahweh called for some modification. The nature

---

[21]cf R. Abba s.vv. *Interpreter's Dictionary of the Bible,* ed. G. Buttrick (Nashville: Abingdon, 1962). The semantic problem which is here briefly outlined can be illustrated from the observations of C. F. D. Moule, *The Sacrifice of Christ* (Philadelphia; Fortress, 1964), 33-35, with editor John Reumann's added notes on pp. vi-vii and a bibliography on p. 46. The theologian is on the one hand bound to express clearly and systematically the meaning of the biblical revelation and still on the other hand to prefer the terminology of sources that used language in a more popular and non-scientific fashion for practical goals. Thus the modern theologian's term, *expiation,* represents quite precisely the central and essential sense of various Hebrew terms derived from *kpr* as these terms were used in connection with the God of Israel. On the other hand, the term *propitiation* may be understood and defined in this precise sense, and it has the advantage (from a philologist's viewpoint) of representing the basic ambivalence of the original term that the biblical authors took up, with its connotation (significant from the theologian's viewpoint) that certain human actions are in some fashion a personal offense against Yahweh. It should be noted that *propitiatio* and its cognates in the Roman liturgy keep the biblical sense of these terms which are as full of risk in Latin as *kpr* in Hebrew or *propitiation* in English (cf S. Lyonnet, *DPR,* II, 98-99). The conciliar documents which use these terms seem to follow this practice also. In both cases the practical, non-speculative goals of the authors kept them closer to the biblical vocabulary, in spite of the risks therein which the theologians rightly advert to and seek to counteract through their own refinement of terminology.

of this latter relationship was dictated by the nature of Yahweh as he had revealed himself. The gods whom the nations worshipped were by and large ill-tempered or at best indifferent. Their worshippers therefore would *appease* or *entreat* them, just as they would a powerful fellow man who was offended or indifferent. Yahweh had revealed himself as chronically good-tempered, by nature merciful and concerned for men (Ex. 34.6-7; the context of this archaic creed should be noted in this connection). This faith left its mark on the use of *kipper* which never takes Yahweh as an object. It does refer as an object to that which must be expunged from Yahweh's presence, all that which is contrary to his revealed will. Thus the term kept the notion of wiping out (covering) that which was offensive to or disruptive of Yahweh's relation to his people while avoiding a use that would imply a god by nature indifferent but made complaint by merely human initiative. Much the same field of meaning is covered in the uses of *hillah,* though the term tends to emphasize prayer rather than sacrificial rites, and it may have the "face of Yahweh" as its object.

According to Dodd[22] the LXX use of *(ex-) hilaskesthai* normally refers to that which delivers man from sin "and it looks in the last resort to God himself to perform that deliverance," i.e., to be gracious, to have mercy, to forgive (cf Lk. 18.13).

To summarize in S. Lyonnet's words,[23] the Hebrew and the Greek OT express in their terminology for expiation an activity of God himself or of his priest essentially ordered to the removal of sin and therefore to reconciling man with God. Even in those few places where the Greek term has God as its object, the rite of expiation is thought of as functioning after the fashion of intercession in which man (moved by grace) disposes himself to receive from God himself that which God has willed for the one who prays or for others. The *hilaskesthai* of Hebr. 2.17 coincides for the most part with this "intercessory" nuance of meaning (cf 5.7-9: 7.25: 9.24 & 12.24).

At 1 Jn. 2.2 and 4.10 the noun *hilasmos* is applied to Jesus: ". . . but if anyone does sin, we have an advocate with the Father, Jesus Christ, the righteous and he is the expiation *(hilasmos)* for *(peri)* our sins and not for ours only but also for the sins of the whole

---

[22]*The Bible and the Greeks* (London: Hodder & Stoughton, 1935) 82-95.

[23]*DPR,* II, 96 (a translation of Lyonnet's summary). For the evidence from Qumran, cf *ibid.* 81-84.

world." Though 1.7 implies that the death of Jesus was indeed the starting point for this affirmation, yet it is so phrased that it is "wide enough to cover the whole work of Christ." From the incarnation to the exaltation it "is an act of expiation, and God is the author of it." [24] The terms used by John here are those used by the LXX to translate the Hebrew *hatta't* (sin-offering). 1 Jn. 4.10 takes up the same imagery with the statement, "In this is love, not that we loved God but that he loved us and sent his Son to be the expiation *(hilasmon)* for *(peri)* our sins."

For Paul, in the eucharistic action, "you proclaim the Lord's death" (1 Cor. 11.26). The development of the words of institution traces the same trajectory as the theological inquiry into the historical death of the Lord. His death and the sacrament of his death are "for many" (Mk.), "for you" (Paul), "for the forgiveness of sins" (Mt.) and finally "for the life of the world" (Jn.).[25]

The link between the Supper and Calvary is not only that both involve the body and blood of Jesus but also that both can be declared to be "for many" or "for you." It appears that an original dominical saying pronounced over bread and wine at the Supper was transferred to the proclamation of the actual death of Jesus. The reason is not far to seek. The historical death of the Lord was hardly different from that of the men crucified with him. If that death contained any other reality it was accessible only to faith, it was attainable only from revelation. That revelation was sought in Jesus' word at the Supper that his imminent death was "for many." Thus the Lord's word and action at the Supper revealed and established a reality in his historical death that called for its interpretation in terms in sacrifice and expiation.

This link between the word of Jesus and his death as sacrifice may be even closer if one accepts the observations of G. von Rad[26] and H. Ringgren[27] on the essential character of the declaratory formulae in OT sacrifices. As the latter puts it,

> "There is reason to believe that every time a sacrifice was offered, the priest had to pronounce a brief formula to declare it acceptable, or not acceptable, to the Lord. The

---

[24] C. H. Dodd, *The Johannine Epistles* (N.Y.: Harper & Row, 1946), 27

[25] *cf* K. Aland, *Synopsis Quattuor Evangeliorum* (Stuttgart: Wuerttembergische Bibelanstalt, 1964) 436 (#311).

[26] *Old Testament Theology* (N.Y.: Harper, 1962) I, 246-247, 261-262.

[27] *SB*, 41-42.

> O.T. has preserved some of these 'declaratory formulae.' In the laws, the clearest examples have a negative form . . . Other formulae contain objective statements concerning the type of sacrifice, such as 'it is a burnt offering' (Lev. 1.9, 13, 17), 'it is a cereal offering' (Lev. 2.6, 15), etc. . . . This proclamation pronounced by the priest on behalf of God was necessary to make the sacrifice complete. It was the divine word spoken by God's representative, the priest, that made it something more than a mere human enterprise. The word of acceptance made it a means of grace provided by God for the benefit of mankind, a way by which man could approach God and receive His grace."

Against this background the interpretative word of Jesus at the Supper would be better described as a declaratory formula. With it, he assumes the role of a priest of Israel and proclaims the sacrificial character of his own imminent death. The crucifixion was to be "more than a mere human enterprise." Hence this formula in the style of a priest who speaks in Yahweh's name illuminates the death of Jesus from within, reveals the event as "a gracious act of God" (von Rad). In this interpretation not only the word but the whole action of Jesus at the Supper is essentially and indissolubly linked with Calvary, and each event in its own way illumines and reveals the content of the other.

LUTHER AND ROMAN CATHOLICISM ON THE MASS AS SACRIFICE *

BY JAMES F. MCCUE

BY way of introduction to his exposition of the Roman Catholic doctrine of the sacrifice of the mass, Johann Adam Moehler made the following assertion:

> The mighty subject [the Roman Catholic doctrine of the mass], which is now about to engage our attention, gave birth to the most important controversies between the Christian communities. All the other distinctive doctrines are here combined, though in a more eminent degree; for although, as has been clearly shown, in every point of difference the whole system of doctrine is mirrored forth, yet here this is more especially the case.[1]

This view of the relationship between conflicting doctrinal systems would seem to rule out the possibility of significant partial identities between Roman Catholic and Lutheran doctrine or theology. If the whole is reflected in every part, and if the whole is a system derived from a set of basic and characteristic principles, then the only way in which the corresponding parts of two systems could be alike would be for the systems themselves to be alike.

However, there seems to be no compelling *a priori* reason for accepting Moehler's thesis. Perhaps it is true, but perhaps it is not; it would seem that the only way to decide the matter would be to carry out a detailed investigation of the two bodies of thought. The assumption that Luther's thought and Roman Catholic doctrine are *systems* of thought is, as the outset at least, open to question; and I think that most would agree that the attempts made so far to articulate the basic (and by implication antithetical) first principles of the systems have not been satisfactory.

***Reprinted from *Journal of Ecumenical Studies;* Vol. 2, No. 2.**

[1] J.A. Moehler, *Symbolism, or Exposition of the Doctrinal Differences Between Catholics and Protestants as Evidenced by Their Symbolical Writings,* tr. J. B. Robertson (New York, 1844), p. 310.

It will be the thesis of the present paper that there is a substantial identity of view between Luther and Roman Catholicism on the understanding of the mass as a sacrifice. I will not attempt to deny that there is much in Lutheran mass piety that seems foreign and perhaps undesirable to Roman Catholics, and *vice versa*. However, on what Luther in 1520 and the Council of Trent in 1562 took to be the central issue—the sacrificial character of the mass—there is substantial agreement. In what follows I shall attempt to do three things: (1) to show that this agreement does exist, (2) to consider certain general features of Luther's and Roman Catholic doctrine which might seem to negate this identity, and (3) to consider how it was possible and how it has remained possible for Lutherans and Roman Catholics to engage in polemics over a point on which they are in agreement.

I

It may seem at the outset that, whatever the general possibility of doctrinal agreements between Luther and Rome, there is and can be no such agreement about the sacrificial character of the mass. The Swedish Lutheran scholar, Yngve Brilioth, has remarked that "at no point was Luther so violently opposed to the mediaeval system as in his repudiation of the Romish doctrine of the mass. This was the spear-point of his assault. . . ."[2] Indeed there are few things which Luther finds more offensive than the Roman understanding of the mass, and the fundamental distortion against which he protests is the idea that the mass is a sacrifice. In 1528, when the passions of 1520 had quieted somewhat and the eucharistic controversy with Zwingli and the "fanatics" had muted the anti-Roman polemic, he could still write in his *Confession Concerning Christ's Supper*: "As the greatest of all abominations I regard the mass when it is preached or sold as a sacrifice or good work. . . . Although I have been a great, grievous, despicable sinner, and wasted my youth in a thoughtless and damnable manner, yet my greatest sins were that I was so holy a monk, and so horribly angered, tortured, and plagued my dear Lord with so many masses for more

---

[2]Y. Brilioth, *Eucharistic Faith and Practice, Evangelical and Catholic* (London, 1930), p. 137. It should be noted that Dr. Brilioth subsequently does suggest that Luther's rejection of "sacrifice" is *simpliste*, and that it would be of considerable value if the question were to be re-examined by Lutherans. Since the time that Dr. Brilioth wrote, some such re-examination has taken place. See P. Meinhold, "Eucharistie and Opfer nach Luther," in *Eucharistie und Opfer*, ed. H. Asmussen (Stuttgart, 1960), for references to the literature.

than fifteen years."[3] Since he introduces the general confession of faith from which this is taken with a warning against those who "shall say after my death, 'If Luther were living now, he would teach or hold this or that article differently, for he did not consider it sufficiently,' "[4] it may seem most temerarious to wish to reopen the question. Undoubtedly Luther knew his own mind in the matter: "Let me say once and for all that by the grace of God I have most diligently traced all these articles through the Scriptures, have examined them again and again in the light thereof, and have wanted to defend all of them as certainly as I have now defended the sacrament of the altar. I am not drunk or irresponsible. I know what I am saying, and I well realize what this will mean for me before the Last Judgment at the coming of the Lord Jesus Christ."[5] Moreover, a recent Roman Catholic student of the subject rejects the suggestion that Luther somehow or other missed the point and was attacking a doctrine of the mass as sacrifice which really was not the doctrine held by Roman Catholics: "It is an unwarranted reflection on some of the keenest minds of the age to suppose that the Reformers' whole protest was based on the crass misapprehension that their opponents really claimed to slay Christ daily."[6] It would seem, therefore, that all that can be done in considering "Luther and Roman Catholicism on the Mass as Sacrifice" would be to catalogue the differences and perhaps to show how these are rooted in more fundamental theological options.

Before we accept this conclusion, however, a rather basic consideration is in order. What sort of disagreement is involved when one man or community says, "The mass is a sacrifice," while another says, "The mass is not a sacrifice"? It is of course quite possible that both parties are in complete agreement as to the meaning of "sacrifice." This is possible, but there are two reasons to *suspect* that such was not the case in Luther's dispute with Roman Catholicism. The first is that, during the two centuries immediately antecedent to Luther's rejection of the mass as sacrifice in *A Treatise on the New Testament, that is, the Holy Mass* (1520) there had

---

[3]"Confession Concerning Christ's Supper," in *Luther's Works* (Philadelphia, 1961), XXXV, 370-371. This series will henceforth be abbreviated as *LW*, followed by the volume and page numbers. All English quotations of Luther are from this series except where otherwise indicated.

[4]*Ibid.*, 360

[5]*Ibid.*, 360-361.

[6]Francis Clark, *Eucharistic Sacrifice and the Reformation* (London, 1960), pp. 102-103. See also pp. 93-95.

been no detailed discussion of the meaning of the mass as a sacrifice.[7] Despite this, neither Luther nor the Council of Trent experienced any need to clarify the sense in which each used the word. The word was used on both sides as though its meaning were immediately evident to all. But was it? This remains to be seen. The second reason for at least questioning the assumption that Luther and Roman Catholicism were using "sacrifice" in precisely the same sense as they fired anathemas at one another is the vigorous, even violent, tone that characterized the religious disputes of the sixteenth century. In an age in which Luther could say to Zwingli, "Listen now, you pig, dog, or fanatic, whatever kind of unreasonable ass you are,"[8] and Zwingli could reply by calling Luther a "fanatic, fool, bumpkin, yes a devil, murderer, and corrupter of souls,"[9] we must reckon with the *possibility* that adversaries would not listen to each other's refinements, clarifications, and extenuations with quite the openness which the seriousness of the subject would seem to require.

In order to determine Luther's position with respect to the Roman Catholic affirmation that the mass is a sacrifice, we must therefore look beyond Luther's simple negation. We shall have to attempt to articulate Luther's understanding of what the mass *is*, and shall try to relate this to the Roman Catholic understanding of the sacrificial character of the mass. This approach, though it has the disadvantage of being round-about, has the advantage of bringing into focus certain aspects of Luther's eucharistic doctrine which, I shall try to show, affirm many of the points affirmed by Trent's doctrine of the mass as a sacrifice.

It is customary and helpful to distinguish three stages in the

---

[7]Cf. E. Iserloh, "Eucharistie und Opfer," in *Eucharistie und Opfer*, p. 79: "Von den 126 Theologen dieses Zeitabschnittes (the 14th and 15th centuries), von denen uns Kommentare zum 4. Buch der Sentenzen vorliegen, habe ich 46, darunter die bedeutendsten, bearbeitet. Bei keinem findet sich eine theologische Behandlung des Messopfers . . . M.a.W. werden nur praktische, rubrizistische oder kanonistische Einzelfragen behandelt. Vom Opfer der Messe ist nicht audsruklich die Rede, auch klingen der Kultcharakter der Eucharistie und ihre Beziehung zum Opfer Christi kaum an." To the same effect, see Clark, *Eucharistic Sacrifice*, pp. 79-80. E. Iserloh, *Der Kampf um die Messe* (Munster, 1952), treats this matter in greater detail. Iserloh's "Bei keinem findet sich eine theologische Behandlung des Messopfers" seems an overstatement in light of Heiko Oberman, *The Harvest of Medieval Theology: Gabriel Biel and Late Medieval Nominalism* (Cambridge, 1963), pp. 271-275, 279-280.

[8]"That these Words of Christ, 'This is my Body,' etc., Still Stand Firm Against the Fanatics," *L.W.* XXXVII, 68.

[9]Quoted from "That these Words . . . Will Always Retain Their Ancient, Single Meaning. Ulrich Zwingli's Christian Answer" in *L.W.* XXXVII, 18, n. 14.

development of Luther's understanding of the eucharist. At each stage the emphasis is different. However—and this is a matter of some importance for the argument of this paper—in the absence of proof to the contrary, the writings of one period ought not to be understood as repudiating those which have gone before.[10] In the earliest of his eucharistic works, *The Blessed Sacrament of the Holy and True Body of Christ, and the Brotherhoods* (December, 1519), Luther conceives of the mass primarily as the sacrament of Christian unity, of the unity of Christians with Christ and with one another. Beginning with *A Treatise on the New Testament, that is, the Holy Mass* (July, 1520), and continuing through *Prelude on the Babylonian Captivity of the Church* (September, 1520), *The Misuse of the Mass* (late 1521) and *The Abomination of the Secret Mass* (1525),[11] his emphasis is on the testament character of the mass. Finally, beginning with *Against the Heavenly Prophets in the Matter of Images and Sacraments* (1525), and continuing through the anti-Zwingli tracts of 1527 and 1528—*That these Words* etc. and *Confession Concerning Christ's Supper*—he is concerned most of all to affirm and defend the physical presence of the body and blood of Jesus in the bread and wine. When Luther asserts the testament character of the mass he is not thereby denying that the mass is the sacrament of Christian unity; in affirming the real presence, he does not deny either the testament or the sacrament of unity. The burden of proof would be upon those who would maintain that the later views are intended as a repudiation of the earlier, and such proof has not been produced.

The Blessed Sacrament of the Holy and True Body of Christ and the Brotherhood (hereinafter referred to as *The Blessed Sacrament*) is the last of a trilogy on what Luther then took to be the three sacraments: penance, baptism, and the eucharist. It is intended as a positive exposition of the meaning of the sacrament, and, as indicated by its subtitle, has been written for the laity.[12] Given the circumstances of the time, it would be too much to expect that

---

[10] On the matter of transubstantiation, for example, there is clear evidence of a change in Luther's views. Even here, however, the change in eucharistic doctrine is less than one might think. See below, n. 14.

[11] This list is not exhaustive. Luther wrote other works on the eucharist during this period—*Receiving both Kinds in the Sacrament* (1522), for example—but they are of decidedly secondary importance for our purposes.

[12] "Fur die Leyen," according to *D. Martin Luthers Werke*. Kritische Gesamtausgabe (Weimar, 1883-), II, 73.9. Reference to this edition of Luther's works will be to *WA*, followed by the volume and page numbers. Reference to the subtitle is to be found in *L.W.*, XXXV, 47, n.2.

the work be entirely unaffected by Luther's conflict with Rome. Nevertheless, the work is substantially non-polemical and is pastoral in tone. Though Luther does not endorse the sacrificial understanding of the mass, neither does he inveigh against it; he develops his analysis of the mass in such a way that the question of the mass as a sacrifice really does not arise. The work is for that very reason of special interest to us.

Luther begins by distinguishing three aspects of a sacrament: "The first is the sacrament, or sign. The second is the significance of this sacrament. The third is the faith required with each of the first two."[13] The sign is "the form or appearance of bread and wine."[14] "The *significance* or effect of this sacrament is fellow-

---

[13]*L.W.*, XXXV, 49.

[14]*Ibid.* When he wrote this work Luther had not yet taken issue with transubstantiation. We may note in passing that Luther never considered transubstantiation in itself to be a matter of primary importance. He states most emphatically in *Confession Concerning Christ's Supper*: "Now, I have taught in the past and still teach that this controversy is unnecessary, and that it is of no great consequence whether the bread remains or not. I maintain, however, with Wycliffe that the bread remains; on the other hand, I also maintain with the sophists [i.e. the scholastics] that the body of Christ is present" (*L.W.*, XXXVII, 296). And later in the same work he writes: "I have often asserted that I do not argue whether the wine remains wine or not. It is enough for me that Christ's blood is present; let it be with the wine as God wills. Sooner than have mere wine with the fanatics, I would agree with the pope that there is only blood" (*ibid.*, 317). This is substantially the view expressed in *The Babylonian Captivity*, "Therefore I permit every man to hold either of these opinions [i.e. transubstantiation or the opinion that the substance of bread remains], as he chooses" (*L.W.*, XXXVI, 30). Luther of course favored the latter opinion, but he is careful to indicate that he does not consider this an essential of the gospel.

Luther is thus less concerned with the eucharistic doctrine in question than with the problem of authority which it involves. Karl Rahner, in an article comparing the Roman Catholic and Luther's conception of the real presence ("Die Gegenwart Christi im Sakrament des Herrenmahles," *Schriften zur Theologie*, IV (Einsiedeln, 1962), 357-385), interprets Trent's affirmation of transubstantiation in the following way: "Der Satz von der Transubstantiation . . . will ja genau das sagen, was Christus sagt: das, was er gibt, ist sein Leib, und nicht mehr Brot, und dies, obwohl Brot da war, dadurch, dass diese seine Erklarung wirksam die Wirklichkeit verandernd das herbeifuhrt, was sie aussagt: die Wirklichkeit des Leibes Christi an Stelle der Substanz des Brotes" (p. 375). Luther's point is to ask why this "und nicht mehr Brot" is insisted upon as a *sine qua non* of orthodoxy.

This question becomes perhaps more difficult to answer if one agrees with Rahner that, "Das Brotsein als solches scheint fur unsere heutige Auffassung gerade in jener Dimension zu liegen, die, scholastisch ausgedruckt, jene der *species* der empirisch-anthropomorphen Erscheinung ist . . ." (p. 383). Rahner adds that he does not believe that this effects the explanation which he has given of transubstantiation. Still, it is difficult to see how in Rahner's view one can distinguish meaningfully between *substantia panis* and *species panis:* and if this is the case, then the dispute between Roman Catholics and Lutherans over transubstantiation demands thorough reconsideration.

ship of all the saints. . . . All the saints, therefore, are members of Christ and of the Church, which is a spiritual and eternal city of God. And whoever is taken into this city is said to be received into the community of saints and to be incorporated into Christ's spiritual body and made a member of him. . . . To receive this sacrament in bread and wine, then, is nothing else than to receive a sure sign of this fellowship and incorporation with Christ and all saints. . . . This fellowship consists in this, that all the spiritual possessions of Christ and his saints are shared with and become the common property of him who receives this sacrament."[15] As he states matters further on: "In this sacrament, therefore, man is given through the priest a sure sign from God himself that he is thus united with Christ and his saints and has all things in common [with them], that Christ's sufferings and life are his own, together with the lives and sufferings of all the saints."[16]

It is this community of all things between Christ and the faithful—a community which is founded in baptism and will be completed only at the resurrection[17]—which the sacrament signifies *and effects.* This last point needs to be stressed, since Roman Catholic scholars as perceptive as Joseph Lortz[18] and Francis Clark[19] either do not notice this or else suppose that Luther does not mean what he says. Luther writes: "So it is clear from all this that this holy sacrament is nothing else than a divine sign, in which are pledged, granted, *and imparted* Christ and all

---

[15]*Ibid.,* 50-51.

[16]*Ibid.,* 52.

[17]It might be helpful in a general way to note the parallel between Luther's theology and New Testament eschatology. In interpreting Luther one must be careful to avoid the extreme alternatives of the sort reached by A. Schweitzer and C.H. Dodd in their reading of New Testament eschatology. For example, one does not do justice to Luther's view of justification if one interprets it in such a way as to exclude the fact that a transformation has already begun, though this transformation will not be unambiguously manifest and perfect until the last day.

[18]J. Lortz, *Die Reformation in Deutschland,* 3rd ed. (Freiburg, [1949]), I, 229: " 'Von der babylonischen Gefangenschaft der Kirche' . . . ist von allem, was Luther schrieb, der theologisch radikalste Angriff: die Kirche wird in Gefangenschaft gehalten durch die bisherige Sakramentenlehre. Das bedeutet vielmehr als einen Angriff nur gegen die Siebenzahl der Sakramente; es geht gegen den uberlieferten Sakramentsbegriff, d.h. also gegen die Objektivitat des in der Liturgie der Kirche tatigen gottlichen Lebens. Hier wird die Auflosung des Christentums in eine Gesinnungs-religiositat gerade an dem Punkt vollendet, der am starksten deren Uberwindung bedeuten sollte. . . . Nicht der Kampf gegen den Papst ist fur die katholische Kirche das Verhangnisvollste am reformatorischen Vorgang, sondern die Entleerung der objektiven Kraftquelle, des eigentlichen Mysteriums."

[19]Clark, *Eucharistic Sacrifice,* p. 106.

saints together with all their works. . . ."[20] The sacrament is not simply an occasion for pious reflection. In the sacrament what is signified is given. If faith is a necessary component in an effective sacrament, it is not the entire sacrament nor does it create the sacrament. Rather it is that wherein the sacrament comes to fruition. It is important, in a Catholic evaluation of Luther's conception of the mass, to point out that there is a substantial identity between the conception which Luther develops here of the relationship between sacrament (or sign) and faith and (for example) Karl Rahner's analysis of the relationship between *opus operatum* and *opus operantis*.[21]

It is only through my faith in the sacrament, or rather my faith in God's word addressed to me here and now in the sacrament, that the sacrament works in me. "Here, now, follows the third part of the sacrament, that is, the *faith* on which everything depends. For it is not enough to know what the sacrament is and signifies. It is not enough that you know it is a fellowship and a gracious exchange or blending of our sin and suffering with the righteousness of Christ and his saints. You must also desire it."[22]

In this first eucharistic treatise Luther says little about the real presence, but what he does say is definite. The body and blood of Christ are really, substantially present in the bread and wine. It might be said that Luther does not make much of the real presence. It is the fellowship-meal that is central, and the presence of Christ in the sacrament serves simply to enhance the meal symbolism: "For just as the bread is changed into his true natural body and the wine into his natural true blood, so truly are we

---

[20] *L.W.* XXXV, 60; emphasis added.

[21] It would be impossible within present time and space limitations to develop this assertion. The relevant literature would be *L.W.*, XXXV, 60-63; XXXVII, 86-87; K. Rahner, "Personale und sakramentale Frommigkeit," in *Schriften zur Theologie*, II (Einsiedeln, 1958), 115-141; especially 119-134. See also K. Rahner, *The Church and the Sacraments* (New York, 1963), pp. 24-33; K. Rahner, H. Vorgrimler, *Kleines theologisches Worterbuch* (Freiburg, 1961), s.v. "opus operatum"; O. Semmelroth, "Opus operatum—opus operantis," in *Lexikon fur Theologie und Kirche*," 3rd ed., VI (Freiburg, 1962), 1184-1186.

[22] *L.W.* XXXV, 60. Cf. E. Schillebeeckx: "Der innere religiose Zustand des empfangenden Subjektes ist keine blosse pro oder parasakramentale Disposition, er geht in das Wesen des fruchtbaren Sakramentes selbst ein. . . . Als Personalbegegnung mit dem himmlischen Kyrios impliziert das vollkommenwahrhafte Sakrament deshalb notwendig den religiosen Einsatz des empfangenen Subjektes." "Sakramente als Organe der Gottesbegegnung," in *Fragen der Theologie Heute*, 2nd ed. (Einsiedeln, 1959), p. 397. For English version see *Christianity Divided*, ed. D. Callahan et al. (New York, 1961), pp. 268-269.

also drawn and changed into the spiritual body. . . ."[23] This playing down of the real presence would itself seem to be a result of polemic. Luther is concerned that the sacrament not be reduced simply to the adoration of Jesus present, but that it effect what it signifies. He writes of those who "fall into such blindness that they do not know what else to do in this sacrament except to fear and honor Christ there present with their own prayers and devotions. When they have done this, they think they have done their whole duty. But Christ has given his whole body for this purpose, that the thing signified by the sacrament—the fellowship, the change wrought by love—may be put into practice. And Christ values his spiritual body, which is the fellowship of his saints, more than his own natural body."[24] Clearly this is not a "spiritualization" of the real presence; just as clearly, the doctrine of the real presence is not yet central in Luther's eucharistic thought.

Though Luther nowhere mentions "sacrifice" in this work, the central thesis will strike a Roman Catholic as being quite relevant to the question of the mass-sacrifice. As I shall subsequently attempt to show, the Roman Catholic understanding of the mass as a sacrifice is rooted in the community or fellowship of Christians with Christ, in the doctrine of the Church as the body—the spiritual or mystical body—of Christ. When a Roman Catholic reads the following passage from *The Blessed Sacrament,* he half expects Luther to go on to speak of the Church as participating in the sacrificial action of Calvary through the sacrifice of the mass.

> When Christ instituted the sacrament, he said, "This is my body which is given for you, this is my blood which is poured out for you. As often as you do this, remember me." It is as if he were saying, "I am the Head, I will be the first to give himself for you. I will make your suffering and misfortune my own and will bear it for you, so that you in your turn may do the same for me and for one another, allowing all things to be common property, in me, and with me."[25]

---

[23]*L.W.*, XXXV, 59. Hans Grass observes: "Aber wenn er dann die Vollkommenheit des Zeichens darin sieht, dass die Elemente verwandelt werden—Luther lehrt in unserem Sermon *[The Blessed Sacrament of the Holy and True Body of Christ]* noch die Transubstantiation—, was wiederum ein Zeichen unserer Verwandlung in den geistlichen Leib Christi ist, dann ist die besondere Bedeutsamkeit von Leib und Blut doch recht kunstlich begrundet." *Die Abendmahlslahre bei Luther und Calvin: eine kritische Untersuchung* (Gutersloh, 1954), p. 22.

[24]*L.W.* XXXV, 62.

[25]*Ibid.*, 54-55.

Of course Luther does not speak of the sacrifice of the mass, but a Roman Catholic may find it difficult to understand why he *could* not have done so. We shall return to this point when we have considered the Roman Catholic understanding of the mass as sacrifice.

Not long after the publication of *The Blessed Sacrament*, Luther was at work on another study of the eucharist, which was published in July, 1520, under the title, *A Treatise on the New Testament, that is, the Holy Mass* (hereinafter referred to as *A Treatise on the New Testament*). By this time he had already published *An Open Letter to the Christian Nobility* (June, 1520), and the ideas which were to find classic expression in *The Freedom of a Christian* (published November, 1520) were firmly in place. Most of the ideas on the eucharist known from the more familiar *Babylonian Captivity* were developed first in *A Treatise on the New Testament.*

The thesis of the work is implicit in its title: the mass is a testament *and therefore not a sacrifice.* The work is thus positively an exposition of the mass as testament and negatively an attack on the Roman doctrine of the mass as sacrifice. A testament, according to Luther, is "a last irrevocable will of one who is about to die, whereby he bequeaths his goods, allotted and assigned to be distributed to whom he will."[26] It is to be noted that Luther draws this idea of testament from its legal use rather than from the biblical "diatheke."[27] Only in a rather artificial way can Luther connect his use of "testament" with the scriptural use: "Therefore wherever in Scripture God's testament is referred to by the prophets, in that very word the prophets are taught that God would become man and die and rise again, in order that his word, in which he promises such a testament, might be fulfilled and confirmed. For if God is to make a testament, as he promises, then he must die; and if he is to die, then he must be a man. And so that little word 'testament' is a short summary of all God's wonders and grace, fulfilled in Christ."[28] However, it is not on this frail basis that Luther's view of the mass as a testament depends, but rather, as we shall see, on Luther's views on grace, faith, and works.

Luther's doctrine of the mass as a testament is epitomized in the following manner:

Now we see how many parts there are in this testament, or

---

[26] *Ibid.*, 84.

[27] Cf. J. Behm and G. Quell, "διαθηκη," in G. Kittel, *Theologisches Worterbuch zum Neuen Testament*, II (Stuttgart, 1935), 106-137.

[28] *L.W.* XXXV, 84.

mass. There is, first, the testator who makes the testament, Christ. Second, the heirs to whom the testament is bequeathed, we Christians. Third, the testament itself, the words of Christ—when he says, "This is my body which is given for you. This is my blood which is poured out for you, a new eternal testament," etc.

Fourth, the seal or token is the sacrament, the bread and wine, under which are his true body and blood. For everything that is in this sacrament must be living. Therefore Christ did not put it in dead writing and seals, but in living words and signs which we use from day to day. And this is what is meant when the priest elevates the host, by which he addresses us rather than God. It is as if he were saying to us, "Behold, this is the seal and sign of the testament in which Christ has bequeathed to us the remission of all sins and eternal life." In agreement with this is also that which is sung by the choir, "Blessed be he who comes to us in the name of God," whereby we testify how [in the sacrament] we receive blessings from God, and do not sacrifice or give to God.

Fifth, there is the bequeathed blessing which the words signify, namely, remission of sins and eternal life. Sixth, the duty, remembrance, or requiem, which we are to do for Christ; that is, that we should preach his love and grace, hear and meditate upon it, and by it be incited and preserved unto love and hope in him. As St. Paul explains it in I Corinthians 11 [:26], "As often as you eat this bread and drink this cup you proclaim the death of Christ." And this is what an earthly testator does, who bequeaths something to his heirs, that he may leave behind him a good name, the good will of men, and a blessed memory, that he should not be forgotten.[29]

At the Last Supper Christ bequeaths to us what is to be won on Calvary; in the mass we receive this inheritance. Within this perspective the meal-symbolism is of subsidiary importance, and the conception of the eucharist is correspondingly more individualistic. Of primary importance are the words of institution, and most particularly the phrase, "which is poured out for you and for many for the forgiveness of sins."[30] The forgiveness of man's sins, spoken through the Word on the Cross, is spoken to me here and now—Christ becomes Christ for me—and insofar as it is received by me in faith it is here and now effective.

---

[29]*Ibid.*, 86-87.

[30]*Ibid.*, 82.

The body and blood of Christ, really present "under the bread and wine," serve as a seal to the words of forgiveness. "This is what Christ has done in this testament. He has affixed to the words a powerful and most precious seal and sign: his own true flesh and blood under the bread and wine."[31] For our purposes we may ignore the problems posed by the idea of the flesh and blood as a sign.[32] The important thing to note is the primacy of the word of forgiveness. Luther can envisage the possibility of someone possessing the word, the testament, apart from the sacrament, and being saved by faith in the word; whereas the bare sacrament, the sacrament without the word of promise and hence without faith in the word of promise, would be "dead and . . . nothing at all, like a body without a soul. . . ."[33]

Here again a Roman Catholic may consider this an attenuation of the "objectivity" of the sacrament. To do so, however, is to misconstrue Luther's point. He conceives the sacramental event as a performative utterance in which God addreses his word of forgiveness to the Christian. Luther's analysis is worked out within the categories of dialogue and could be termed personalistic. In the sacrament God addresses the participants; and he speaks to them not simply to inform them or remind them of an already accomplished state of affairs, but addresses them efficaciously: "Your sins are forgiven." It is quite true that this analysis does not try to translate the sacrament into the categories of substance and accident and efficient and formal causality, but unless one insists upon hopelessly rigid conceptions of "subjectivism" and "objectivity" this cannot be construed as subjectivism. It is to be hoped that the recent development within Roman Catholicism of a more personalistic understanding of the sacraments will help to create a greater sympathy for and appreciation of Luther's sacramental theology.

Luther here emphasizes two points which must be understood together. First, God speaks to the Christian in a properly celebrated sacrament. Second, faith is a necessary part of God's

---

[31]*Ibid.*, 86.

[32]Cf. the remark of Hans Grass, *Abendmahlslehre*, p. 28: "Hat Luther es in der Schwachheit unseres Fleisches, d.h. psychologisch, besser seelsorgerlich begrunden konnen, dass ein Zeichen zur Bestatigung der Verheissung Not ist, so ist weit weniger einleuchtend, dass gerade Leib und Blut dieses Zeichen sein sollen. Dazu fehlt ihnen ein wesentliches Merkmal, namlich die Sichtbarkeit und Sinnenfalligkeit. Dass Luther ihnen trotzdem diese Funktion zuschreibt, zeigt, mit welcher Selbstverstandlichkeit er die Realprasenz von Leib und Blut im Abendmahl annimmt."

[33]L.W. XXXV, 91.

efficacious action. Without faith God's word does not affect me; I am not forgiven unless in faith I accept God's word. But it must be stressed that Luther is emphatically opposed to the idea that it is my faith which somehow or other makes the bread and wine to be the body and blood of Christ and which makes the word of forgiveness addressed by the celebrant to the community to be God's word of forgiveness. Rather it is Christ's promise and the power of God which makes of certain earthly realities the instruments of God's action on his people. If the *opus* is *operatum* according to the institution of Christ, then he is present and active according to his promise.

It is because Luther considers the word of forgiveness to be the heart of the sacrament that Luther now opposes the Roman conception of the mass as a sacrifice. If the mass is essentially the reception in faith of the forgiveness of sins promised at the Last Supper and won on Calvary, then it is, Luther charges, a basic distortion to make of the mass something that we offer to God. If the mass is a receiving it is not a giving, if a testament it is not a sacrifce. Making of the mass a sacrifice of this sort denies two basic facts about the Christian life: it is God who gives to us; we have nothing to give and can thus only receive.

It is here that Luther's general thesis on the relation of grace, faith, and works shapes his understanding of the mass. He attacks "sacrifice" as synonymous with "work."[34] The dichotomy between giving and receiving is insisted upon uncompromisingly. Either we have nothing to give or Christ's sacrifice was not unique and adequate.

A Treatise on the New Testament is especially important for our purposes because, though in it Luther says essentially the same things about the mass as he does in *The Babylonian Captivity*, his vocabulary is still fluid enough for him to admit a certain sense in which the mass could be called a sacrifice. I quote the following lengthy passage because it shows that Luther's position is not as simple—from the point of view of the Roman Catholic understanding of the mass-sacrifice—as it might appear only from the better known *Babylonian Captivity*.

> We should, therefore, give careful heed to this word "sacrifice," so that we do not presume to give God something in the sacrament, when it is he who in it gives us all things. We should bring spiritual sacrifices, since the external sacri-

[34]*Ibid.*, 93.

fices have ceased and have been changed into the gifts to churches, monastic houses, and charitable institutions. What sacrifices, then, are we to offer? Ourselves, and all that we have, with constant prayer, as we say, "Thy will be done, on earth as it is in heaven" [Matt. 6:10]. With this we are to yield ourselves to the will of God, that he may make of us what he will, according to his own pleasure. In addition we are to offer him praise and thanksgiving with our whole heart, for his unspeakable, sweet grace and mercy, which he has promised and given us in this sacrament. And although such a sacrifice occurs apart from the mass, and should so occur—for it does not necessarily and essentially belong to the mass, as has been said—yet it is more acceptable when it takes place with the multitude and in the assembly, where men encourage, move, and inflame one another to press close to God and thereby attain without any doubt what they desire.

. . . To be sure this sacrifice of prayer, praise, and thanksgiving and of ourselves as well, we are not to present before God in our own person. But we are to lay it upon Christ and let him present it for us, as St. Paul teaches in Hebrews 13[:15], "Let us continually offer up a sacrifice of praise to God, that is, the fruit of lips that confess him and praise him"; and all this "through Christ." For this is why he is also a priest—as Psalm 110[:4] says, "You are a priest for ever after the order of Melchizedek"—because he intercedes for us in heaven. He receives our prayer and sacrifice, and through himself, as a godly priest, makes them pleasing to God. Again St. Paul says in Hebrews 9[:24], "He has ascended into heaven to be a mediator in the presence of God on our behalf"; and in Romans 8[:34], "It is Christ Jesus, who died, yes, who was raised from the dead, who sits on the right hand of God, who also makes intercession for us."

From these words we learn that we do not offer Christ as a sacrifice, but that Christ offers us. And in this way it is permissible, yes, profitable, to call the mass a sacrifice; not on its own account, but because we offer ourselves as a sacrifice along with Christ. That is, we lay ourselves on Christ by a firm faith in his testament and do not otherwise appear before God with our prayer, praise, and sacrifice except through Christ and his mediation. Nor do we doubt that Christ is our priest or minister in heaven before God. Such faith, truly, brings it to pass that Christ takes up our cause, presents us and our prayer and praise, and also offers himself for us in heaven. If the mass were so understood and for this reason called a sacrifice, it would be well. Not that we offer the sacrament, but that by our praise, prayer, and sacrifice we move him and give him occasion to offer himself for us in heaven and ourselves with him. It is as if I were to say, I had brought a king's son to his father as an offering, when actually I had done no more than induce that son to present my need and petition to the king and made the son my mediator.

Few, however, understand the mass in this way. For they suppose that only the priest offers the mass as a sacrifice before God. Actually this is done and should be done by everyone who receives the sacrament—yes, also by those who are present at the mass but do not receive the sacrament. Furthermore such an offering of sacrifice every Christian may make, wherever he is and at all times, as St. Paul says [Heb. 13:15], "Let us continually offer up a sacrifice of praise through him," and Psalm 110[:4], "You are a priest for ever." If he is a priest for ever, then he is at all times a priest and is offering sacrifices without ceasing before God. But we cannot be continually the same; therefore the mass has been instituted that we may there come together and offer such sacrifice in common.

Now whoever understands the mass otherwise or would use it otherwise than as a testament and sacrifice of this kind, let him take heed how he understands it. I understand it, as has been said, to be really nothing else than this: we receive the testament and at the same time we admonish ourselves to be intent upon strengthening our faith and not to doubt that Christ in heaven is our priest that he offers himself for us without ceasing, and presents us and our prayer and praise, making all these acceptable. It is just as if I wished to offer the physical, earthly priest as a sacrifice in the mass and to appoint him to present my need and my praise of God, and he were to give me a token that he would do it. Just as in this case I would be offering the priest as a sacrifice, so it is that I also offer Christ, in that I desire and believe that he accepts me and my prayer and praise and presents it to God in his own person. And in order to strengthen this faith of mine he gives me a token that he will do it. This token is the sacrament of bread and wine. Thus it becomes clear that it is not the priest alone who offers the sacrifice of the mass: it is this faith which each one has for himself. This is the true priestly office, through which Christ is offered as a sacrifice to God, an office which the priest, with the outward ceremonies of the mass, simply represents. Each and all are, therefore, equally spiritual priests before God.

From this you can see for yourself that there are many who observe the mass and make this sacrifice properly, yet themselves know nothing about it. Indeed they do not realize that they are priests and can hold mass. Again there are many who take great pains and who apply themselves with all diligence, thinking that they are observing the mass quite well and making sacrifice properly; and yet there is nothing right about it. For all those who have the faith that Christ is a priest for them in heaven before God, and who lay on him their prayers and praise, their need and their whole selves, presenting them through him, not doubting that he does this very thing, and offers himself for them—these people take the sacrament and testament, outwardly or spiritually, as a token of all this, and do not doubt that all sin is there forgiven, that God has become their gracious Father, and that everlasting life is prepared for them.

All such, then, wherever they may be, are true priests. They truly observe the mass aright and also obtain by it what they desire. For faith must do everything. Faith alone is the true priestly office. It permits no one else to take its place. Therefore all Christian men are priests, all women priestesses, be they young or old, master or servant, mistress or maid, learned or unlearned. Here there is no difference, unless faith be unequal. On the other hand all who do not have such faith but who presume to make much of the mass as a sacrifice, and perform this office before God, are anointed idols. They simply observe the mass outwardly and do not themselves know what they are doing. They cannot be well pleasing to God, for without true faith it is impossible to please him at all, as St. Paul says in Hebrews 11[:6]. Now there are many who, hidden in their hearts, have such true faith and do not themselves know about it. And there are many who do not have such true faith; and of this, too, they are unaware. . . .

I will gladly agree that the faith which I have called the

true priestly office is truly able to do all things in heaven, earth, hell, and purgatory; and to this faith no one can ascribe too much. It is this faith, I say, which makes us all priests and priestesses. Through it, in connection with the sacrament, we offer ourselves, our need, prayer, praise, and thanksgiving in Christ and through Christ; and thereby we offer Christ to God, that is, we move Christ and give him occasion to offer himself for us and to offer us with himself.[35]

I have found no evidence that indicates that Luther ever repudiated the view of the mass expressed here. If he subsequently becomes more reluctant to speak of the mass as a sacrifice, I take it that this is not because of a change in his understanding of the eucharist, but rather because, as he puts it, "Few . . . understand the mass in this way," few understand sacrifice as he here describes it. To continue to speak of the mass as a sacrifice would be to lend support to distortion.

We shall return to a more detailed analysis of this passage after we have seen something of the Roman Catholic understanding of the mass as sacrifice, in order to determine what agreement there is between the view expressed here and Roman Catholic views.

I would call attention to one final point. Luther says that it is legitimate to pray for the dead and for a variety of other intentions. He allows that such prayer is offered to God. However, he argues that though these prayers are said *at* mass, and with this he has no quarrel, they are not part of the mass. They surround the mass but are distinct from it. Thus though it is a praiseworthy thing to pray for the dead, this is not the same as to offer the mass for them. To suppose that we can offer mass for some such intention is to misunderstand the mass profoundly. The mass is not offered to God for some end; it is received from him through faith.

The section on the eucharist in *A Prelude on the Babylonian Captivity of the Church* (hereinafter referred to as *The Babylonian Captivity*) does not significantly alter the doctrine presented in *A Treatise on the New Testament*. However, it clarifies and expands the ideas of the earlier work, introduces the subsidiary topics of communion under both kinds and transubstantiation,[36] and integrates all

[35]*Ibid.*, 98-101.

[36]Here too we may note that Luther's criticism of the Roman practice of withholding the cup from the laity is more directly concerned with the problem of authority in the Church than with eucharistic doctrine. Luther does not attack communion under one kind as such; he recognizes that it is a legitimate way of receiving communion. However, he objects strenuously to the view that the hierarchy—and most

of this into a broad attack against the Roman system of sacraments and authority. Though the treatment of the eucharist is no more radical or anti-Roman than that of *A Treatise on the New Testament,* it is now part of a whole which is of much more far-reaching significance than were any of the earlier exclusively eucharistic treatises.

First, it brings the contrast between testament and sacrifice into closer relationship with the doctrine of justification by grace and faith. The mass-sacrifice is more consistently identified as a good work. "*The third captivity of this sacrament* is by far the most wicked abuse of all, in consequence of which there is no opinion more generally held or more firmly believed in the church today than this, that the mass is a good work and a sacrifice."[37] The mass-sacrifice is something that we do, which automatically *(ex opere operato)* exerts an influence upon God. "Out of the sacrament and testament of God, which ought to be a good gift received, they have made for themselves a good deed performed, which they then give to others and offer up to God."[38]

Luther's objection to the sacrificial conception of the mass is therefore basically the same as his objection to what he takes to be the Roman Catholic doctrine of works. Both doctrines change the Christian into one who *earns* his salvation from God, whereas Luther insists that the Christian life is from beginning to end a reception in faith of the forgiveness of a gracious God. Instead of coming to the mass to receive from God through Christ, Roman Catholics come to the mass to give something to God in order to win his favor. The Roman view, according to Luther, obscures the fact that God is already gracious to us, and that if he were not, there would be nothing that we could do about it.

As in *A Treatise on the New Testament* the word still has a functional primacy over the body and blood of Christ. "The mass is a promise of the forgiveness of sins made to us by God."[39] What was won in principle on Calvary is made effective here and now as God addresses me with his word of forgiveness; and if this word is received by faith it is effective. The forgiveness of sin, won on Cal-

---

particularly the pope—may, according to its own good pleasure, outlaw reception under both kinds. For a Roman Catholic study of the matter which in many ways approaches Luther's position, see James J. Megivern, *Concomitance and Communion: A Study in Eucharistic Doctrine and Practice* (New York, 1963), especially pp. 246-257.

[37] *L.W.* XXXVI, 35.

[38] *Ibid.,* 49.

[39] *Ibid.,* 38.

vary, is distributed, made actual in the lives of the faithful, in the sacrament of the altar. "The whole power of the mass consists in the words of Christ, in which he testifies that forgiveness of sins is bestowed on all those who believe that his body is given and his blood poured out for them."[40] In the mass it is God's word that I hear and Christ's body and blood which I receive. But unless I hear and receive God's word with trust, the sacrament works to my condemnation; if I receive in faith, it affects forgiveness of sins.

Anyone who will place this analysis of the eucharist alongside *The Freedom of a Christian Man* will immediately note that Luther has in *The Babylonian Captivity* made of the mass a model of the Christian life as outlined in the later work. The activity of God is all sufficient in the work of our justification, and the faith-act in which God's activity is fulfilled in analyzed in such a way as to avoid speaking of it as man's act. In the mass it is God's word, sealed by the body and blood of the Saviour, that is alone efficacious; the faith-act, though its importance is stressed by Luther, is essentially a receiving: "be it done unto me according to thy word."

The third group of Luther's writings on the eucharist add nothing new from our present point of view. Though these writings are of considerable intrinsic interest, it is clear that at the time that he wrote them Luther considered the battle of the mass as sacrifice to be finished. From time to time he may reiterate his previously developed position, but he feels no need to develop it further. We may therefore proceed directly to a consideration of the Roman Catholic position.

II

Though Roman Catholics are generally agreed *that* the mass is a sacrifice, the consensus breaks down when it comes to the detailed explanation of what is meant by "sacrifice." And though certain common views do emerge from a consideration of the variety of Roman Catholic *Messopfertheorien,* one is not justified in taking these common views as the essentials of each position and relegating the points of disagreement to the limbo reserved for accidentals. Accordingly, it will not be possible to detail a theory of the sacrifice of the mass and to say that this is *the* Roman Catholic understanding of the matter.

However, the situation is not altogether disparate. The Council of Trent did say some definite things, so that if we develop what was

---

[40]*Ibid.,* 43.

defined at Trent, and do this along lines taken in some of the more recent Roman Catholic literature on the subject, we shall at least be able to work out *a* Roman Catholic understanding of the mass as sacrifice. How this view is related to the various other Roman Catholic views developed during the last several centuries is a question which we can legitimately leave unanswered here.[41]

The Council of Trent spoke in the following manner on the sacrifice of the mass:

> Quia tamen per mortem sacerdotium eius extinguendum non erat [Hebr. 7, 24-27], in coena novissima, *qua nocte* tradebatur, ut dilectae sponsae suae Ecclesiae visible (sicut hominum natura exigit) relinqueret sacrificium [can. 1], quo cruentum illud semel in cruce peragendum repraesentaretur eiusque memoria in finem usque saeculi permaneret [1 Cor. 11, 23 sqq.], atque illius salutaris virtus in remissionem eorum, quae a nobis quotidie committuntur, peccatorum applicaretur.
>
> Et quoniam in divino hoc sacrificio, quod in Missa peragitur, iden ille Christus continetur et incruente immolatur, qui in ara crucis *semel se ipsum* cruente obtulit [Hebr. 9, 27]: docet sancta Synodus, sacrificium istud vere propitiatorium esse [can. 3], per ipsumque fieri, ut, si cum vero corde et recta fide, cum metu ac reverentia, contriti ac poenitentes ad Deum *accedamus, misericordiam consequamur et gratiam inveniamus in auxilio opportuno* [Hebr. 4, 16]. Huius quippe oblatione placatus Dominus, gratiam et donum poenitentiae concedens, crimina et peccata etiam ingentia dimittit. Una enim eademque est hostia, idem tunc in cruce obtulit, sola offerendi ratione diversa. Cuius quidem oblationis (cruentae, inquam) fructus per hanc incruentam uberrime percipiuntur: tantum abest, ut illi per hanc quovis modo derogetur [can. 4]. Quare non solum pro fidelium vivorum peccatis, poenis, satisfactionibus et aliis necessitatibus, sed et pro defunctis in Christo, nondum ad plenum purgatis, rite juxta Apostolorum traditionem offertur [can. 3]. . . .
>
> Can. 1. Si quis dixerit, in Missa non offerri Deo verum et proprium sacrificium, aut quod offerri non sit aliud quam nobis Christum ad manducandum dari: A.S. . . .
>
> Can. 3. Si quis dixerit, Missae sacrificium tantum esse laudis et gratiarum actionis, aut nudam commemorationem sacrificii in

---

[41] **For the period from Trent down to the 1920's, see M. Lepin, *L'Idee du sacrifice de la Messe d'apres les theologiens depuis l'origini jusqu'a nos jours* (Paris, 1926), pp. 335-758.**

cruce peracti, non autem propitiatorium; vel soli prodesse sumenti; neque pro vivis et defunctis, pro peccatis, poenis, satisfactionibus et aliis necessitatibus offerri debere: A.S.

Can. 4. Si quis dixerit, blasphemian irrogari sanctissimo Christi sacrificio in cruce peracto per Missae sacrificium, aut illi per hoc derogari. A.S.[42]

We may summarize this by means of the following propositions:

1. The mass is a visible sacrifice.
2. The mass makes present (this is the sense of *repraesentaretur*) the sacrifice of the Cross, and serves for all times as a memorial thereof.
3. In the mass the salutary power of Calvary is applied for the remission of our sins.
4. The mass is a propitiatory sacrifice because in it Christ is contained and offered.
5. The mass is rightly offered for both the living and the dead.
6. The mass in no way takes away from Calvary.

We may note first of all that Luther would have no quarrel with the second, third, and sixth propositions: they express a substantial part of his thought. He would, however, object that the sixth would be incompatible with the first, fourth, and fifth, and would reject these latter as serious deformations. In what follows I shall be primarily concerned with these three propositions. Can and does Roman Catholic theology understand them in a way which is compatible with the sixth proposition?

As stated previously, the Council of Trent did not define the sense in which it uses the word "sacrifice." The Council doubtless supposed that the meaning was well enough defined by the usage of the time. As already noted, however, the usage of the time was not without ambiguity. An attempt has been made to elaborate a composite definition of "sacrifice" from the views expressed by individual participants in the Council,[43] but though this may be helpful it can hardly stand as a definitive pronouncement.

---

[42]H. Denzinger—A. Schonmetzer, *Enchiridion Symbolorum*, 32nd ed. (Freiburg, 1963), nn. 1740, 1743, 1751, 1753-1754 (=nn. 938, 940, 948, 950-951 in 31st ed.) Hereinafter referred to as Dz. followed by the differing numbers of the 32nd and 31st editions.

[43]Emile Joumelle, "Le sacrifice eucharistique au concile de Trente," *Nouvelle Revue Theologique* 67 (1945), 520-521: "Cependant, en totalisant le meilleur de leurs apports respectifs, on obtient un enonce qui n'est pas a proprement parler une definition, mais plutot la somme des traits fondamentaux qui de tout temps ont servi a decrire un sacrifice. Le voici: le sacrifice est un acte de religion (Trisi, de Vellosillo), signe exterieur d'un acte spirituel (Pendasio), pose par un ministre officiel, le

The following "definition" is in agreement with at least many of the views expressed at Trent and at least some more recent Roman Catholic opinion. When it is said that the mass is a visible sacrifice it is meant that the liturgical action itself is an act in which Jesus Christ, present in the sacrament, is offered to the Father by the celebrating community.

It will straightaway be noted that I have here merely replaced one difficult word, "sacrifice," by another, "offer." If anything, "offer" is even more problematic. What after all does it mean to say that we offer something to God? Or more to the point, what does it mean to say that we offer some*one* to God, someone who has already offered himself to God on our behalf to effect our salvation, our reconciliation with God? Clearly it does not mean that we take Christ, as a pre-Christian might take a sacrificial animal, and "slay" him (even symbolically) as a sign of our dependence on God or our desire for community with him, to appease his wrath, to gain forgiveness of sins, to obtain good weather, or the like. But if it does not mean this—and I take it that in part it was in order to rule out such conceptions that Luther attacked the idea of the mass as a sacrifice—what does it mean?

An adequate discussion of the meaning of "to offer Jesus to the Father" would require a long detour through Christology and an explicit theory of the atonement. We must, therefore, content ourselves here with an inadequate discussion. We shall take as our point of departure—not denying that this point of departure is not simple and entirely unproblematic—the familiar New Testament conception of Jesus offering his life—himself—on behalf of men in obedience to his Father, thus establishing the final covenant between God and mankind. His death is an offering to the Father on our behalf, and in this respect he is our High Priest before the Father.

Through baptism the Christian is rooted in Christ's priestly act, and lives in anticipation of the fulfillment of the new covenant presaged by Christ's resurrection and exaltation. Through baptism he has been made one in whom Christ's sacrifice on Calvary has become

---

pretre (doctrine du 6 aout), qui consiste a rendre saint (Sancio), a benir, consacrer, offrir (doctrine du 6 aout, Ballani, Cornejo, Salmeron, Cuesta) a Dieu une chose sensible (doctrine du 6 aout), que l'on immole, boit ou mange (Casal, d'apres saint Thomas) ou sur laquelle on exerce une action (Corrionero, d'apres saint Thomas) et qui a pour but de le louer et de le remercier (Sancio), d'unir notre ame a lui (de Paiva, Ramirez, Pendasio d'apres saint Augustin) et d'unir les offrants entre eux (Pendasio). Par lui, nous accomplissons notre devoir de referer tout a Dieu duquel tout bien derive (Pendasio) et nous expions pour les vivants et pour les morts (de Burgonovo)."

efficacious. He has been included—taken up—in Christ's offering. Christ did not give only himself to the Father; he presented at the same time his body the Church. As a member of this body, the Christian is made part of the one offering, the one sacrifice, of the new covenant. When Christ gives himself to the Father in obedience and love, he does this in order that men may be able to give themselves in obedience and love. Christ offers the Church—the community of the faithful—along with himself. There is an intended identity between Christ and those on whose behalf he offers himself.

The life of the Christian community is shaped by all this. Its existence is structured by the one sacrifice of Calvary. The faith-act in which the community, celebrating the eucharistic memorial of Calvary, acknowledges and receives what was done for it and to it on Calvary, is itself an offering. That is, we *receive* the fruits of Calvary in an act in which we say yes to Calvary by offering ourselves along with Christ to the Father. Note that this does not make of the mass a repetition of Calvary. The mass does not replace Calvary, nor does it reduce Calvary to the status of *primum inter paria.* The sacrifice of Calvary has consequences for the entire Christian life, which consequences are most perfectly realized in the eucharistic sacrifice. Within this perspective the antithesis between receiving and giving, between testament and sacrifice, proves to be overly simple. Christ's offering is "received" in the Church's offering.

What is perhaps the chief difficulty with this conception is that its vocabulary tends to suggest what it nevertheless energetically denies. I have thus far been speaking of Calvary as "the one sacrifice of the new covenant." Yet I also have been speaking of a mass celebrated at a particular time and place as a sacrifice. This ambiguity can be clarified by considering further the central idea of Christ's high priestly offering. Does not such an offering require as part of its full realization the involvement of the Christian people? There is simply the one sacrifice of Christ in the new covenant, but the faith-act wherein the Christian community is most fully taken up into this one sacrifice is itself sacrificial in structure.[44]

---

[44]Cf. the following passage from K. Rahner, "Die vielen Messen und das eine Opfer," *Zeitschrift fur katholische Theologie*, 71 (1949), 266-267: "Wir wissen aus der Lehre der Kirche, dass das Messopfer eine *repraesentatio* des Kreuzesopfers Christi ist. Es kann hier nicht naher darauf eingegangen werden welches der genauere Sinn dieses dunklen Begriffes nach der Auffassung des Konzils ist. Soviel aber durfte mindestens sicher und allgemein annehmbar sein: Das Messopfer ist zunachst einmal *repraesentatio sacrificii crucis* dadurch dass der kultische Vorgang als solcher in den Konsekrationsworten und der Doppeltheit der Gestalten auf das Kreuzesopfer zuruckweist; zweitens dadurch, dass der *Christus passus* real gegen-

So much for the general statement that the mass is a visible sacrifice. Before comparing this with Luther we must consider the two further points which may at first seem to undercut everything which I have thus far been saying. Trent affirms that the mass is a propitiatory sacrifice, and that it is rightly offered for the living and the dead.

In what sense is the mass a propitiatory sacrifice? First of all it must be stated very plainly that the mass is not propitiatory in the sense that it somehow wins over a hostile God. As it has been stated quite forcefully:

> If the proposition is true (and in fact it is dogma) that the sacrifice of the mass is only the application of the fruit of the sacrifice of the cross, then the following is thereby clearly affirmed: The sacrifice of the mass creates no new gracious and saving will in God vis-a-vis the world, which did not already exist through the cross (and only through the cross!); but it is only a way in which the constantly and definitively present saving will of God encounters man visibly and concretely in the here and now of history and takes hold of him. We can speak of "moving" God to forgiveness, reconciliation, mercy, assistance, etc., through the sacrifice of the mass (insofar as it is—qua visible, ceremonial sacrifice—distinct from the sacrifice of the cross) only in the following sense: the gracious will of God, founded exclusively on the reconciliation of the cross, becomes visible in the sacrifice of the mass and comes to man in his concrete situation, and man takes to himself this gracious will in and through its visible appearance. This gracious will is not newly constituted in the sacrifice of the mass, it is appropriated; which is not to deny that in the particular case the concrete results of this saving will would not come about if man did not take it to himself in this sacrificial way.[45]

---

wartig ist unter den sakramentalen Zeichen; und drittens dadurch, dass er unter diesen sakramentalen Gestalten durch die von Christus bevollmachtigte Kirche dem Vater als der dargebracht wird, der gelitten hat und gestorben ist. Diese letztere Darbringung selbst hat wieder eine zweifache Schicht (wenn wir so sagen durfen): sie ist zunachst eine kultisch-rituelle (. . .*offerimus* . . .), d.h. eine in Worten und Gebarden sich vollziehende; sie ist weiter (oder soll sein)—was sie von der Gesamtheit der Kirche her gesehen auch immer ist—eine innere, existenielle: das glaubige innere Ja des Menschen zu der Bewegung des Liebesgehorsams Christi hin zum Vater."

[45]*Ibid.*, 288. "Wenn der Satz richtig ist (und er ist eigentlich Dogma), dass das Messopfer nur Zuwendung der Opferfrucht des Kreuzes Christi ist, dann ist damit doch offenbar folgendes gesagt: Das Messopfer schafft keinen neuen Gnaden—und Heilswillen Gottes der Welt gegenuber, der nicht schon durch das Kreuz (und es allein!) da ware, sondern ist nur eine Weise, in der der schon immer und endgultig

Thus the mass is propitiatory in that it effects—as Luther and Trent both insist—the forgiveness of sins of those who participate by faith.

The difficulty thus focuses on the offering of mass for the absent living and the dead. It will be recalled that Luther carefully distinguishes between the mass proper and whatever prayers might be said by the community assembled to celebrate the eucharist. Though he insists that prayer for the living and dead is a Christian responsibility, and though he is willing to allow that we offer such prayer to God in Christ's name, he wants this clearly distinguished from the mass. He does not want our understanding of the mass to be determined by the fact that in connection with our celebration of the eucharist we offer prayers for the dead.

It is unfortunate that though the mass intention plays a very large role in Roman Catholic mass piety, it is generally given only passing attention by theologians. For this reason I find it difficult to say precisely how (or whether) Luther and Roman Catholicism differ in this matter. Because Roman Catholic theologians do not agree with Luther that prayer differs from the mass in that the former is man's word (in Christ) to God and the latter God's word to man, they would not agree that the mass should be separated from the prayer. Prayer—for the entire Church, for those whom the celebrating community has special responsibilities—is a part of the one harmonious liturgical celebration. A mass "offered" for a dead person (for example) is a mass in which the celebrating community, in

---

vorhandene Heilswille Gottes konkret im Hier und Jetzt der Geschichte sichtbar dem Menschen begegnet und ihm ergreift. Von einem 'Bewegen' Gottes zur Vergebung, Versohnung, zum Erbarmen zur Hilfe usw. durch das Messopfer (insofern es als kultisch sichtbares Opfer vom Kreuzesopfer verschieden ist) Kann im Gegensatz zum Kreuzesopfer somit nur in dem Sinn die Rede sein, dass der auf der Versohnung am Kreuz allein beruhende gnadige Wille Gottes durch das Messopfer sichtbar zur Erscheinung kommt und sich auf den Menschen in seiner konkreten Situation hinbewegt, und der Mensch diesen gnadigen Willen in und durch seine sichtbare Erscheinung sich zu macht. Dieser Gnadenwille wird im Messopfer nicht neu konstituiert, sondern angeeignet, womit durchaus nicht geleugnet ist, dass im Einzelfell die konkrete Wirkung dieses Heilwillens Gottes im Menschen unter Umstanden nicht eintrate, wurde der Mensch ihn sich nicht gerade auf diese Weise des Opfers aneignen." The question of the appropriateness and the value of calling the mass a propitiatory sacrifice should not be confused with the question of the possibility of calling it such. Trent should, I think, be interpreted as insisting upon the *possibility*: an orthodox interpretation can be given to the expression. However, it may well be that the interpretation which "propitiatory sacrifice" would seem to suggest *prima facie* is *not* orthodox, and that for this reason the expression may be an unfortunate one. Though I think that this is a very important issue, I do not pretend to decide it here.

virtue of its baptismal solidarity with the sacrificing Christ, prays for that person.[46]

Though certain aspects of current Roman Catholic practice suggest the contrary—the use of black vestments and the requiem mass, the practice of announcing at the beginning of mass that this mass is being offered for x—the specific intention is not primary in the mass. That is, mass is not celebrated in order that we may have something with which to ransom the suffering dead. Rather, as we come to participate more deeply through the mass in Christ's one sacrifice, we offer prayer for all and especially for those most directly committed to our care.[47]

III

Thus far then I have considered those statements of Trent which were in fact directed most uncompromisingly against Luther. I have argued that, if rightly understood, they do not have the fell consequences which Luther thought that such views must have. I propose by way of conclusion to do two things: first, to consider in more detail than was possible in our initial survey of Luther's position the extent to which the Roman Catholic doctrine is in fact present, albeit in disguised form, in Luther's own thought; and second, to consider how it was possible for Luther to misconstrue the Roman Catholic position, and furthermore how it was possible for this misconstruing to go unnoticed by the Roman Catholics of that time and since.

We have seen that the Roman Catholic view is rooted in the idea of the Church as the body of Christ, and thus in the idea that Christ is not only God's word to mankind but simultaneously the representative high priest of mankind before God. In Luther's earliest work on the eucharist, *The Blessed Sacrament*, this conception is central. We share all with Christ through the mass; we are the spiritual body of which he is the head. He writes there: "Thus in the sacrament we too become united with Christ, and are made one body with all the saints, so that Christ cares for us and acts in our behalf. As if he were what we are, he makes whatever concerns us to concern him

[46]Once again it is important to note that the appropriateness of the expression "to offer mass for so-and-so" is not presently at issue. It is my personal opinion that it is most inappropriate, but that is not presently the point. I am concerned to show here that what Roman Catholic doctrine and theology do mean by the expression is not something antithetical or even foreign to Luther. If this can once be agreed upon, we will be in a better position to discuss the appropriateness, value, and dangers of the expression.

[47]*Cf. ibid.*, 287-296, 307-315, for a more detailed discussion and for reference to some of the standard literature.

as well, and even more than it does us. In turn we so care for Christ, as if we were what he is, which indeed we shall finally be—we shall be conformed to his likeness."[48] We share with Christ and are at least inchoatively conformed to him. Luther does not go on to add that, since the mass is our participation in Calvary, our sharing with and being conformed to Christ takes the form first of all of joining ourselves with him in the sacrificial act which is the center of his as of our life. Luther does *not* add this; but I do not see that he *could* not have done so; and if he had, he would have been saying substantially what Trent was to say.

However, *The Blessed Sacrament* was written in 1519, the attack on the doctrine of sacrifice began in 1520. Is it not possible that Luther thereby repudiated his 1519 position, that on this point he was still a Roman Catholic in 1519 but a Lutheran in 1520? In answer to this question we may first note that, though first published in 1519, *The Blessed Sacrament* went through thirteen additional German editions and one Latin edition by 1525.[49] That is, it was immensely popular among Luther's followers during the period in which he was most bitterly attacking the abomination of the sacrifice of the mass. We must conclude, therefore, that Luther's early associates in the Reformation did not consider *The Blessed Sacrament* to have been repudiated by the subsequent development of Luther's thought. And the fact that Luther did not object to the republication of this work leads one to the conclusion that Luther shared this view.

Moreover, even in *A Treatise on the New Testament* we still find that the main elements of the Roman Catholic doctrine of the mass as a sacrifice are being affirmed at the same time that Luther is launching his attack against it. Let us reconsider the long passage already quoted from this work (above, pp. 57-60). Though Luther insists "that we do not offer Christ as a sacrifice, but he offers us," at the same time he asserts what a Roman Catholic would think is thereby denied. That is, in the mass we offer "ourselves, and all that we have." And this sacrifice "we are not to present before God in our own person. But we are to lay it upon Christ and let him present it for us." "That is, we lay ourselves on Christ by a faith in his testament and do not appear otherwise before God with our prayer, praise, and sacrifice except through Christ and his meditation." "So it is that I also offer Christ, in that I desire and believe that he accepts me and my prayer and praise and presents

[48] *L.W.*, XXXV, 59.
[49] *Ibid.*, 48.

it to God in his own person. . . . Thus it becomes clear that it is not the priest alone who offers the sacrifice of the mass; it is the faith which each one has for himself." "For all those who have the faith that Christ is a priest for them in heaven before God, and who lay on him their prayers and praise, their need and their whole selves, presenting them through him, not doubting that he does this very thing, and offers himself for them . . ." And finally, "through it [faith], in connection with the sacrament, we offer ourselves, our need, prayer, praise, and thanksgiving in Christ and through Christ; and thereby we offer Christ to God. . . ."[50] So far as I can see there is nothing which the Roman Catholic position requires that Luther does not here maintain. The dogmatic assertion that the mass is a sacrifice is simply a compendium of all of this.

We are thus led to the paradoxical result that in the very work in which Luther launched his famous attack on the doctrine that the mass is a sacrifice he was in fact holding that doctrine. Furthermore, though the ideas expressed in the material just quoted are less prominent in *The Babylonian Captivity*, there is no reason whatsoever to suppose that between July and September of 1520 Luther did an abrupt about-face. Hence we can extend our paradoxical conclusion to the central reformation treatise.

While it is true that in Luther's later theology we hear less of the Christology underlying these earlier works—specifically, less of the Church as the spiritual body of Christ—this must be regarded as a shift in emphasis rather than a break with the past. It is worth noting that in *The Confession Concerning Christ's Supper* Luther is still able to speak with ease of the Church as the "one spiritual body of Christ."[51]

Thus far I have argued that the position which Luther attacked was not the one which Roman Catholicism was defending, and that in substance Luther was actually holding the Roman Catholic position. Are we to conclude then that this was simply a case of mutual misunderstanding which can readily be cleared up? Unfortunately I do not think that the situation is quite that simple.

The distinction between doctrine and practice is, on the surface

---

[50] The concluding phrase, "that is, we move Christ and give him occasion to offer himself for us and to offer us with himself," could give rise to the same kind of distorted view of the mass that Luther is so much against, and as such would be objectionable to a Roman Catholic and, one would think, to Luther himself.

[51] *L.W.*, XXXVII, 275.

of it, a simple one; and one might conclude that Luther's differences with Rome concern practice rather than doctrine. Luther was vehement against the multiplication of masses for the dead, against the silent mass, the Latin mass, the private mass, the "buying" and "selling" of masses. All of these are, of course, matters of practice, and it cannot seriously be maintained that change in these practices could not be made without change in doctrine. Nevertheless, to Luther it did seem that such practices were related to Roman Catholic doctrine. They are all dependent upon a view of the mass as primarily something to be used, a means to an end. Men want things from God and the mass is *the* means of obtaining them. The mass is an offering (a sacrifice) which, if correctly performed by the priest, influences God automatically *(ex opere operato).*

It is not quite enough to say that this is a caricature of the Roman Catholic understanding of the mass. It is a caricature, but it was not created by Luther or the other reformers. It is a caricature that developed within Roman Catholicism, and which to some extent is still to be found there. Luther took Roman Catholic practice as a genuine incarnation of Roman Catholic doctrine: the meaning of the mass as "sacrifice" he read off from the lived piety of his day. In this he erred I think; but the way was prepared by the indifference of Roman Catholic theologians to the problem of the relation of theology to the concrete life of the Church. When theologians who defend the sacrificial concept of the mass seem not to be disturbed by the development of a sub-Christian understanding of sacrifice within Roman Catholic piety, then there is at least some justification for thinking that the piety does express the doctrine. It is a very natural assumption, though in a surprising number of cases it turns out to be false, that practice and doctrine will agree, and that the meaning of the latter is best understood by means of the former.

Thus one may conclude that Luther misconstrued the Roman Catholic doctrine of the mass as sacrifice, and that what he was really attacking were certain aspects of popular Catholicism. But the fact that Roman Catholic theologians—both before Luther and after him—did not think that it was an essential part of their theological responsibility to criticize the *status quo* in light of the Church's norm and ideal helped to create a situation in which such misconstruction was possible.

In recent years there have been significant developments from both sides. Among Roman Catholics, the liturgical movement has taken seriously the responsibility of making practice express doctrine.

Even after Vatican II's decree on the liturgy there is a long way to go, [52] but a significant beginning has been made. It is neither fortuitous nor a sign of heretical tendencies on the part of liturgists, that practically all of the changes made have been in the direction called for by Luther. On the Lutheran side, there has been something of a rehabilitation of the idea of the mass as sacrifice—i.e., as the re-presentation of Christ's unique sacrifice. To date there remains a continued unwillingness to speak of the mass as the sacrifice of the celebrating community.[53] It is not possible here to consider the objections raised by these most ecumenical of Lutheran theologians. However, if it is true, as argued above,[54] that in *The New Testament* Luther was still asserting everything that a Roman Catholic asserts when he says that the mass is the sacrifice of Christ and the community, then there would seem to be grounds for hoping that the present impasse will not be permanent.

---

[52] The silent Latin canon is but one instance of a practice which, even after Vatican II, tends to distort doctrine.

[53] See the article by Meinhold cited in note 2.

[54] Cf. pp. 71-72

THE WORDS OF INSTITUTION

By Bertil E. Gartner

THIS presentation is focused on the Words of Institution (WI) in relation to the 4 contexts: 1) real presence, 2) sign, 3) consecration, and 4) change. A certain overlapping cannot be avoided as the 4 contexts are intertwined.

1) *Real presence*

The idea of real presence is complex in the NT. The WI seem to contain two ideas which are of particular importance. At the Last Supper a) Jesus, the Son of God, is as a human being present and b) the body of Jesus as sacrificed is proleptically present in the bread and wine. These two ideas occur also in other eucharistic NT texts but never combined. a) The meal of the Kingdom of God was manifested at many occasions during Jesus' public ministry. It began with the meals in Galilee—Jesus had table fellowship with sinners, gave the multitude bread and celebrated the Passover meal with his disciples. This table fellowship continued in the period between Jesus' resurrection and his exaltation, the 40 days. It is a meal *together with* Jesus, the Risen Lord—Acts 10:41 *synesthio,* Lk. 24:29-30 (the prepositions *meta* and *syn* stress the idea of together with Jesus), Jn. 20:19 *eis to meson,* and Jn. 21:9-10.

In the period *after Jesus' exaltation* the same idea occurs once in the NT, namely Rev. 3:20 *deipneso met'autou kai autos met'emou.* This passage is not only a reference to the eschatological communion but it is an expression of the presence of Christ at the eucharist on earth in terms of "together with Jesus." (It is possible, as scholars have said, that Acts 2:46 also reflects this idea.) The resurrection traditions containing the idea of table fellowship with the Risen Lord were used in the Primitive Church not only as narratives of events during the 40 days but also as expressions of an important aspect of the presence of Christ at the eucharist. The eschatological sayings of Jesus on the messianic banquet, e.g., Mt. 8:11; 25:10, and traditions on Jesus eating with the disciples, the people, the sinners were also regarded as expressions of Jesus' presence at the eucharistic meal. Jesus was still together with his disciples.

b) It is, however, obvious that the WI, as well as Paul's (1 Cor. 10-11) and John's (6:53ff.) interpretations of the WI, also expressed another idea of the presence: The bread and wine are the flesh and blood of the Lord. The origin of this idea is difficult to find.

Is it likely that a) and b) originally represented two different ideas which later were combined and b) becoming the dominating idea? Or was a) the first stage of the idea of Christ's presence and b) a more developed form built upon theological re-interpretations? Or did they exist from the beginning as two parallel expressions of the same idea?

2) *Sign*

When I say "real presence" I refer particularly to three different traditions in the NT: a) "This is my body"—"This is my blood" ("the blood of the covenant") in the WI, b) "a communion, *koinonia,* with the blood of Christ," "with the body of Christ," 1 Cor. 10:16, and to eat and drink in an unworthy manner means to be guilty of profaning "the body and blood of the Lord," 1 Cor. 11:27, c) "you eat the flesh of the Son of man and drink his blood," Jn. 6:53. In what manner are bread and wine signs in these texts?

a) *soma* and *haima* in the WI refer to Jesus as giving his life on the cross. The sacrificial terminology of the WI shows that his death was interpreted as a sacrifice for sins. Bread and wine are signs of what Jesus' body stood for on the cross. What is present under the signs are the fruits of the death of Christ as a sacrifice.—"This is my body" can be understood in the light of the Semitic *dabar*-thinking the close relationship between a word, a thing, and an action. The bread is not only an external sign, representing, symbolizing something, but it is what it symbolizes. To eat the bread means to receive the fruits of the death of Christ. A further definition of the *estin* in "This *is* my body" is mere speculation.

b) From the context of the WI in 1 Cor. 10-11 we can learn that Paul understood the WI as expressing the idea of real presence, even if we are not able to give the exact meaning of Paul's statement that the elements are the flesh and blood of the Lord. Paul used, however, a new term to show what he meant with the presence, namely *koinonia,* which seems to stress a communion within a spiritual realm. To eat and drink is to take part in a new spiritual dimension. This is clear from 1 Cor. 10:17 "Because there is one bread, we, though many, are one body. For we all partake of the one bread." On *koinonia* as a term expressing a communion within a spiritual realm see 1 Cor. 1:9, 2 Cor. 13:13, Phil. 2:1. (Compare 1 Cor. 11:27-29, to sin against "the Lord's body and blood," and 1 Cor. 8:12, to "sin against Christ" when committing sins against a fellow Christian.)

c) John's interpretation of the WI in ch. 6 should be understood as an apology of the real presence in the elements, that had been denied by some Christians. John has a sharper and more realistic terminology than Paul, but it is still uncertain how to define the presence of Christ when eating the bread-*sarx*. But in the light of John's theology as a whole I think it is possible to come to a certain definition. The word of God, *logos,* became *sarx,* 1:14. God's "presence," *Shekinah,* dwells in Jesus—a man. God created in him—a man an earthly vehicle conveying to man a share in the divine world, life, salvation. Through Jesus' words and actions the new dimension entered our world. When Jesus after his death was exalted, the Spirit replaced him. The Spirit continued to use earthly vehicles for bringing to man the life of God, water—baptism, ch. 3, bread and wine—the eucharist, ch. 6, man—forgiveness, 20:22. The church uses these signs-vehicles to receive life-salvation. In the three mentioned traditions the Spirit plays a dominating role, 3:5; 6:63a; 20:22, (6:63a seems to be John's especial answer to the objections against the presence). The signs are as earthly things "of no avail." It is the Spirit that gives life.—To this can be added Jn. 4:23-24, where it is said that the worship of the church takes place "in the Spirit," and 6:63b, where it is said that the words of Jesus are spirit and life.

3) *Consecration*

The NT material does not allow us to form any exact conclusion about the function of the WI in the Primitive Church. The form of the 4 pericopes of the Last Supper show that they had a liturgical Sitz im Leben. It is difficult to find any clue to understand the function of them in terms of consecration. Let me, however, present an hypothesis that can establish a connection between the WI and the idea of consecration.

Mt., Mk., and Lk. present the following liturgical order: The bread: a) *labon,* b) *eulogesas* or *eucharistesas,* c) *eklasen,* d) *edoken,* e) *eipen*—The wine: a) *labon,* b) *eucharistesas,* c) *edoken,* d) *lego.*

Paul's version of the WI includes (to the bread) a), b), c), and e), and (to the cup) a), b), and d). That means the word for the distribution is omitted both at the bread and the cup. The formula "This is my body" is thus linked closer to the *eucharistesas* and seems to be part of the *eucharistia.* The same is the case with the formula "This cup is the new covenant in my blood." The Synoptic versions follow the Jewish liturgical order. The only addition is the two formulas connected with the distribution and not with the *eucharistia.*

The Pauline version of the WI, connecting the formulas with the *eucharistia,* seems to be behind 1 Cor. 10:16, where the apostle speaks of "the cup of blessing which we bless," *to poterion tes eulogias ho eulogoumen.*

Didache 9:1-3 links the prayer of *eucharistia* with the cup and the bread but there is no mentioning of the WI. Justin, in his Apology I, 66, 3, comes closer to Paul's version when he writes "Jesus took the bread, praised (God), *eucharistesanta,* and said: Do this in remembrance of me. This is my body. And in the same way he took the cup and praised (God) and said: This is my blood." There is no word of distribution in Justin's text.

Is it posible to say that Paul's version of the WI shows that the two—a) the *berakah—eucharistia* and b) the formula at the distribution—had been combined in one of the NT teaching traditions at an early stage? Is this combination reflected in Didache 9:5 and Ignatius, Smyrna 7:1, and Ephesians 13:1, where *eucharistia* means the consecrated elements? The prayer of *eucharistia* was combined with the WI and the consecration took place within this praising of God and the elements therefore were denoted by the term *eucharistia* (?)

If this hypothesis is not accepted, I must conclude that NT does not indicate at all what the function of the WI was. The moment of consecration cannot be identified. The *hoc facite* has nothing to do with the consecration.

4) *Change*

"Change" is in my opinion a word connected with later philosophical attempts to find an exact definition of the sign as the body of Christ and has no counterpart in the NT traditions. In the material presented above there is no hint at any interest to discuss the problem that is connected with the theological word "change." Not even John who presents the most "realistic" interpretation of the WI in his ch. 6 has any word or expression that can be related to the later discussion of "change." The NT traditions teach the real presence in different ways but there is no evidence of a discussion of "change."

When discussing the WI in relation to the 4 contexts the problem that we face is the interpretation of how the "Heilsgeschehen" that belonged to one particular historical event in the past, *passio Christi,* can be made present here and now. How is it possible that an *ephapax* event, that belongs to the past, can be made present without loosing its singularity in the plurality (the repeated eucharist)? How to combine *factum passionis* and *usus passionis*? Does the cultic repetition of Jesus' words and action at the Last Supper in our eucharist abolish the distinct "Einmaligkeit des Heilsgeschehen"? I think that John is the only one in the NT that really thought in these categories and tried to present a solution—his theology of the Spirit as the vehicle. John gives an answer to the problem of how to make present the absent Christ, present in the world, in the Church and in the sacraments. I am more uncertain when I read Paul. Was the concept of the spiritual body of Christ Paul's solution of the same problem?

'SACRAMENTAL SIGN' IN THE LUTHERAN CONFESSIONS

By Warren A. Quanbeck

THERE are three dominating elements in Lutheran thought concerning the Lord's Supper: the centrality of the Word of God, the communion-meal character of the sacrament, and stress on the unity of the "action" of the Supper. These elements appear first in the writings of Martin Luther and then in the confessional writings of the Lutheran church as they develop between 1530 and 1580.

1. The biblical concept of the Word of God is central to the reality and understanding of the Lord's Supper. In the thought of the writers of scripture God's Word or address is the means He uses to relate Himself to His world. Through His Word He created the world; He addressed Israel through His Word on the lips of the prophets; in the fullness of time the Word of God became Incarnate in Jesus of Nazareth; in the era of the church God continues to reveal Himself in His Word, now defined further as the gospel, the announcement of what He has done in Jesus Christ; through the Word of the gospel God continues to work in the church, sending it into the world as the continuation of the redemptive mission of His Son. The Lord's Supper is a visible, dramatic form of the Word of God, rooting in its institution by Jesus Christ, receiving its authority and efficacy through the coming together of God's Word and the created things used in accordance with the institution and purpose of God. Through it God continues to speak, reminding men dramatically of His saving deed in Christ, who through the sacrament becomes effectually present among His people and gives to them the benefits of His death and resurrection.

The character of the Supper as an act in the history of salvation is pointed out in the Formula of Concord, Solid Declaration VII 75 ff: "For the truthful and almighty words of Jesus Christ which he spoke in the first institution were not only efficacious in the first Supper but they still retain their validity and efficacious power in all places where the Supper is observed, and the body and blood of Christ are truly present, distributed and received by the virtue and potency of the same words which Christ spoke in the first Supper. For wherever we observe his institution and speak his words over the bread and cup and distribute the blessed bread and cup, Christ himself is still active through the spoken words by the virtue of the first institution, which he wants to be repeated. . . . Thus it is not our work or speaking but the command and ordinance of Christ that, from the beginning of the first Communion until the end of the world, make the bread the body and the wine the blood that are daily distributed through our ministry and office." It is the consciousness that the Supper is an act in the history of salvation as well as the conviction that its efficacy is based upon the Word of God that causes the Reformers to stress the propriety of speaking or singing the words of institution "distinctly and clearly before the congregation." They "are under no circumstances to be omitted." (FC VII 79)

The connection between the Supper and the Word of God is put very simply in the Large Catechism: "God's Word . . . is the chief thing to be considered. For the Lord's Supper was not invented or devised by any man. It was instituted by Christ without man's counsel or deliberation. Therefore, just as the Ten Commandments, the Lord's Prayer, and the Creed retain their nature and value even if we never keep, pray, or believe them, so also does this blessed sacrament remain unimpaired and inviolate even if we use and handle it unworthily" (LC V 5). The same point is urged strongly in the Formula of Concord to strengthen the faith of those who are disturbed by questions as to how Christ can be present in the Sacrament, and also to affirm the validity and efficacy of the Supper even though administered by an unworthy minister. (FC VII 24)

One effect of this has been to discourage theological speculation as to the way in which Christ is present in the sacrament. Since His presence is an act of God effected through His word, it is not accessible to man's understanding or to his powers of observation. Persistent questions, however, especially by the Swiss Reformers impelled Luther and his followers to develop an apologetic for their position, whose main lines are discussed below.

2. A second prominent element in Lutheran reflection on the Lord's Supper stresses its character as a meal and as a communion. Luther's sacramental thought is remarkably rich and diverse, developing many different aspects of the meaning of the Supper: memorial,

sacrifice, a sign of faith among men, a sign of God's will toward us, an awareness of its eschatological dimension, the importance of man's response in faith and obedience, but the element which provides the structure for his thought is his insistence that the sacrament is above all a meal, a communion of the believer with Christ and with his fellow christians. Because of this he insisted that the Supper be celebrated only when communicants were present and that communion be administered in both kinds. Here Luther is conscious of the institution and commandment of Christ and also aware of the danger of distorting or losing sight of the meal-character of the supper through neglect or omission of essential aspects of the liturgical actions.

3. The third main thrust of Lutheran teaching on the Lord's Supper is emphasis upon the form of the sacrament as a series of actions which comprise a liturgical unity. The service properly includes the reading and exposition of the Word of God in scripture, confession of faith, the blessing of the elements, their distribution and their reception by the communicants. Lutheran theologians insist that at least three of these elements are necessary to the proper administration of the Supper: the consecration, the distribution, and the reception. The Formula of Concord summarizes this point in the rule: "Nothing has the character of a sacrament apart from the use instituted by Christ, or apart from the divinely instituted action (that is, if one does not observe Christ's institution as he ordained it, it is no sacrament). (FC VII 85)

The Formula of Concord goes on to define "action." "In this context 'use' or 'action' does not primarily mean faith, or the oral eating alone, but the entire external and visible action of the Supper as ordained by Christ: the consecration or words of institution, the distribution and reception, or the oral eating of the blessed bread and wine, the body and blood of Christ. Apart from this use it is not to be deemed a sacrament." (FC VII 86,87). "But the command of Christ, 'Do this,' which comprehends the whole action or administration of this sacrament (namely that in a Christian assembly we take bread and wine, consecrate it, distribute it, receive it, eat and drink it, and therewith proclaim the Lord's death), must be kept integrally and inviolately." (FC VII 84)

The unity of the action of the Sacrament finds expression in all of the confessional documents of the Lutheran church. It is less explicit in the earlier confessions, but the constitutive elements are enumerated, e.g. Augustana X: "The true body and blood of Christ are really present in the Supper of our Lord under the form of bread and wine and are there distributed and received." The same elements are affirmed in the Apology of the Augsburg Confession X, the Smalcald Articles VI, and the two catechisms. In each of these documents the same complex of elements is presented: the body and blood of Christ, bread and wine, the distribution and reception. The Smalcald Articles become more specific with reference to the distribution of bread alone: "Administration in one form is not the whole order and institution as it was established and commanded by Christ." (SA VI)

4. The word "sign" is used in the Lutheran confessions primarily of the sacrament in the unity and totality of its action. It is a sign of profession among men, but, more important, it is a sign of God's will toward us. (Apology 24) In the Formula of Concord, where Calvinist and Zwinglian interpretations of the Supper are discussed at length, there is necessarily more concentration upon the elements of bread and wine, especially concerning the problem of their relation to the body and blood of Christ in the sacrament. But even this concentration upon the problem of the elements and the concern for the proper interpretation of the term "sign" as applied to them, does not move the discussion out of the earlier context. The Formula uses the term "sign" both of the total sacramental action and of the elements of bread and wine. The lengthy discussion of the unity and integrity of the sacramental action (FC 83-86, 108, 110) also serves to remind the reader that bread and wine as signs are to be seen in the context of the total liturgical action as sign.

5. Lutheran argumentation concerning the fact and mode of the real presence follows four main lines, which are here summarized briefly.

6. The first line of argument moves from the words of Institution to the assertion of the real presence. Lutheran theologians of the 16th and 17th centuries maintain that the proper starting point for the discussion of the Supper is in the passages which describe its institution. They reject other starting points, even from the scriptures, as being less central and less clear, and therefore involving the danger of imposing upon the interpretation of the Supper ideas not centrally related to it, or ideas torn out of context. They especially oppose the use of the discourse in John 6 as a starting point. (Zwingli had found the passage John 6:63, "It is the spirit that gives life; the flesh is of no avail," very congenial to his views of the Supper.)

They affirm repeatedly and in various ways that the literal sense of the words is the obvious meaning. Jesus chose His words with care; the Evangelists and Paul transmit them with accuracy. When Jesus said that the bread was His body and the wine His blood, He meant precisely what He said; He does not lie, equivocate or deceive. His saying so is sufficient, for He speaks the Word of God which is able to accomplish the purpose God intends. Therefore since our Lord has said so, and His word is sufficient to accomplish His purpose, theologians ought not to multiply objections but simply accept the authority of the Word. The fact of the presence of Christ in the Supper is established by the word and promise of God; how it takes place is a supernatural event which surpasses our understanding and eludes our ability to explain.

7. The arguments of the Calvinists and the Zwinglians nevertheless push Lutheran theologians to attempt an apologetic for their contention that the whole Christ is present in the Sacrament with His body and blood "as the words declare." The Swiss Reformers maintained that the presence of Christ in His body and blood in the Sacrament was impossible because of the personal union of the two natures in Christ. The union of divinity and humanity is so complete and enduring that even after the ascension Christ is still possessed of a (glorified) human body. Since it is not an attribute of a human body to be in more than one place at a time, the human body of Christ is limited spatially to heaven, where He sits at the right hand of the Father. The believer's participation in the body and blood of Christ must therefore be understood either as faith's reception of the bread and wine as symbols of Christ's body and blood, or else as the act of the Holy Spirit who elevates the believer to heaven, there to hold communion with the risen Christ.

The Lutherans rejected both alternatives and used the language of christological formulations as an instructive analogy to make their position persuasive. The so-called *communicatio idiomatum* speaks of the communication of the two natures in the person of Christ. Since the union of the two natures is a personal one, and not like a chemical mixture or the joining of two boards with glue, the two natures communicate with each other in three different ways:

a. The *genus idiomaticum* in which the attributes of each of the two natures are predicated of the entire person of Christ. The *idiomata* of the divine nature as well as those of the human nature belong to the person of Jesus Christ.

b. The *genus apotelesmaticum* in which the attributes of both natures are ascribed to the one person in accomplishing the work of redemption. None of the influences proceeding from Christ can be attributed to only one of the two natures. The Swiss reformers accepted these points; the argument arose concerning the third.

c. The *genus majestaticum* in which through the personal union the human nature has become partaker of the attributes of the divine nature. Thus the man Jesus participated in the omniscience of the Logos, a participation of which, however, he did not avail Himself during His earthly ministry. Now, in His glorified state the person of Christ can be present in many places simultaneously, inasmuch as the communication of attributes enables His glorified humanity to participate in the omnipresence of the divine nature.

8. The Formula of Concord amplified this teaching concerning ubiquity (FC VII 98-103) by a quotation from Luther (WA, 26: 335 ff.).

"The one body of Christ has three different modes, or all three modes, of being at any given place.

1. "The comprehensible, corporeal mode of presence, as when he walked bodily on earth and vacated or occupied space according to his size. He can still employ this mode of presence when he wills to do so, as he did after his resurrection, and as he will do on the Last Day."

2. "There is, secondly, the incomprehensible, spiritual mode of presence according to which he neither occupies nor vacates space but penetrates every creature, wherever he wills. . . . He employed this mode of presence when he left the closed grave and came through locked doors, in the bread and wine in the Lord's Supper."

3. "Thirdly, since he is one person with God, the divine, heavenly mode, according to which all creatures are indeed much more penetrable and present to him than they are according to the second mode. . . . But who can explain or even conceive how this occurs? We know indeed that he is in God beyond all creatures and is one person with God. But how this happens, we do not know; it transcends nature and reason, even the comprehension of all the angels in heaven, and is known only to God. Since this is true, even though unknown to us, we should not give the lie to his words until we know how to prove certainly that the body of Christ cannot in any circumstances be where God is and that this mode of being is a fiction."

"I do not wish to have denied by the foregoing that God may

have and know more modes whereby Christ's body can be anywhere. . . . For I do not want to deny in any way that God's power is able to make a body be simultaneously in many places even in a corporeal and comprehensible manner."

9. Another analogy drawn from christological thought suggests that the presence of Christ in the Supper is like the presence of the Logos in the man Jesus. Just as in Jesus Christ the two natures co-exist without either nature being absorbed or changed into the other, so in the sacrament the body and blood of Christ are *under, with* and *in* the bread and wine. The reformers note that there is a significant difference: the union of the two natures in the person of Christ is a *personal* union; that of the body and blood of Christ with bread and wine is a *sacramental* union. (FC VII 35 ff.)

10. The terms sacramental presence and sacramental union become key terms in the Lutheran interpretation of the Supper. They become irritating to non-Lutherans because they are defined mainly in negative terms, but illustrate what was noted above, the Lutheran preference for asserting the reality of the presence without defining the mode of the presence. Sacramental presence is distinguished from coarse, material ideas of the presence as capernaitic eating and also from spiritualizing ideas of presence as in Zwingli. Lutherans did not respond favorably to Calvin's language of a *real, spiritual* presence, suspecting that it meant an unreal, ethereal presence. They also rejected the language of *impanation, invination,* or *consubstantiation,* seeing in them too substantial a conjunction of bread and wine with the body and blood of Christ. As against *transubstantiation* they maintained that bread and wine remain bread and wine, remarking, mildly enough, that this understanding seems to accord better with scripture, as in I Cor. 10:16: "The bread which we break, is it not a participation in the body of Christ?" Sacramental presence becomes thus a formula seeking to avoid materialistic or spiritualistic interpretations of the Supper, trying to find another option to objective and subjective understandings of the presence. As they recognize, the term is more effective in rejecting what is seen to be wrong than in finding adequate formulations of a right interpretation.

THE DOCTRINE OF TRANSUBSTANTIATION FROM BERENGAR THROUGH THE COUNCIL OF TRENT *

BY JAMES F. MCCUE

IT will be the purpose of this paper to trace the doctrine of transubstantiation down through the Council of Trent. Trent is chosen as the *terminus ad quem* because, as I shall try to show, it is the first conciliar response to a dispute over the doctrine of transubstantiation. The *terminus a quo* is more difficult. It would be helpful to trace the doctrine of the eucharist from its origins, but that would be impossible here. Somewhat arbitrarily (but I hope not completely so), I shall begin at the point at which the vocabularly and theory of transubstantiation begins to take shape within the discussion of the presence of Christ in the sacrament of the altar. I take it for granted that the focus of interest at this point in time was not precisely what it had been in earlier centuries; nor do I wish to imply that this shift in focus can easily or entirely be subsumed under the heading of development.[1] I have no intention of settling these larger issues here.

I

As is well known, the two principal patristic sources of the eucharistic controversies which took place from the ninth through the eleventh centuries were Ambrose and Augustine. From the thoroughly orthodox Ambrose came a strong emphasis on the change of the bread and wine into the actual body and blood of Christ. From the equally orthodox Augustine came a strong emphasis on the non-identity of the bread and wine and the body and blood of Christ, and on Christ's presence in the eucharist in spirit and in power. Twentieth century scholarship may be able to harmonize

* With permission of the *Harvard Theological Review*.

[1] The work of P. Battifol, *L'Eucharistie. La presence reele et la transsubstantiation (Etudes de theologie positive, 2)*, 9th ed. Paris, 1930, strikes me as altogether too optimistic in this regard.

the two views; the ninth and tenth had no little difficulty. It is not necessary for us here to articulate precisely what Augustine and Ambrose did think about the eucharist. We need but note that they served as the principal patristic sources for two conflicting tendencies in later centuries.

There were, in the ninth, tenth, and eleventh centuries a number of theologians, largely Augustinian in their inspiration, who seemed to some to be evacuating the eucharist of its content and substance. Their opponents, deriving more from Ambrose, seemed to the "Augustinians" to be guilty of theological crudity and of a grotesquely physical conception of the eucharist. Here again, the precise details and evaluations need not detain us, for it is what emerges from the dispute rather than the dispute itself that is of importance for our problem.

The debate came to a climax and to an end in the career of Berengar of Tours. Whether or not he was a Zwinglian *avant la lettre* is here beside the point; so he was understood in his day and immediately thereafter. The profession of faith required of Berengar at the Synod of Rome (1059) may be taken as a decisive triumph of "Ambrosian" over "Augustinian" tendencies:

". . . Consentio autem sanctae Romanae Ecclesiae et Apostolicae Sedi, et ore et corde profiteor de sacramento dominicae mensae eam fidem me tenere, quam dominus et venerabilis papa Nicolaus et haec sancta Synodus auctoritate evangelica et apostolica tenendam tradidit mihique firmavit: scilicet panem et vinum, quae in altari ponuntur, post consecrationem non solum sacramentum, sed etiam verum corpus et sanguinem Domini nostri Iesu Christi esse, et sensualiter, non solum sacramento, sed in veritate, manibus sacerdotum tractari et frangi et fidelium dentibus atteri, iurans per sanctam et homousion Trinitatem et per haec sacrosancta Christi evangelia. Eos vero, qui contra hanc fidem venerint, cum dogmatibus et sectatoribus suis, aeterno anathemate dignos esse pronuntio." Dz-S. 690.

For the next several centuries, eucharistic realism and change after the manner of Ambrose would be the common meeting-ground of almost all Latin theologians, and it was in this setting that the doctrine of transubstantiation would emerge. In another confession of faith imposed on Berengar in 1079 we have the following expression: "Ego Berengarius corde credo et ore confiteor, panem et vinum, quae ponuntur in altari, per mysterium sacrae orationis et verba nostri Redemptoris substantialiter converti in veram et propriam ac vivificatricem carnem et sanguinem Iesu Christi Domini nostri." (Dz. S. 700.)

The transition from "substantialiter converti" to "transsubstantiari" is, as Hans Jorissen has recently pointed out, a matter of terminology and does not in itself constitute a substantive advance beyond 1079.[2] Jorissen is unable to find "transsubstantiatio" or "transsubstantiari" prior to the work of Roland Bandinelli, who died in 1181 as Pope Alexander III.

Jorissen, after tracing the development of the vocabulary of transubstantiation during the century after Berengar, considers the varying assessments of the status of the doctrine in the last years of the twelfth and the first years of the thirteenth century. On one side are those—Balduin of Ford and Alan of Lille most notably—who consider the doctrine to be an *articulus fidei;* on the other side are theologians like Peter of Capua who hold that it is not.

Jorissen's juxtaposition of views is, however, a bit too simply conceived. It is true that some earlier writers had rejected as heretical a doctrine of consubstantiation even while recognizing that it was not equivalent to a denial of the real presence.[3] But such is not the situation in the ca. 1200 writers whom Jorissen cites in this connection. Balduin of Ford and Alan of Lille are both speaking of transubstantiation over against what they take to be a complete denial of the doctrine of the real presence. They are not discussing transubstantiation as one of several possible ways of asserting the real presence. Balduin, for example, does not get involved in explanatory subtleties but simply maintains that eucharistic realism requires that we believe that what was bread becomes, by the power of Christ's word, the body of Christ. It ceases to be bread.

Consider the following statement of position:

"Dilingenter intuentibus quid acceperit Jesus Christus, et quid dederit, mutatio panis facta demonstratur, panem quippe accepit, re et nomine panem; et benedicens et frangens, corpus suum dedit. Unde creditur secundum pietatem fidei, mutatio panis facta, etsi ipso mutationis nomine ab evangelista non sit expressa. Et quoniam corde

[2] Hans Jorissen, *Die Entfaltung der Transsubstantiationslehre bis zum Beginn der Hochscholastik* Munster, 1965), p. 7.

[3] "Nunc contra illos habenda est ratio qui, Ecclesiae rationibus expugnati, jam quidem negare nequeunt substantiam corporis Christi cibo inesse Dominico, panem tamen et vinum per verba Salvatoris in carnem ejus et sanguinem verti nequaquam credentes, sed Christum pani et vino commiscentes, tanquam subtiliori ratione haeresim alteram condiderunt." Guitmundus archiepiscopus .aversanus (d. 1079), *De corporis et sanguinis Christi veritate libri tres, PL,* 149, 1480-1481. It may be that Guitmund is here identifying what I have called consubstantiation with the theory of impanation. For a rejection of this latter as heretical in terms reminiscent of Guitmund see *PL,* 180, 342; *ibid.* 754.

creditur ad justitiam, ore autem confessio fit ad salutem (*Rom.* x), ut, sicut mutatio vere facta firmissime tenetur in fide cordis, sic constanter teneatur in confessione oris; confitetur Ecclesia, sicut ex traditione orthodoxorum Patrum indubitanter apparet, quod panis virtute divinae benedictionis efficitur corpus Christi, vel fit corpus Christi: et transsubstantiatur, vel mutatur, vel convertitur in corpus Christi: multisque modis aliis loquendi melius fide institutum explicat. Et cum in hac fidei confessione multa sit verborum diversitas, una est tamen fidei pietas, et individua confessionis unitas." *Liber de sacramento altaris, PL,* 204, 662.

In other places (e.g. *ibid.* 667) one finds the explicit affirmation that the bread ceases to be bread. But the entire affirmation is part of the larger affirmation of the actual presence of Christ in the sacrament. Balduin never picks up the question of whether real presence and transubstantiation are necessarily connected or whether it might be possible to have the former without the latter. He does not suppose that he is describing how this all takes place, only that it takes place:

"Simpliciter ergo et confidenter, firmiter et constanter, teneamus, credamus, et confiteamur, quod substantia panis, in substantiam carnis Christi mutatur, manente tamen specie panis, mirabiliter, et ineffabaliter, et incomprehensibiliter. Indubitanter credimus, quod ita est: quomodo autem hoc sit, adhuc simpliciter ignoramus. Nondum de modo scimus; sciemus autem postea, cum virtus hujus mysterii in nobis fuerit consummata." *Ibid.* 679f.

So far as I have been able to ascertain, none of the writers of this period who insist on transubstantiation as an article of faith do this in opposition to those who would maintain the possibility of other alternatives within the doctrine of the real presence. Instead, they identify transubstantiation and real presence as two sides of a single coin.

The question being asked in Peter of Capua is significantly different. Peter considers the doctrine of the real presence to be an article of faith, but the way in which this comes about is a matter of theological debate:

"De conversione triplex est opinio. Quidam dicunt quod non est ibi aliqua mutatio, sed remanente substantia panis et substantia vini ad prolationem illorum verborum incipit sub eisdem speciebus esse caro et sanguis Christi, cum prius non esset ibi nisi substantia panis et vini, et ubicumque legitur aliquid de conversione, sic intelligitur: ubi prius erat tantum panis et vinum, incipit esse etiam caro Christi et sanguis.

"Alii dicunt quod substantia panis et vini penitus adnihilatur et manentibus speciebus eisdem incipit ibi esse sola caro et sanguis Christi, et simili modo exponunt conversionem illam.

"Nos dicimus et expositores hoc asserunt, quod ipsa substantis panis convertitur in carnem Christi veram quam traxit de Virgine, et substantia vini in verum sanguinem, et manentibus prioribus speciebus incipit ibi esse caro et sanguis Christi. Nec est articulus fidei credere quod sic vel sic fiat illa conversio, sed tantummodo credere quod corpus Christi ad prolationem illorum verborum sit in altari."[4]

For purposes of convenience I shall call the three positions set forth here, respectively, consubstantiation, annihilation, and transubstantiation. Peter is simply asserting that any one of these *can* be used to assert the real presence; and though he himself favors transubstantiation as an account of how the presence of Christ comes about, he states quite clearly that the other alternatives are not in his judgment heretical. Thus Peter cannot be accused of trying to make room within orthodoxy for his own heterodox views. I think that one is forced to conclude from what he says, and from the easy way in which he says it, that he does not suppose that this is a question that has been settled or that needs to be settled.

In a similar manner, Lothar of Segni, who as Innocent III was to preside over the Fourth Lateran Council, quite clearly favors a doctrine of transubstantiation in his *De sacro altaris mysterio;* yet where he discusses consubstantiation (=cons.) he does indeed reject it, but simply as something erroneous with which he disagrees, not as something heretical. He writes:

"Solet a multis inquiri, sed a paucis intelligi quid Christus tunc in mensa fregit, et quid sacerdos in altari nunc frangit. Fuerunt qui dicerent quod, sicut post consecrationem vera panis remanent accidentia, sic et vera panis substantia, quia sicut subjectum non potest sine accidentibus existere, sic accidentia non possunt existere sine subjecto. Accidents esse non est aliud quam inesse. Sed panis et vini substantiis permanentibus, ad prolationem illorum verborum corpus et sanguis Christi veraciter incipiunt esse sub illis, ita quod sub eisdem accidentibus utrumque vere sumitur panis et caro, vinum et sanguis, quorum alterum probat sensus, reliquum credit fides . . . Hi facile solvunt quaestionem illam, qua quaeritur quid a mure comedi-

---

[4]Text as in Jorissen, p. 24. According to Jorissen, the work quoted here was completed in 1201 or 1202.

tur, cum sacramentum cor roditur, comeditur secundum illos illa panis substantia, sub qua corpus Christi esse mox desinit."[5]

He goes on to work out an alternative which is obviously to take the place of the view described here; but it is important to note that there is no suggestion that the view is heretical or subversive of orthodoxy. In contrast, he quite straight-forwardly labels a merely symbolic interpretation of the eucharist heretical: "Quod ergo panis fuerat cum accepit, corpus suum erat cum dedit. Panis itaque mutatus erat in corpus ipsius, et similiter vinum in sanguinem. Non enim ut haereticos sapit, sed desipit, ita debet intelligi, quod Dominus ait: *Hoc est corpus meum,* id est hoc signat corpus meum, sicut quod dicit Apostolus: *Petra autem erat Christus,* id est petra significabat Christian."[6]

Lothar of Segni and Peter of Capua were, of course, both writing before 1215. In that year the Fourth Lateran Council met. Since the time of Scotus, as we shall see, the confession of faith of this council has been interpreted as a formal definition of transubstantiation over against cons.[7] It is, however, worthy of note that for a generation after 1215 theologians continued to express views similar to those of Peter of Capua without any apparent realization that they were thereby contradicting a council. Moreover, even those who, around 1250, began to argue that transubstantiation alone was orthodox did not refer to Lateran IV in support of their position.

The Fourth Lateran Council had, among its aims, the repudiation of certain heresies, the most important of which was Albigensianism. It is the definition of faith *contra Albigenses et Catharos* that contains the affirmation of transubstantiation. The relevant portion is as follows:

"Una vero est fidelium universalis Ecclesia, extra quam nullus omnino salvatur, in qua idem ipse sacerdos est sacrificium Iesus Christus, cuius corpus et sanguis in sacramento altaris sub speciebus

---

[5]*De sacro altaris mysterio,* IV, ix, *PL,* 217, 86lf. Jorissen dates this work before 1198.

[6]*Ibid.* 860.

[7]We need not complicate our considerations here by a prolonged consideration of the ecumenicity of Lateran IV. F. Dvornik, in "Which Councils are Ecumenical"? *Journal of Ecumenical Studies,* III (1966), 314-328 (esp. 325), would seem to be correct in asserting that at Florence the Latins did not claim ecumenicity for the medieval Latin councils over against the East. But this notwithstanding, Latin theologians both before and after Florence seem to have treated Lateran IV as an ecumenical and binding council. To limit the question to the matter at hand, I know of no 14th, 15th or 16th century writer who challenged the dogma of transubstantiation on the grounds that the council cited for its support was not ecumenical.

panis et vini veraciter continentur, transsubstantiatis pane in corpus, et vino in sanguinem potestate divina: ut ad perficiendum mysterium unitatis accipiamus ipsi de suo, quod accepit ipse de nostro." Dz.-S. 802.

In the pre-1215 anti-Albigensian polemic one finds commonly enough a repudiation of the denial of the real presence, and commonly it is the doctrine of transubstantiation that is opposed to this denial. The general problematic is similar to that of Alan of Lille or Balduin of Ford.[8] But so far as I know, there was never any discussion in this literature of the alternatives presented by Peter of Capua. Nor does there appear to have been any discussion at the Council itself of Peter of Capua's problem. The language, it is true, is that of one of Peter's three alternatives; but it is not unreasonable to suppose that this language is being used without any intention of canonizing one of the three alternatives to the exclusion of the others. This suggestion will seem less artificial if we bear two considerations in mind: a) prior to 1215 writers who favored one of Peter of Capua's first two alternatives could still quite easily use the language of transubstantiation; and b) as already mentioned, no one for 85 years after the council supposed that it had canonized transubstantiation.

In support of the first of these assertions we may begin by noting what Peter Lombard has to say about the advocates of cons.: "Alii vero putaverunt ibi substantiam panis et vini remanere, et ibidem corpus Christi esse et sanguinem, et hac ratione *dici illam substantiam fieri istam*, quia ubi est haec, est et illa. . . ."[9] Though it is necessary to handle an indirect quotation such as this with considerable caution, the most obvious interpretation of this passage is that advocates of cons. could use the vocabulary of transubstantiation without strain. The word itself, of course, is not used here, and so far as we know it may not yet have been coined; but *illam substantiam fieri istam* would seem to imply the entire doctrine of transubstantiation, and according to Peter Lombard the expression was used by some who did not hold that explanation of the real presence. It is difficult to get the defenders of cons. to speak for themselves, since they are very difficult to find. I presume that there were some, that the position was not simply made up by its opponents for the sake of symmetry, yet I have not found any treatises from this period which actively

---

[8]See *PL*, 195, 84; *PL*, 204, 782.
For further literature, see art. "Albigeois", *DTC*, I, 686; art. "Cathares", *DTC*, II, 1997-1998.

[9]*Sententiarum libri quatuor*, IV, dist. xi, *PL*, 192, 862; emphasis added.

champion cons. The disagreement was rather between advocates of transubstantiation and succession. Among at least some of the latter the vocabulary of transubstantiation was used. Roland Bandinelli, in whose writings we first find the word "trans-substantiatio," favored succession rather than what we have been calling transubstantiation.[10]

In support of the second assertion we may note first the *Glossa ordinaria* to the Decretals of Gratian. The gloss was written shortly after 1215, and was reworked some thirty years later.[11] It favors succession, and we still have Peter of Capua's three alternatives recognized as possible ways of asserting the real presence. The alternatives are not juxtaposed as orthodoxy and heresy.

De eo tamen quod dicitur quod panis convertitur in corpus Christi, variae sunt opiniones. Una asserit, quod illa substantia, quae fuit panis primo, postea est caro et sanguis Christi . . . Secunda opinio tenet, quod substantia panis et vini ibi desinit esse et remanet accidentia tantum, scilicet sapor, color, pondus, et similia, et sub illis accidentibus incipit esse corpus Christi. Tertia tenet, quod remanet ibi substantia panis et vini, et in eodem loco, et sub eadem specie est corpus Christi . . . Quaelibet tamen opinio fatetur ibi esse corpus Christi. Secunda opinio verior est.[12]

To stress the post-1215 toleration of consubstantiation is not to say that it was at all popular or widely held. Indeed it was often quite vigorously criticized, especially as we draw near to mid-century; but apparently it is not until Thomas Aquinas that any one labels the position heretical.[13]

William of Auxerre, writing between 1220 and 1222, attacks cons. in the following terms: "Alii vero dicunt quod idem est: panis transit in corpus Christi: quod corpus Christi incipit esse ubi panis est; unde dicunt quod panis manet. Sed ex hoc sequitur quod transitus ille non est miraculosus: quia corpus glorificatum naturaliter potest esse cum corpore non glorificato in eodem loco: dicunt autem sancti quod transitus ille miraculosus est.[14] It should be noted that cons. is criticized not because of any alleged philosophical impossibility

[10]Cf. Jorissen, 7, 27.

[11]See Jorissen, p. 29.

[12]*Corpus Juris Canonici*, ed. A. Friedberg, Leipzig, 1879, I, 1314; quoted in Jorissen, p. 30, n. 78.

[13]Thus, owing to a number of complications of which I am sure he knew nothing, Luther's charge that Aristotle and Aquinas were responsible for the introduction of transubstantiation was not without an element of truth.

[14]Summa aurea, Paris, 1500, 257vb, quoted in Jorissen, p. 40, n. 111.

but, to the contrary, because it is too simple and non-miraculous. Cons. along with succession he characterizes as "minus fideles."

Hugh of St. Cher, writing ca. 1232, repeats William of Auxerre's line of argument in much the same terms. After citing a number of authorities on behalf of transubstantiation, Lateran IV not among them, he concludes: "Propter has auctoritates et multas alias sanctorum videtur nobis, quod propriė duae opiniones minus verae sint et forte minus catholicae; de secunda [cons.] non est dubium. Ideo concedimus simpliciter, quod tertia est vera, dicentes quod panis transsubstantiatur in corpus Christi et vinum in sanguinem."[15]

Alexander of Hales, in his *Glossa in quatuor libros sententiarum* (1223-1227), advances as traditional a criticism which we have not seen yet.

"Quaeritur, si caro Christi est salvatrix nec Deus vult aliquid perire, cum sit causa permanendi in omnibus, et corpus Christi glorificatum potest simul esse cum corpore non glorificato: propter quid desinit esse panis, cum idem effectus posset esse sine desinitione et cum?—Respondet Magistri quod, si panis haberet esse completum, non esset simpliciter ductivum in aliud; ut ergo simpliciter esset ductivum in aliud, remansit species sensibilis sine substantia. Praeterea, ut non quaereretur ibi refectio corporalis, sed spiritualis."[16]

In his *Quaestiones disputatae 'antequam esset frater'* (prior to 1236), Alexander does label heresy a position which at first appears to be cons., but it turns out that the position is in fact a denial of the real presence.

Ioannes Damascenus, in fine sui tractatus, multa dixit circa hoc. Basilius enim videbatur dicere quod panis et vinum remanent, et haec essent ductiva ad corpus Christi et sanguinem. Unde hoc est haeresis quod dicit; sic *Hoc est corpus meum*, id est ductivum ad corpus meum; similiter *Hic est sanguis meus*, id est ductivus in sanguinem Christi.[17]

William of Militona, another Franciscan, adopts a similar approach in his *Quaestiones de sacramentis* (probably written between 1245 and 1249). A considerable number of arguments and authorities are heaped up in favor of transubstantiation against consubstantiation; but it is noteworthy that 1) the arguments are directed

[15]Quoted in Jorissen, p. 41, n. 112: Ms. Leipzig, Univ. Bibl., lat. 573, f. 230rb.

[16]*Glossa in quatuor libros sententiarum Petri Lombardi* (Quaracchi, 1957), IV, dist. xi, n. 6, *Bibliotheca Franciscana Scholastica Medii Aevi*, XV, 173.

[17]*Quaestiones disputatae 'antequam esset frater'* q. 51, disp. 3, memb. 1, n. 72, (Quaracchi, 1960), II, 921-922, (*Bibl. Frans. Schol.*, XX)

toward showing the appropriateness (not the necessity) of transubstantiation,[18] 2) Lateran IV is not among the authorities, and 3) cons. is not called a heresy.

In the *Sentence Commentary* of Albert the Great (written 1246-1248) the situation remains basically the same. To deny the real presence is *expresse contra fidem.*[19] Transubstantiation is preferable to succession or cons. for a variety of reasons. His first argument is based upon the words of institution: "Si substantia panis manet: tunc falsus est sermo Domini, dicens: 'Hoc est corpus meum': quia tunc substantia panis per sua accidentia oculis subiecta demonstratur per pronomen."[20] The point is that if the substance of bread had remained, Jesus would have said "*Hic* est corpus meum," or "*Hic panis* est corpus meum." So far as I know Albert is the first to argue for transubstantiation over against consubstantiation directly from the New Testament.

He argues secondly that cons. does not suit the sacramental character of the eucharist. "Dicendum, quod licet corpus gloriosum et praecipue corpus Domini possit esse cum pane in eodem loco, tamen ratio sacramenti, non ratio loci repugnat . . . quia accidens non duceret nisi in substantiam propriam, et sic caderet a ratione signandi.[21] It should be noted here that, in contrast to the position soon to be adopted by Thomas Aquinas, Albert expressly allows the possibility of cons. Moreover, in his argument from authorities there is no reference to Lateran IV. He concludes the discussion: "Dicendum quod ista opinio his rationibus multis et fere omnibus falsa videtur, sicut et secunda: tamen cum prima sit fere omnium et totius Ecclesiae: secunda habet adhuc aliquos defensores: tertia autem, ut puto. nullum.[22] That Albert does not consider transubstantiation to be a dogma, and that the question is still in some measure open, is clear from the following: "Dicendum hic videtur *sine praeiudicio melioris sententiae*, quod in sacramento isto est transmutatio, quae proprie transsubstantiatio vocatur."[23]

---

[18]"Respondeo: multiplex est ratio quare *decuerit divinim sapientiam* quod res huius sacramenti, scilicit corpus Christi, contineretur sub specie non exsistente in subiecto." Guillelmi de Militona, *Quaestiones de sacramentis* (Quarrachi, 1961), II, *(Bibl. Frans. Schol.*, XXIII), 615.

[19]IV, d. 10, a. 1 *(Opera Omnia*, Paris, 1890-1899, XXIX, 244); quoted as in Jorissen, p. 46.

[20]*Ibid.* d. 11, a. 8 (XXIX, 286); as in Jorissen, p. 46, n. 137.

[21]*Ibid.* ad. 1 (XXIX, 287) ; quoted as in Jorissen, p. 46, n. 140.

[22]*Ibid.* d. 11, a. 8 ad 1 (XXIX, 287); quoted as in Jorissen, p. 46, n. 141.

[23]*Ibid.* d. 11, a. 1, sol. (XXIX, 266-267); quoted as in Jorissen, p. 47.

Albert is much stronger in his criticism of cons. in his later *De corpore domini* (written in the 1260's, in all likelihood). Jorissen speaks of "einen Fortschritt in der Zensurierung."[24] While only a denial of the real presence is heretical, cons. is the next thing to it. Of the view that Christ "non continetur nisi sub signo sacramentali," he writes: "illa opinio non est opinio, sed haeresis manifesta et condemnata, et deberet comburi liber in quo continetur."[25] As to cons.: "dico sine praeiudicio, quod numquam mihi placuit ista opinio, quae quamvis non iudicetur esse haeretica, tamen est valde incauta, et haeresi valde vicina."[26] And again: "Et ideo subtiliter inspiciendo hanc opinionem, dico quod est valde incauta, et valde vicina haereticae pravitati: et ideo videtur mihi abjicienda."[27]

In a later passage in the same work, referring back to this discussion, he asserts that cons. "super quoddam non Catholicum fundatur fundamentum . . .: fundatur enim super hoc quod panis in Corpus Christi non transsubstantietur, neque vinum in sanguinem . . . Et hoc est contra Catholicam veritatem. . . . "[28] Thus, though to the end Albert deliberately refrains from labelling cons. heretical, he does consider it suspect and the next thing to heresy. To what extent this hardening of view was the result of the influence of his younger contemporary, Thomas Aquinas, I do not presently know.

Bonaventure is also firm in his rejection of cons., but his opposition does not go beyond that of the writers whom we have already considered. To deny the real presense, "Christum esse in Sacramento altaris secundum vertitatem" is "error pessimus et contra pietatem fidei" as well as "contra Sacramenti dignitatem et excellentiam."[29]

To deny transubstantiation, on the other hand, "contraria est Sanctorum auctoritati et rationi."[30] The holy fathers to whose authority he refers are Ambrose, Eusebius of Emesa, and John Damascene. There is no reference to Lateran IV. The unreasonableness of cons. is argued as follows:

"Sed haec positio contraria est Sanctorum *auctoritati* et *rationi*. *Rationi* quidem, quia aufert Sacramenti *veritatem, congruitatem* et *utilitatem: veritatem* quia ponit ex hoc falsitatem in forma; ponit

---

[24] Jorrissen, p. 47.

[25] *De corpore domini*, dist. 3, tr. 3, c. 1., n. 1; *Opera* XXXVIII, 306.

[26] *Ibid.* n. 4; *Opera*, XXXVIII, 308.

[27] *Ibid.* 307.

[28] *Ibid.* dist. 4, tr. 2, c. 1, n. 6 (XXXVIII, 369).

[29] *In IV Sent.* dist. x, art. un., q. 1; *Opera* (Quarrachi, ed.), IV, 217.

[30] *Ibid.* dist. xi, art. un., q. 1; *Opera*, IV, 242.

etiam mutationem circa Christi substantiam, sicut probatum est in opponendo. *Congruitatem* tollit, quia, cum manet ibi panis, non est adeo ductivum in alterum, sicut cum manent sola accidentia, quae dependent et per se stare non possunt. *Utilitatem* etiam, quia, dum possibilitatem et rationem quaerit, minuit meritum fidei.

"Propter hoc igitur haec positio est reprobanda et neminem habet ex doctoribus defensorem; immo communiter tenet Ecclesia, quod est ibi conversio panis in corpus Christi, non, inquam, in partem corporis, sed in totum."[31]

The first argument on the basis of *veritas* and the argument from *congruitas* we have already seen in Albert the Great. That it would be less a challenge to our faith we have seen in William of Auxerre. Perhaps original is the argument that cons. would require a (local) change in Christ. None of these points is developed very far by Bonaventure, but the *utilita (s)* argument at least suggests the view taken by the leading 14th century Franciscans that cons. was philosophically a more plausible position.

Jorissen states that Bonaventure condemned cons. as heretical;[32] but he adduces no evidence for this, and I have been able to find none. For the reasons given Bonaventure considers cons. to be false, but he does not seem to move significantly beyond the position of many of the earlier opponents of the position or beyond even the earlier work of Albert the Great.

In Thomas Aquinas the situation is significantly different. So far as I have been able to determine. Aquinas is the first 13th century writer to label cons. heretical and the first one to consider it impossible. In his early *Commentum in IV libros Sententiarum* he takes the following position:

Solutio I.—Respondeo dicendum ad primam quaestionem, quod haec positio, quae ponit substantiam panis ibi remanere post consecrationem simul cum vero corpore, incompetens est huic sacramento, impossibilis, et haeretica. Incompetens quidem, quia impediret venerationem debitam huic sacramento: esset enim idolatriae occasio, si hostiae veneratio latriae exhiberetur, substantia panis ibi remanente. Esset etiam contra significationem sacramenti: quia species non ducerent in verum corpus Christi per modum signi, sed magis in substantiam panis. Esset etiam contra usum sacramenti: quia jam

---

[31] *Ibid.* Emphasis in printed text. In the *Breviloquim*, only the argument from local motion is used: "Et quia Christus sub illis speciebus esse debebat non secundum mutationem factam in ipso, sed potius in eis; ideo . . ." VI, c. 9, n. 4.

[32] Pp. 50-54.

cibus iste non esset pure spiritualis sed etiam corporalis. Sed quod sit impossibile, patet ex hoc quod impossibile est aliquid esse nunc cum prius non fuerit nisi ipso mutato vel aliquo in ipsum: nec posset etiam per miraculum fieri, sicut nec quod esset animal rationale mortale, et non esset homo: aliter enim se habere nunc et prius est idem quod moveri vel transmutari. Si ergo corpus Christi verum esset sub sacramento nunc et non prius, oporteret aliquem motum vel mutationem intervenisse. Sed nulla mutatio est ex parte panis facta secundum hanc positionem. Ergo oportet quod corpus Christi sit mutatum saltem localiter, ut dicatur quod corpus Christi est hic, quia per motum localiter huc venit; quod omnino esse non potest: quia cum simul et semel in diversis locis corpus Christi consecretur, oporteret quod simul et semel ad diversa loca unum numero moveretur corpus, quod est impossibile: quia contingeret simul contrarios motus inesse eidem, vel saltem diversos ejusdem speciei. Quod autem sit haeretica, patet ex hoc quod contradicit veritati Scripturae; non enim esset verum dicere: 'Hoc est corpus meum.' sed: 'Hic est corpus.'[33]

In the *Summa Contra Gentiles* Aquinas uses almost exactly the same arguments against either of the alternatives to transubstantiation. He does not here expressly call these positions impossible or false, but instead uses the milder formula: "Ex hoc autem apparet falsam esse opinionem."[34] However, since in the *Summa Theologiae* he once again speaks of cons. as heretical—"Unde haec positio vitanda est tanquam haeretica"[35]—it seems unlikely that the wording of the *Contra Gentiles* reflects a change in position.

It should be noted that Aquinas does not argue for transubstantiation from the metaphysical impossibility of the simultaneity of two substances in one concrete entity. Cons. is impossible because it would involve the local motion of the body of Christ to many different places simultaneously.[36]

---

[33]Lib. IV, dist. xi, a. 1, solutio 1. (Vives ed., X, 254).

[34]IV, 62.

[35]III, 75, a. 3.

[36]I would note in passing that the particular difficulty ascribed here to cons. could just as readily be advanced against the position subsequently developed by Scotus, Bellarmine, and DeLugo; yet though their position is often enough criticized by other Roman Catholic theologians it is not ordinarily judged heretical. See M. Schmaus, *Katholische Dogmatik* IV/1, 6th ed. (Munich,1946) 348-350.

We might also note here that Pierre de Tarantaise, a Dominican contemporary of Aquinas (died 1276 as Pope Innocent V—*Sentence Commentary*, 1257-1259), opposed cons. on the ground that it would require a local change in the body of

Richard of Mediavilla, a Franciscan writing probably in the last decade of the 13th century, argues against cons. on by now familiar grounds: "hoc est" rather than "hic est" in the words of institution; the communion fast would otherwise be broken and reception of communion more than once thus prohibited; and the fathers—Ambrose, Eusebius of Emesa, and Peter of Lombard are cited—speak against it. Still there is no reference to Lateran IV, and nothing is said about heresy or impossibility.[37]

It is with Scotus that the important change comes, because with Scotus the doctrine of transubstantiation comes to be more a question of the authority of the post-apostolic Church than of the understanding of the eucharist. There are two crucial points on which Scotus differs from the earlier tradition. First, he interprets the confession of faith of the Fourth Lateran Council as a dogmatic affirmation of the doctrine of transubstantiation over against cons. or any other alternatives within the doctrine of the real presence. Thus transubstantiation is a dogma of the Church, having been solemnly defined by a council; and it is a dogma separate from the dogma of the real presence. Secondly, Scripture does not favor transubstantiation over consubstantiation, and on philosophical grounds cons. would be more plausible. The theologian, if left to his own devices, would come down in favor of cons.; but in light of the Church's formal definition to the contrary, he will hold transubstantiation. This does not mean that the theologian will be forced to deny what his reason tells him is absolutely and necessarily true. As one might suspect from a consideration of the 13th century arguments pro and con transubstantiation, the arguments on either side were hardly overwhelming. In Scotus' view the balance of the arguments—apart from the conciliar definition—favored cons.; but Lateran IV quite decisively showed that in fact transubstantiation was the case.

Scotus begins his discussion of the question "Utrum panis convertitur in corpus Christi in Eucharistia," by describing the familiar three positions in the same order and in much the same terms as had Peter of Capua. After presenting arguments on behalf of each of the first two positions he introduces arguments from a "quidam Doctor," whom Scotus' editors identify as Thomas Aquinas. These

---

Christ. He does not label cons. heretical (he does so label the denial of the real presence) nor does he cite Lateran IV. See *In IV libros sententiarum commentaria*, dist. 10, q. 1, a. 1.

37 *In IV Sent.* d. xi, a. 1; *Ricardi de Mediavilla Super IV libros sententiarum quaestiones subtilissimae*, Brescia, 1591, IV, 131-132.

objections to cons. and succession Scotus sets out to refute in detail: "Quidquid sit de opinionibus (cons. and succession) istae rationes non videntur eas efficaciter improbare."[38]

But after he turns back the arguments directed against these two positions, Scotus repudiates them himself and adopts transubstantiation:

Quantum ergo ad istum articulum, quid scilicet sit tenendum, respondeo, quod communiter tenetur, quod nec panis manet, contra primam opinionem; nec annihilatur vel resolvitur in materiam primam, contra secundam opinionem, sed convertitur in corpus Christi. Et ad hoc multum expresse videtur loqui Ambrosius, cujus duae auctoritates supra adductae sunt, et plures habentur de consecrat. dist. 2. et ponuntur a Magistro dist. 10. et dist. ista. Principaliter autem videtur movere, quod de Sacramentis tenedum est, sicut tenet Sancta Romana Ecclesia, sicut habetur Extra de haereticis, ad abolendam. Nunc autem ipsa tenet panem transubstantiari in corpus et vinum in sanguinem, sicut manifeste Una vero, ubi dicitur: Ipse Jesus Christus Sacerdos est, et sacrificium, cujus corpus et sanguis in Sacramento altaris sub speciebus panis et vini veraciter continetur; et sequitur statim: Transubstantiatis pane in corpus, et vino in sanguinem potestate divina.

Ad hoc etiam est una congruentia, quia Ecclesia non errat, cum dicit: Fiat commixtio et consecratio corporis et sanguinis Domini nostri Jesu Christi, etc. Alia est congruentia, quia non jejunus non potest congrue celebrare; sed percepta Eucharistia adhuc potest Sacerdos iterum celebrare, sicut habetur Extra de celeb. Miss. Consuluisti: Excepto (inquit) die Nativitatis Domini, nisi tamen necessitas superveniat, sufficit Sacerdoti semel in die Missam celebrare; et ex hoc innuit, quod in die Nativitatis Domini, et quando necessitas ingruit, licet plures Missas celebrare in die.[39]

The arguments ex congruentia are, as Scotus certainly realizes, not compelling. The decisive factor is the definition by the Church. Any one of the three proposed alternatives is possible, and it is difficult to see that one is clearly more fitting than the others. It is thus not so much a question of what must be the case, but of what in fact is the case:

Ad argumenta pro prima opinione et secunda. Ad primum, concedo quod etiam in creditis non sunt plura ponenda sine necessitate,

---

[38] *In IV Sent.*, d. xi, q. 3, n. 9 (Vives ed. XVII, 357).

[39] *Ibid.* n. 13; p. 372.

nec plura miracula quam oportet. Sed cum dicitur in minori, veritas Eucharistiae posset salvari manente pane vel sine transubstantiatione, dico quod bene fuisset Deo possibile instituisse, quod corpus Christi vere esset praesens, substantia panis manente, vel cum accidentibus, pane annihilato, et tunc fuisset ibi ritas Eucharistiae, quia et signum verum et signatum verum; sed hic non est modo tota veritas Eucharistiae, non enim sic instituit, ut dicunt auctoritates adductae. Et cum dicitur, quod ad veritatem Eucharistiae nihil requiritur nisi verum signum et verum signatum; respondeo, verum est eo modo quo signum est institutum, et quo sibi debet correspondere signatum, quod non est nunc praecise, quod corpus sit cum aliquo, scilicet cum pane, vel cum accidentibus panis indistincte; sed institutum est nunc, quod signatum sit tantum sub accidentibus, ut sub signo.

Ad secundum, dico quod non est aliquis articulus arctandus ad intellectum difficilem, nisi ille intellectus sit verus; sed si verus est, et probatur evidenter esse verum, oportet secundum illum intellectum tenere articulum, quando inquiritur in speciali, quia nullus alius intellectus specialis verus est; sic autem supponitur de intellectu hujus articuli ex auctoritatibus allegatis.

Et tunc ad tertium, ubi stat vis, dicendum quod Ecclesia declaravit istum intellectum esse de veritate fidei in illo Symbolo edito sub Innocentio III. in Concilio Lateranensi, Firmiter credimus, etc. sicut allegatum est superius, ubi explicite ponitur veritas aliquorum credendorum, magis explicite quam habebatur in Symbolo Apostolorum, vel Athanasii, vel Niceni. Et breviter, quidquid ibi dicitur esse credendum, tenendum est esse de substantia fidei, et hoc post istam declarationem solemnem factam ab Ecclesia.

Et si quaeras quare voluit Ecclesia eligere istum intellectum ita difficilem hujus articuli, cum verba Scripturae possent salvari secundum intellectum facilem et veriorem secundum apparentiam de hoc articulo; dico, quod eo spiritu expositae sunt Scripturae, quo conditae. Et ita supponendum est, quod Ecclesia Catholica eo Spiritu exposuit, quo tradita est nobis fides, Spiritu scilicet veritatis edocta, et ideo hunc intellectum eligit, quia verus est. Non enim in potestate Ecclesiae fuit facere istud verum, vel non verum, sed Dei institutentis; sed intellectum a Deo traditum Ecclesia explicavit, directa in hoc, ut creditur, Spiritu veritatis.[40]

Because Lateran IV has so defined matters, transubstantiation is "de substantia fidei"; and yet "verba Scripturae possent salvari

---

[40]*Ibid.* nn. 14-15 (XVII, 375-376).

secundum intellectum facilem et veriorem secundum apparentiam de hoc articulo." Transubstantiation is of the substance of the faith not, it seems fair to say, because its importance—its substantiveness is apparent: it would seem that absolutely nothing would be changed had God decided to leave the substance of the bread. It is of the substance of the faith because it has been defined and thus must be of the substance of the faith. And the Church was guided in the choice of transubstantiation over consubstantiation by the same Spirit that gave us the Scriptures.

Luther will see the matter in more negative terms than does Scotus; yet Scotus has already conceded most of what Luther will claim: that the dogma of transubstantiation has no purpose and no support other than the authority of the Church. The doctrine of the real presence is altogether independent of it, and neither Scripture nor reason requires it; yet one cannot be an orthodox Christian unless one maintains it. Transubstantiation has no discernible origin and no appreciable end; but anyone who would deny it is anathema.

The situation is much the same in Ockham. Ockham's position is developed in closer conjunction with his metaphysics, and his metaphysics leads him to make a stronger case for consubstantiation. Moreover, though he refers and submits to the *determinatio ecclesiae* of Lateran IV, he holds that cons. is a tenable position.

"Quantum ad primum potest dici quod transsubstantiatio in proposito est successio substantie ad substantiam desinentem esse simpliciter in se sub aliquibus accidentibus propriis substantie precedentis. Possibilitas illius apparet, quia non repugnat potentie diuine destruere substantiam in se & conseruare accidentia, & quod aliqua alia substantia eisdem accidentibus eam non informantibus immediate coexistat.

Quantum ad secundum dico quod in altari est vera transsubstantiatio corporis Christi. Sed hoc potest multis modis poni. Uno modo ponendo quod remaneat ibi substantia panis et cum hoc quod corpus Christi coexistat substantie illi, ita quod prima substantia sit deserens accidens secunda non, sed tantum coexistens. Alio modo quod recedat substantia panis subito de illo loco ad alium locum et remaneant accidentia et eis coexistat corpus Christi. Tertio quod redigatur in materiam vel per se stantem vel aliam formam recipientem, et hoc siue in eodem siue in alio, & tunc illi materie et accidentibus coexistat corpus Christi. Quarto quod substantia panis redigatur in nihil.

Primus modus patet, quia hoc potest fieri per simplicem coexistentiam veri corporis Christi substantie panis quia non minus repugnat quantitas quantitati vel substantia quantitati quam substantia substantie. Sed quantitas potest coexistere in eodem loco cum quantitate alia. Patet de maioribus corporibus existentibus in loco eodem. Similiter substantia potest coexistere quantitati in eodem loco. Patet de corpore Christi. Igitur aliud est possible. Sed utrum corpus Christi ibi possit coexistere per unionem et assumptionem dubium est & potest divi quod si sit possibile unam creaturam sustinere aliam (ut dicunt aliqui; & credo quod non includit contradictionem, nec potest probari per rationem naturalem quod corpus Christi* posset assumere substantiam panis per unionem) et tunc natura sustentans erit suppositum —et alia erit sustentata a supposito & aliq . . . (?) non quia utraque potest inniti alicui supposito.

Secundus modus patet, quia sicut non est impossibile deo subito facere corpus Christi hic sub speciebus hostie, ita potest facere quod substantia subito sit alicubi remanentibus speciebus in eodem loco, & quod illi coexistat corpus Christi.

Tertius modus patet per idem.

Quartus modus patet quia in potestate dei est esse substantie sub specie panis & non esse eius.

Primus modus potest teneri quia non repugnat rationi nec alicui auctoritati biblie & est rationabilior & facilior ad tenendum inter omnes modos, quia pauciora inconvenientia sequuntur ex eo quam ex aliquo alio modo. Quod patet quia inter omnia inconvenientia que ponuntur sequi ex isto sacramento maius est quod accidens sit sine subiecto. Sed ponendo primum modum non oportet illud ponere. Igitur & c. Si dicis quod maius est duas substantias corporeas esse simul. Contra. Non est maius inconveniens nec magis mirabile duas substantias corporeas esse simul quam substantiam et quantitatem, quia non plus compatitur illa species hostie secum aliam hostiam quam substantia cum speciebus eius aliam substantiam; quia videmus quod illa species expellit aliam hostiam non consecratam sicut si esset ibi substantia panis, & hoc non convenit sibi ratione corporis Christi—quia corpori Christi non repugnat alia quantitas sicut nec ista. Ita videtur quod nullum inconveniens sequitur ex primo modo ponendi quod non sequatur ex secundo modo.

Quia tamen determinatio ecclesie in contrarium existit, sicut patet extra de summa trinitate et fide catholica & de celebratione missae et commuiter doctores tenent quod ibi non remanet sub-

---

***40a Perhaps a "non" added here would make the text more coherent.**

stantia panis, ideo etiam teneo quod non remanet substantia panis sed illa species et quod illi coexistat corpus Christi. & quod hoc sit possibile patet, quia, in ista transsubstantiatione non includitur nisi quod species ibi realiter maneant & quod substantia non maneat in se realiter, & quod ibi sit realiter corpus Christi non quantitative; sed quodlibet istorum est possibile. igitur & c.[41]

In Ockham's later writings on the eucharist, the *De sacramento altaris* (part II) and the *Quodlibeta,* Ockham no longer says that cons. can be held ("potest teneri"). His position is now more exactly like that of Scotus.

Tertia opinio esset multum rationabilis, nisi esset determinatio ecclesiae in contrarium, quia illa opinio salvat et vitat omnes difficultates, quae sequuntur ex separatione accidentium a subiecto, nec contrarium illius habetur in canone bibliae nec includit aliquam contradictionem.[42]

This position, or a position very much like it, seems to have become rather commonplace from about Ockham's time, and apparently remained so down to Luther's time[43] Durand of Saint-Pourcain (d. 1334) differs perhaps in tone but not in content.

After listing the familiar alternatives, and after mustering most of the traditional arguments for transubstantiation, he concludes:
Si autem iste modus cons. esset verus de facto, multae dubitationes quae occurrunt circa hoc sacramentum (tenendo quod substantia panis non remaneat) essent solutae. Dubitatur enim qualiter ex hoc sacramento potest aliquid nutriri, & quomodo species possunt corrumpi, et ex eis aliquid generari: quae omnia salvarentur naturaliter eo modo sicut salvarentur si naturae panis & vini non assumerentur ad naturam sacramenti, ponuntur enim manere post consecrationem sicut ante. Sed quia hic modus non debet teneri de facto, cum ecclesia

---

[41]*In IV Sent.* IV, q. 6. Guillelmus de Occam, *Opera Plurima* (Lyons 1494-1496), IV, no pagination. It should be noted that all but the first book of Ockham's Sentence Commentary is a *reportatio*, and thus does not owe its final form to Ockham's own hand. I have amplified the frequent word abbreviations and added some punctuation in the interests of intelligibility.

[42]Quodl. IV, 30 (35). Text as in Erwin Iserloh, Gnade und Eucharistie in der philosophischen Theologie des Wilhelm von Ockham: Ihre Bedeutung fur die Ursachen der Reformation (Wiesbaden, 1956) p. 158, n. 45. For the dating of Ockham's writings on the eucharist, see pp. 12-26.

[43]I would simply note that this constitutes two-thirds of the period of scholasticism or university theology. The common classification of Ockham and even of Scotus as "late scholastics" may obscure the fact that all the writers who are commonly reckoned major figures in scholasticism wrote within a fairly short period of time.

determinaverit oppositum quae non praesumitur errare in talibus, ideo tenendo de facto aliam partem.[44]

Thomas of Strasbourg, mid-14th century general of the Augustinians, holds much the same position. His discussion of cons. concludes: "Unde semper, salvo meliori iuditio, non videtur mihi, quod ante determinationem sanctae matris ecclesiae, quam superius recitavi, ista opinio fuerit haeretica reputanda."[45]

The last important pre-Reformation discussion of these issues takes place in connection with Wycliff. The Council of Constance (May 4, 1415) lists as the first of the "errores Iohannis Wyclif": "Substantia panis materialis et similiter substantia vini materialis remanent in sacramento altaris." (Dz.–S. 1151)

We may here abstract from the question of precisely what were Wyclif's views on the eucharist. There would seem to be reason to assert that his views were of the "symbolist" variety, not greatly unlike those of Zwingli, and that his assertion of a *remanentia panis post consecrationem* was part of this overall view.[46] But by the time of Wyclif or Constance "remanentia panis" did not have to be part of something else to be considered heretical. Lateran IV had already declared such a doctrine heretical. As an early historian of the Council of Constance writes: "Cet Article est déclaré *faux*, *erronè*, & *heretique*, & cette qualification est confirmée par le Concile de Latran, & par l'autorite de St. *Ambroise*."[47] Thus it seems fair to say that a mistaken understanding of an earlier conciliar text was now generating new conciliar decisions. The pattern will be repeated at Trent.

---

[44]*In IV Libros Sententiarum*, IV, dist. xi, q. 1, n. 15 (Venice, 1571; II, 318vb). The difficulty which later Roman Catholics have had in understanding this quite common late medieval position is illustrated by Stephanus Ehses, the editor of the fifth volume of the *Concilium Tridentinum*. Ehses informs us, after referring to the material just cited that Durand "respondetur affirmative ad alteram partem [scil. utrum cum corpore Christi remaneat substantia panis], quia haec solutio minus difficultatis habeat." *Conc. Trid.*, V, 928, n. 6.

[45]*Commentaria in IV libros sententiarum*, lib. iv, dist, xi, a. 2 (Venice, 1564), IV, 93v.

[46]See Paul DeVooght, "La presence reelle dans la doctrine eucharistique de Wiclif," in *Hussiana*, Louvain, 1960, 292-299.

[47]Jacques Lenfant, *Histoire du concile de Constance*, 2nd ed., Amsterdam, 1727 (ist ed. 1714), I, 208. Lenfant says that he is following H. von der Hardt, *Magnum oecumenicum Constantiense Concilium* (Leipzig, 1697-1700), IV, 150, who in turn was using a Leipzig ms. which purported to give a "courte Censure de 45. Articles de Wiclef par les Theologiens de Constance." Unfortunately the von der Hardt volumes were not available to me in the preparation of this paper.

II.

We turn then to Luther. I do not propose to describe Luther's total understanding of the eucharist. Rather, as far as this is possible, I wish to confine myself to the single question of his attitude toward the doctrine of transubstantiation. My overall interpretation is simple: (1) Luther maintained a doctrine of the real presence by a most emphatic reiteration of the most traditional medieval vocabulary. (2) He denied that there was any necessary connection between the doctrines of the real presence and transubstantiation. (3) He found transubstantiation a most unattractive doctrine and favored a doctrine of copresence not greatly unlike what we have been calling cons. And (4) he objected not to others holding transubstantiation, but rather to its being made a dogma, a *sine qua non* of orthodoxy. Only on this last point can he be said to differ significantly from a large segment of 14th, 15th, and 16th century Roman Catholic theology; though Luther urges his objections to transubstantiation (the third point) much more vigorously than had any of the scholastics.

(1) It should not be necessary to belabor the point that Luther held (or at the very least thought that he held and intended to hold) a traditional real presence doctrine. This was an issue over which he was willing to split the ranks of the Reformers. Though many Roman Catholics find the language of the Berengarian confession of 1059 a bit too materialistic for their taste, Luther could write (against the Zwinglians):

"Therefore, the fanatics are wrong, as well as the gloss in Canon Law, if they criticize Pope Nicolas for having forced Berengar to confess that the true body of Christ is crushed and ground with the teeth. Would to God that all popes had acted in so Christian a fashion in all other matters as this pope did with Berengar in forcing this confession."[48]

In Luther's first published work on the eucharist, *Eyn Sermon von dem Hochwirdigen Sacrament, des heyligen waren Leychnams Christi*, we read toward the end: "Besides all this, Christ did not institute these two forms solitary and alone, but he gave his true natural flesh in the bread and his natural true blood in the wine, that he might give a really perfect sacrament or sign."[49] To the same effect we read in his next work on the eucharist: "This is what Christ has done in this testament. He has affixed to the words a

---

[48]*Confession Concerning Christ's Supper, AE,* 37, 300-301 *(WA,* 26, 442-443).

[49]*AE,* 35, 59 *(WA,* 2, 749). This work was published in 1519.

powerful and most precious seal and sign: his own true flesh and blood under the bread and wine."[50]

It is in *The Babylonian Captivity of the Church* that Luther first explicitly rejects the doctrine of transubstantiation; but at the same time that he is doing this he is careful to state that he holds the traditional doctrine of the real presence: "it is real bread and real wine, in which Christ's real flesh and real blood are present in no other way and to no less a degree than the others assert them to be under their accidents."[51] Seen in the context of the medieval discussions of transubstantiation there is nothing especially incomprehensible about this position, and nothing in *The Babylonian Captivity* that would furnish grounds for calling into question the genuineness of Luther's conviction here.[52]

(2) Luther denied that there was any necessary connection between the doctrines of the real presence and transubstantiation. In this he was simply taking over the verdict of many Catholic theologians before him, and of not a few after:

Some time ago, when I was drinking in scholastic theology, the learned Cardinal of Cambrai gave me food for thought in his comments on the fourth book of the *Sentences*. He argues with great acumen that to hold that real bread and real wine, and not merely their accidents, are present on the altar, would be much more probable and require fewer superfluous miracles—if only the church had not decreed otherwise. When I learned later what church it was that had decreed this, namely the Thomistic—that is, the Aristotelian church—I grew bolder, and after floating in a sea of doubt, I at last found rest for my conscience in the above view, namely, that it is real bread and real wine, in which Christ's real flesh and real blood are present in no other way and to no less a

[50] *A Treatise on the New Testament, that is, the Holy Mass, AE*, 35, 86, (*WA*, 6, 359); published July, 1520.

[51] *AE*, 36, 29 (*WA*, 6, 508)

[52] Would a fuller consideration of Luther's discussion of the real presence in his later writings and in the Lutheran Confessional writings erode the rather simple realism of Luther's assertion here? I think not, but the matter is too complicated for an already complicated paper. In any event, the question is not central for the purpose of this paper. I am concerned here with the question which Luther poses to the medieval and Roman Catholic doctrine of transubstantiation and not with the questions which Roman Catholicism might want to raise with respect to Luther's total doctrine of the eucharist. Many 14th and 15th century theologians, as well as many theologians and bishops at the Council of Trent, would find nothing inconceivable or impossible in Luther's position: it just happened, as a matter of fact to be wrong.

degree than the others assert them to be under their accidents. I reached this conclusion because I saw that the opinions of the Thomists, whether approved by pope or by council, remain only opinions, and would not become articles of faith even if an angel from heaven were to decree otherwise (Gal. 1:8). For what is asserted without the Scriptures or proven revelation may be held as an opinion, but need not be believed. But this opinion of Thomas hangs so completely in the air without support of Scripture or reason that it seems to me he knows neither his philosophy nor his logic. For Aristotle speaks of subject and accidents so very differently from St. Thomas that it seems to me this great man is to be pitied not only for attempting to draw his opinions in matters of faith from Aristotle, but also for attempting to base them upon a man whom he did not understand, thus building an unfortunate super-structure upon an unfortunate foundation.[53]

(3) Not only did Luther want to relegate transubstantiation to an opinion; he considered it a not very attractive opinion, and favored a doctrine of cons.[54] Following the statement just quoted, he marshalls a number of arguments against transubstantiation and in favor of consubstantiation.

a) But there are good grounds for my view, and this above all—no violence is to be done to the words of God, whether by man or angel. They are to be retained in their simplest meaning as far as possible. Unless the context manifestly compels it, they are not to be understood apart from their grammatical and proper sense, lest we give our adversaries occasion to make a mockery of all the Scriptures. Thus Origen was rightly repudiated long ago because, ignoring the grammatical sense, he turned the trees and everything else written concerning Paradise into allegories, from which one could have inferred that trees were not created by God. Even so here, when the Evangelists plainly write that Christ took bread (Matt. 26:26; Mark 14:22; Luke 22:19) and blessed it, and when the Book of Acts and the Apostle Paul in turn call it bread (Acts 2:46; 1 Cor. 10:16; 11:23; 26-28), we have to think of real bread and real wine, just as we do of a real cup, (for even they do not

---

[53]*Ibid.* 28-29. *(WA, 6, 508).*

[54]There seems to be considerable objection to describing Luther's position with this term. It is, doubtless, a more scholastic turn of phrase than Luther ordinarily uses, and more appropriate designations might be found. However, there is an obvious similarity between Luther's view here and Peter of Capua's first position, and I use the word "cons." to draw attention to this similiarity.

say that the cup was transubstantiated). Since it is not necessary, therefore, to assume a transubstantiation effected by divine power, it must be regarded as a figment of the human mind, for it rests neither on the Scriptures nor on reason, as we shall see.[55]

b) Moreover, the church kept the true faith for more than twelve hundred years, during which time the holy fathers never, at any time or place, mentioned this transubstantiation (a monstrous word and a monstrous idea), until the pseudo philosophy of Aristotle began to make its inroads into the church in these last three hundred years.[56]

c) Perhaps they will say that the danger of idolatry demands that the bread and wine should not be really present. How ridiculous! The laymen have never become familiar with their fine-spun philosophy of substance and accidents, and could not grasp it if it were taught to them. Besides, there is the same danger in the accidents which remain and which they see, as in the case of the substance which they do not see. If they do not worship the accidents, but the Christ hidden under them, why should they worship the (substance of the) bread, which they do not see?[57]

d) And why could not Christ include his body in the substance of the bread just as well as in the accidents? In red-hot iron, for instance, the two substances, fire and iron, are so mingled that every part is both iron and fire. Why is it not even more possible that the body of Christ be contained in every part of the substance of the bread?[58]

e) Thus, what is true in regard to Christ is also true in regard to the sacrament. In order for the divine nature to dwell in him bodily (Col. 2:9), it is not necessary for human nature to be transsubstantiated and the divine nature contained under the accidents of the human nature. Both natures are simply there in their entirety, and it is truly said: 'This man is God; this God is man.' Even though philosophy cannot grasp this, faith grasps it nonetheless. And the authority of God's Word is greater than the capacity of our intellect to grasp it. In like manner, it is not necessary in the sacrament that the bread and wine be transubstantiated and that Christ be contained

[55]*Ibid.* 30-31 (WA, 6, 509).

[56]*Ibid.* 31. (WA, 6, 509).

[57]*Ibid.* 31-32. (WA, 6, 509-510). This is in answer to arguments such as the third advanced by Thomas Aquinas, S.Th. III, 75, 2c.

[58]*Ibid.* 32 (WA, 6, 510)

under their accidents in order that the real body and real blood may be present. But both remain there at the same time, and it is truly said: 'This bread is my body; this wine is my blood,' and vice versa.[59]

(4) Luther did not object to others holding transubstantiation, but only to its being made a dogma. He concludes the paragraph just quoted with the following:

Thus I will understand it for the time being to the honor of the holy words of God, to which I will allow no violence to be done by petty human arguments, nor will I allow them to be twisted into meanings which are foreign to them. At the same time, I permit other men to follow the other opinion, which is laid down in the decree, *Firmiter*, only let them not press us to accept their opinions as articles of faith (as I have said above).

So far as I can ascertain, Luther never considered the eucharistic issue involved in all this as being very important. It was the very triviality of the *doctrine* of transubstantiation which made its *dogmatization* so very important. In posing the problem as he does he brings to the surface a problem that had been latent in scholasticism at least since the time of Scotus: Is it a legitimate exercise of papal or conciliar authority to define as true and a *sine qua non* of communion a proposition which is admittedly not required by scripture or reason and which seems to make no difference whatsoever to anything? This may seem a prejudicial way of posing the question, but the theology of the two centuries prior to Luther could hardly deny its appropriateness.

III.

Some thirty years separate Luther's attack on the doctrine of transubstantiation and the reply of the Council of Trent. During that period a sizable controversial literature developed, and doubtless this literature would be of some relevance to the general problem under consideration here. However, owing to time and library limitations I am unable to bring this material into focus here, I would just note the response of two Roman Catholics to Luther.

Erwin Iserloh summarizes Eck's reply to Luther's attack on transubstantiation in the following terms:

Bei der Behandlung der Transsubstantiation beschrankt sich Eck also darauf, die bloss Tatsache, dass das Brot in den Leib Christi bezw. der Wein in das Blut Christi verwandelt werden,

---

[59] *Ibid.* 35 (*WA*, 6, 511-512)

aus der Schrift und der Lehre der Vater zu beweisen und weiter die Moglichkeit einer solchen Verwandlung und ihre Vereinbarkeit mit dem Sprachgebrauch der Schrift aufzuzeigen. Wir vermissen hier eine eigentliche theologische Verarbeitung und Darstellung. Wir erfahren z.B. nichts uber das Verhaltnis der Gestalten zum Leib Christi. Auch wird nicht der geringste Versuch gemacht, die Bedeutung dieses Dogmas von der Transsubstantiation fur die Lehre von der Eucharistie uberhaupt darzulegen. Vor allem aber vermissen wir die Auswertung fur das religiose Leben. Diese unterbleibt nicht nur im Enchiridion sondern auch in den Predigten.[60]

The second has to do with the Roman Catholic appraisal of Luther's doctrine of the real presence. Johann Hoffmeister, writing in 1539, seems to have accepted Luther's assertion of the real presence at its face value. How typical this was of the controversialists of the day I cannot say, but at least a good many of the participants at Trent agreed with this appraisal. In Hoffmeister's view the entire difference has to do with the status of the bread, not with the question of presence of Christ.

Dann (noch meinem kleinen verstand) so will die Luthersch sect der kirchen zu fil geben, namlich leib und brot, und die Zwinglisch rott zu wenig, namlich allein das brott, wie sie dan ihr ertz prophet Luther uberzeuget. Derhalben will die kirch nitt des Luthers brot mitt dem leib und nitt des Zwinglisch brot on denn leib. Was dan? Den waren leib Christi, wie Luther sagt, unnd das kein brot darbey sey, wie Zwinglin unnd Oecolampadius geschryben hand.[61]

The Council of Trent discussed transubstantiation twice: in 1547 and again in 1551. The 1547 deliberations were begun at Trent and continued at Bologna whither the Council had fled to escape plague, but no final results were reached prior to the suspension of the Council. When the Council reconvened in 1551, the discussion of the proposed canons *de eucharistia* was begun again and this time seen through to completion. In the present state of publication of the *Concilium Tridentinum* we are dependent almost entirely on the brief summaries of statements of theologians and bishops made by the council's secretary, Angelo Massarelli. The publication of the second part of the seventh volume of *CT*, which is to contain the

---

[60] *Die Eucharistie in der Darstellung des Johannes Eck: Ein Beitrag zur Vortridentinischen Kontroverstheologie uber das Messopfer* (Munster, 1950), p. 315.

[61] *Drei Schriften gegen Luthers Schmalkaldische Artikel von Cochlaus, Witzel und Hoffmeister (1538 und 1539)*, ed. Hans Volz *Corpus Catholicorum*, XVIII (Munster, 1932), p. 167.

texts of the statements of a number of the bishops,[62] may change the general picture which I shall present here to some degree. It seems unlikely, however, that the picture will change very drastically.

The proposition on transubstantiation discussed in 1547 is as follows:

In Eucharistia esse quidem corpus et sanguinem D.N. Iesu Christi, sed simul cum substantia panis et vini, ita ut non sit transsubstantiatio, sed unio hypostatica humanitatis et substantiae panis et vini.[63]

The text of the 1551 proposition is slightly expanded:

In Eucharistia esse quidem corpus et sanguinem D.N. Iesu Christi, sed simul cum substantia panis et vini, ita ut non sit transubstantiatio, sed unio hypostatica humanitatis et substantiae panis et vini, ita ut verum sit dicere: Hic panis est corpus meum, et: Hoc vinum est sanguis meus.[64]

It may be said at the outset that everyone who spoke on the subject agreed that the proposition was heretical. However, the arguments used against it differed, and were in some instances contradictory one of another.

An argument very common among the theologians[65] in 1547 and again in 1551 was that the neuter pronoun in "Hoc est corpus meum" requires that the substance of bread no longer exist. If the substance of bread were still present, Jesus would have said, "Hic panis est corpus meum," or at the very least, "Hic est corpus meum." The entire discussion of this point, to judge from Massarelli's report, was based on an analysis of the Latin text. One finds this argument in Oleastro, Salmeron, Leoninus,[66] Lombardellus, Navarra, and Ioannes Consilii in 1547; and in Ioannes de Ortega in 1551. Others refer more vaguely to scripture, but whether their argument is ultimately the same as this is not clear. Since the only scholastic arguments from the words of institution to transubstantiation are

[62]*Concilium Tridentinum: Diariorum, actorum epistularum, tractatuum nova collectio*, VII/1, ed. T. Freudenberger (Freiburg, 1961), vii-viii.

[63]*CT*, V, 869.

[64]*CT*. VII/1, 112.

[65]It should be noted that the procedure at Trent was for the theologians to discuss a proposed set of propositions, to form judgments about them, and then to pass the propositions with their judgments along to the bishops, who would then discuss the matter further and finally come to some decision in the matter.

[66]Since 16th century non-English names can be Englished in such a variety of ways, I have permitted myself the luxury of simply using these names in the form in which they are found in *CT*.

of this type or else are based upon the metaphysical impossibility of anything but transubstantiation as a concommitant of the doctrine of the real presence, I would assume that the grammatical argument lay behind many of the simple references to scripture. In 1551 the following bishops explicitly adopt the grammatical argument in their repudiation of the thesis under discussion: Balthasar Waneman (Bishop of Missene), Christophorus de Rojas (Oviedo), and Nicolaus Psalmaeus (Verdun).

This argument would at least seem to be open to the interpretation that transubstantiation is not *necessarily* connected with the doctrine of the real presence. We know that transubstantiation is the case because of the wording of scripture; but presumably if the wording were different something other than transubstantiation could be the case.

In the 1547 discussion the question of the absolute necessity of transubstantiation was posed when two Franciscan theologians asserted the impossibility of the presence of the body of Christ along with the substance of the bread. Massarelli reports Franciscus Salazar's criticism of the 1547 proposition: "3. haereticus est, et cum maneat corpus Christi substantialiter, impossibile est, quod substantia panis maneat, ut unum duo sint eisdem remanentibus."[67] And Ludovicus Carvaial argues to the same effect: "3. etiam haereticus est; immo impossibile est, quod non sit haereticus, quia cum in Eucharistia sit corpus Christi, ut superior articulus fatetur, impossibile est, ut ibi sit substantia panis, cum duae substantiae non possint esse in eodem subiecto uno tempore."[68]

However, another Franciscan, Ioannes Consilii, objected strenuously to this in the course of a very lengthy oration, the text of which has been preserved. The relevant passage is as follows:

"Porro autem hic neutiquam sunt audiendi, qui putant, hanc fidem ex iure humano et non ex evangelio ipso natam, quamadmodum quidam eorum, qui ante me dixerunt, existimasse videtur.[69]

Nec praeterea sunt admittendi ullo pacto, qui stultissime, ne aliud dicam, putant, corpus Christi cum substantia panis per Dei potentiam esse non posse. Manifestum est enim, non plus divinae potentiae repugnare, uti sit cum substantia panis, quam ut sit cum accidentibus.

---

[67]*CT*, V, 902.

[68]*Ibid.* 931.

[69]Consilii is here taking issue with those who, like Sebastianus de Castello (quoted below), denied the validity of the argument from scripture.

Neque Pighius ipse huic assertioni ulla ex parte vult aut potest refragari. Est igitur corpus Christi in Eucharistia sine substantia panis, non quia Deus facere non potuit, ut cum substantia esset, sed quia non voluit."[70]

To judge from Massarelli's reports, the debate was not taken up by other theologians; nor is there any echo of it in the reports of the bishops' statements, either in 1547 or in 1551. In view of the importance of this question in much of the subsequent Roman Catholic writing on the subject,[71] it may seem puzzling that such should be the case. The reason why this question could be left unsettled was, I think, two-fold.

First, most (perhaps all) of the theologians and bishops seem to have been of the opinion that the fact that the doctrine was traditional and that it had been defined by solemn councils was enough to settle the question of the orthodoxy of the proposition. The following, from Sebastianus de Castello (also a Franciscan) is a fairly typical statement of position: "3. art. haereticus est, quia realiter fit transsubstantiatio, ex pane corpus etc., quae tamen transsubstantiatio non habetur expresse in evangelio, sed iure positivo, ut in concilio Ephesino, Lateranesi, Constantiensi etc."[72] The argument could be most decisively settled by an appeal to tradition, and there was no need to iron out all the differences between various theological schools in order to agree that transubstantiation was a necessary ingredient in the orthodox faith.

The second reason why the question of the necessary or nonnecessary connection between real presence and transubstantiation was not settled was that the proposition as originally put forth for discussion did not limit itself exclusively to the question of consubstantiation versus transubstantiation. As Aegidius Fuscararius (Bishop of Modena) pointed out, the proposition contained several distinct points.[73] And it was the "unio hypostatica humanitatis et substantiae panis et vini" that, again to judge from Massarelli's report, occasioned the greatest number of extended comments by both theologians and bishops. This was the focus of the remarks of Franciscus Visdomini,

---

[70]*Ibid.* 946.

[71]E.g., the entire point of what Karl Rahner has to say about transubstantiation is that it is a necessary pre-requisite to the doctrine of the real presence. See "Die Gegenwart Christi im Sakrament des Herrenmahles," *Schriften zur Theologie*, IV Einsiedeln, 1962), 357-385.

[72]*Ibid.* 913.

[73]*CT*, VII/1, 168.

Georgius a Vosmediano, and Georgius a S. Iacobo in 1547; and of Franciscus de Toro, Melchior a Vosmediano (apparently the same person as the Georgius of 1547), Franciscus de Heredia, Petrus Frago, Ioannes Fonseca (Bishop of Castellamare), Georgius Flach (Bishop of Salona), and Christophorus Patavinus (General of the Hermits of St. Augustine) in 1551. Thus a good bit of the discussion of the proposition never really dealt with what was eventually to be the sole point of the canon. However, as Martinus Perez de Ayala (Bishop of Cadix) rather disconcertingly pointed out: "Quod tamen dicitur de unione hypostatica, non est error praesentis temporis."[74] Subsequently (and I suppose consequently) the reference to impanation and hypostatic union was omitted in the penultimate and ultimate texts of the canon. But because there were several quite different matters being discussed throughout the entire debate, it is not surprising that a matter that was at most ancillary to one of the points should be left unsettled.

Though Lateran IV is not the only authority cited on behalf of the doctrine of transubstantiation—far from it—it is the authority cited most often and would seem to be (perhaps along with Constance and Florence) the crucial witness.[75]

The only one to question the solidity of the argument from Lateran IV was Melchior Cano.

> Quo igitur ad tertium, de transsubstantiatione, eum haereticum esse declaravit. Responditque ad ea, quae in contrarium ab adversariis adducuntur, scil. quod ea sit vox nova in ecclesia. (Quod licet vox videatur nova, in re tamen semper ecclesiae convenit. Neque enim inconveniens est, quod de nova suborta haeresi nova etiam vocabula ad eam damnandam inveniantur, ut respondet Augustinus de nomine Donatistarum et non Donatianorum, ut etiam de Homusion et de aliis. Quo verbo usum fuit concilium Lateranense, et idem sancti patres in sententia asseruerunt, dum dicunt, panem in Christi corpus transmutari vel panem Christi corpus fieri et similia. Monuit tamen, esse advertendum, qua forma iste articulus damnetur, quia, licet in cap. Firmiter de ipsa transsubstantiatione fiat mentio, tamen

---

[74]CT, VII/1, 163.

[75]A judgment of this sort is obviously in large part a matter of impression and does not lend itself readily to demonstration. It was not the scholastic way—and it was not the way of those at Trent—to label one argument crucial and the others only supportive. Their method of argument was cumulative. I single out Lateran IV because it is the most frequently used, is often used all by itself, and of course because in late medieval theology it was the crucial, often the only witness.

illa non videtur pertinere ad fidem, ut pari modo dicitur de natura angelorum. Et quae habentur in concilio Florentino, non credit, omnia ita astringi ad fidem, ut ea negantes haberi verti in corpus Christi. Quod ecclesia semper tenuit et habetur ex traditionibus et ex patribus, ut Gregorio et Cypriano in expositione orationis Dominicae.)[76]

The speaker following Cano. Ioannes de Ortega, based his support of transubstantiation on the *auctoritatibus per alios adductis.* Since the only speaker to speak before Cano had referred only to Lateran IV and Florence, one wonders if Cano's point had got across at all. There seems to have been no discussion of Cano's point by any of the subsequent speakers. One wonders if the importance of the issue was understood.

Two final matters should be noted. Thomas Campegius (Bishop of Feltre) seems to have urged that the entire canon be dropped because it was already contained in the first canon, the one asserting the real presence. Such at least is what we read in Masserelli's final version of Campegius' statement. "3. articulus etiam haereticus est; sed quia continetur in primo, cuperet eum dimitti." However, the earlier version is quite different: "3. articulus etiam haereticus est; cum vere fiat transsubstantiatio et non unio hypostatica. 5. articulus: Cuperet dimitti, quia sat est quod damnetur haec assertio in primo articulo." Though the *CT* editor regularly favors Masserelli's final version of the proceedings, in this case the earlier version would seem to fit more naturally into the context of the conciliar discussion. Most would not agree that transubstantiation was contained in the first proposition; but the fifth proposition, on the cult appropriate to the eucharist, would seem to be a consequence of the thesis on the real presence.[77]

Campegius had also urged, in 1547, that instead of "transsubstantiatio" the word "conversio" be used; and the Bishop of Vienna, in his final comment a few days before the final ratification of the canons in 1551, urged that the word "transsubstantiatio" be eliminated: "Sed ex 2^{0} vellet expungi *transsubstantiatio,* quia iam ponitur in primo.[78] In reply to this, the Bishop of Bitonto, "(qui curam suscepit respondendi nomine sacrae deputationis obiectionibus, quae opponuntur) respondit, quod in primo canone ponitur, quomodo

---

[76]CT, VII/1, 124-125. An alternate version of the bracketed passage is given in the critical apparatus of CT. The sense of the other version is not significantly different from that of the version preferred by the editor.

[77]CT, VII/1, 149.

[78]CT, VII/1, 188.

sit, in 2^0 quomodo fiat transsubstantiatio, et quia haeretici eam vocem damnant."[79]

I have thus far focused entirely on the canons of Trent. In addition to the canons, however, there is also the *decretum* or *doctrina de ss. eucharistia*. The relevant text is as follows:

Quoniam autem Christus Redemptor noster corpus suum id, quod sub specie panis offerebat, vere esse dixit, ideo persuasum semper in ecclesia Dei fuit, idque nunc denuo sancta haec synodus declarat, per consecrationem panis et vini conversionem fieri totius substantiae panis in substantiam corporis Christi Domini nostri et totius substantiae vini in substantiam sanguinis eius. Quae conversio convenienter et proprie a sancta catholica ecclesia transsubstantiatio est appellata.[80]

The question naturally arises whether this paragraph should be taken as the key to the connection between the canon on the real presence and the canon on transubstantiation. Here transubstantiation is taken as the other side of the coin of real presence. But before we too easily adopt this procedure, we should note several points. The decree was drawn up on the afternoon of October 9, 1551, just two days before the solemn ratification of the chapters and canons. Discussion of the document was completed in the afternoon and evening sessions of October 10, and even in these two meetings it had to share the agenda with the canons on reform. To judge from Massarelli's account, not a word was said about the fourth chapter of the decree on the eucharist. To interpret the "Quoniam" as teaching that the "conversio totius substantiae panis" is a necessary consequence of the real presence is to find in it a sense which a number of the participants at the council had already repudiated. Had the chapter been so understood at Trent, it would presumably have precipitated some sort of discussion.

Though on the face of it it might seem a more reasonable procedure to interpret the canons in light of the decree, since it was the canons that really drew that attention of the council participants it would seem that these should not be reinterpreted against the intentions of their framers on the basis of the rather casually prepared and briefly considered decree.

The interpretation of Trent which I have presented here differs so considerably from that presented by E. Schillebeeckx in an

---

[79] *Ibid.*

[80] *Ibid.* 201.

important article on "The Presence of Christ in the Eucharist," that it may be not inappropriate here to consider the major points of disagreement.[81]

Schillebeeckx distinguishes what he calls three levels in the Tridentine dogma:

Thus there are three levels in the Tridentine dogma:

1. Central Position: There is a specific-proper eucharistic 'real presence,' namely by the real presence of Christ's body and blood under the sacramental form of bread and wine, which is to be understood in such deep reality, that Jesus can say: 'this here, that is my body; I give it to you to eat, so that you may have communion with me.' Therefore Christ is 'vere, realiter and substantialiter' present and not simply 'as in a sign' or only 'in virtute' (canon 1) and not only in the communicating but also before (after the liturgy of consecration) and after; this insistence upon the permanence of the eucharist/'real presence' points directly to the specificness of the reality of this presence.

2. This Eucharistic real presence cannot be meaningfully understood by the council of Trent except in terms of a transformation of the substance of bread and wine into the substance of the body and blood of Christ (canon 2).

3. This transformation of bread and wine is very fittingly called transsubstantiation (conclusion of canon 2).[82]

The crucial point here is Schillebeeckx's assertion that "Eucharistic real presence and transubstantiation are, in the minds of the council fathers, two identical affirmations." That it was in the minds of some, I have no doubt; that it was not in the minds of others would seem equally clear.[83] While Schillebeeckx is correct in noting that more bishops connect the two canons, it must also be noted that there was no attempt made to decide finally how these were connected. And as a perusal of the 1547 and 1551 discussions makes clear, transubstantiation was *not* being defined because the "Eucharistic real presence cannot be meaningfully understood by the council of Trent except in terms of a transformation of the substance of

---

[81] "Christus' tegenwoordigheid in de Eucharistie", *Tijdschrift voor Theologie*, 5 (1965), 136-173. The English quotations are from a partial, unpublished translation of the Dutch. The present writer has checked the crucial passages against the original, and as far as he can see (which in this matter is not very far) the translation is accurate.

[82] *Ibid.* 151-152.

[83] *E.g.*, Christophorus Patavinus, the Augustinian General.

bread, etc." The already referred to statement (*CT*, V. 946) about the *possibility* of cons., simply does not fit in with this assessment of the situation. And though the *subsequent* course of Roman Catholic theology fits in rather nicely with this assessment, the *antecedent* state of theology makes it quite implausible. When Schillebeeckx asserts that "the error condemned in canon 2 is not ascribed to anyone different from that of canon 1,"[84] he would seem to be passing over a considerable amount of evidence. In the texts which served as the basis of the theologians discussions in 1547 and 1551, the errors in the first proposition are expressly ascribed to Zwingli and Oecolampadius, those of the third (our second canon) to Luther. Moreover, at the end of the discussion of the proposed propositions by the bishops in general session, the papal legate summed up the views expressed as follows:

Deinde sententias patrum in summa retulit, videlicet: Primus articulus est Oecolampadii, qui ab omnibus patribus iudicatur damnandus; (aliqui tamen dixerunt ex eo delendum, quod dicitur de divinitate quasi superfluum; id tamen ab eisdem haereticis asseritur.) 2. articulus etiam ab omnibus damnatur, licet quidam censuerint omittendum, (quasi non haberet auctorem), sed est error Buceri et omnino damnandus est, (neque continetur in primo), quia hic de sumptione fit mentio, (quae in primo non habetur). 3. etiam omnes damnarunt et est error Lutheri, et ita eum intelligunt Roffensis et Ekhius."[85]

What skews Schillebeeckx's entire article is his failure to note that in the theological milieu out of which Luther comes, real presence and transubstantiation are connected by ecclesiastical *fiat* rather than by inner necessity. Schillebeeckx writes: "In the Medieval intellectual milieu of Aristotelianism one could not fully assert the properly Catholic notion of the presence of Christ without affirming transubstantiation."[86] This simply does not correspond to the state of the question in much of 14th and 15th century scholasticism.[87]

---

[84]*Ibid.* 151.

[85]*CT*, VII/1, 176.

[86]"Christus tegenwoordigheid," 158.

[87]It would, of course, greatly simplify the problem of continuity or identity in faith amid changes in theological statement if the "essence" of the second Tridentine canon could be reduced to the first, and I take it that one reason why Father Schillebeeckx works so hard at his interpretation of the past is to enhance the responsibility and freedom of the Church in the present. My contention, however, is that the texts are a good bit more recalcitrant than he allows, the work of distilling essences much more problemmatic.

IV.

If at least the major contentions of this paper have been correct, then the Tridentine response to Luther's rejection of transubstantiation *as a dogma* missed the point of that rejection altogether; and the question posed by Luther has remained unanswered, indeed unnoticed.

Luther was correct in his contention that the doctrine of transubstantiation as it had been elaborated in the Church was not connected in a necessary or even particularly significant way to what both Luther and his Roman Catholic opponents regarded as the more important doctrine of the real presence.

It is, of course, possible and somewhat tempting to view this as simply another instance of the general way in which Scotus and Ockham corrupted scholaticism and brought about the Reformation. But this solution seems to ascribe an almost canonical status to Thomas Aquinas, a status which certainly was not his in the medieval and Tridentine periods. Incidentally, it grants the substance of Luther's charges; for to insist that the theologies most prominent in the Church had been corrupt since the early 14th century is to differ only in degree with the charge that the corruption had taken place somewhat earlier. Also, this solution does not take sufficient note of the extent to which the participants at Trent accepted the problem in the terms in which it had been posed by late scholasticism and by Luther. If it was *really* the doctrine of the Church that transubstantiation was simply a corollary of the doctrine of the real presence, then we must at least note that the assembled theologians and bishops at Trent seem to have been singularly unaware of this.

It would perhaps have clarified matters if Luther had, like a good many 13th century but unlike most 14th and 15th century theologians, preferred transubstantiation. For his question was whether the Church should, indeed whether it can, require as a *sine qua non* of communion the confession of a doctrine that is neither necessary nor important.

Indeed, if my analysis of the pre-Tridentine materials has been correct, the question is even more difficult than this; for it has been my contention that the *determinatio ecclesiae* to which Luther objected was never deliberately made: like Topsy, it just growed. The anti-Albigensian confession of faith of Lateran IV was not interpreted as a dogmatic exclusion of all theories of the real presence other than transubstantiation until eighty-five years after that council. Thus what Luther was objecting to would seem to have come about through inadvertance and misunderstanding. Fourteenth and fifteenth century theologians considered themselves bound by a decree which they misinterpreted. This misunderstanding is understandable enough and one could perhaps find other instances similar to this; but the question inevitably arises: is Roman Catholicism to consider itself bound by this series of events? Are the theologians of the 14th and 15th centuries and the council of the 16th to be taken as the crooked lines with which God has written straight, or is the Roman Catholic self-understanding and its understanding of the nature and function of dogma such that it can reopen this question in a more basic way than thus far it has done?

DIGESTS OF RECENT AMERICAN AND EUROPEAN LUTHERAN DISCUSSIONS OF THE SACRAMENT OF THE ALTAR

By Arthur Carl Piepkorn

THE fourteen digests of recent American and European discussions of the sacrament of the altar contained in this paper are not intended to be *complete* summaries. They propose to highlight the issues of consecration and change in which we are immediately interested. In the process of condensation some of the inevitable duplication has been eliminated.

In addition to the references that the summaries cite, the following passages are of interest.

1. At the Colloquy of Regensburg the Lutherans declared: "Nos enim adfirmamus corpus vere praesens esse, converti autem seu mutari panem mutatione mystica, id est, qua iam vera fit exhibitio praesentis corporis post consecrationem. Et intelligimus mutationem mysticam non tantum significativam sed eam qua corpus Christi fit praesens." (CR 4,263)

2. John Gerhard, *Loci theologici*, locus XXI, caput xii, para. 135: "Quod enim toties Bellarminus urget, 'verba Christi, accipite, edite, hoc est corpus meum, aut veram (essentialem) mutationem panis aut metaphoricam tantum inferre,' in eo *to elleipes* committit, datur enim tertium, quod videlicet panis mutatus fuerit sacramentaliter." Para. 136: "Hanc sacramentalem panis mutationem vel potius unionem corporis Christi cum pane (quia mutatio illa sacramentalis in eo unice consistit, quod panis eucharisticus per benedictionem a communi usu sequestratur, ut sit *ochema, organon* ac medium, per quod, cum quo et in quo corpus Christi distribuatur, exhibeatur, manducetur) . . ." (ed. Preuss, V, 135.)

3. David Hollazius, *Examen theologicum acroamaticum*, pars III, sectio II, caput v, quaestio 15, observatio: "Dist [ingue] inter

mutationem essentialem et accidentalem. Quando sancti Patres scripserunt quod panis et vinum in Eucharistia per consecrationem mutentur, aut transelementantur, non intellexerunt mutationem essentialem, sed accidentalem, nempe ratione officii et usus mystici, id est, evectionem elementorum in nobiliorem statum, ita ut panis sit et maneat ratione essentiae idem, qui ante consecrationem fuit, sed juxta institutionem atque promissionem Christi omnipotente ipsius virtute fiat Symbolum corporis Christi communicativum, cum ante consecrationem esset panis vulgaris."

Sasse, Hermann. *This Is My Body: Luther's Contention for the Real Presence in the Sacrament of the Altar.* Minneapolis: Augsburg Publishing House, 1959. (Except where noted, the following material is condensed from a section headed "Consecration," comprising pp. 164-176 of part 3 of chapter 4, "The Great Controversy.")

P. 37: "The danger does not lie so much in the use of the words 'conversio,' 'mutatio,' etc., which for many might not mean anything more than an attempt to express in human language the incomprehensible mystery that the elements after consecration are really the body and the blood of Christ. The danger is rather that such words are understood as a sort of explanation of what happens in that miracle, an explanation which requires more explanations." A footnote recalls that Apology 10 describes the Greek Orthodox eucharistic canon as praying "ut mutato pane ipsum corpus Christi fiat"; that Vulgarius (Theophylact of Ohrid) said "panem non tantum figuram esse, sed vere in carnem mutari"; that in the quotation from St. John Chrysostom in Formula of Concord, Solid Declaration, 7,76 *metarhythmyzein* is reproduced with *consecrare;* and that other Greek synonyms for *metaballo* are *metapoieo, methistemi, metaskeuazo* and *metastoicheo.*

Sasse sees the difference between the Lutheran and the Swiss positions in this that the Reformed Churches, as their classic liturgies attest, do not really believe in a consecration at all, whereas Luther can assert that "our bread becomes and is Christ's body" (WA 18,206,21). The difference between the Lutheran and the Roman Catholic position in Sasse's view is that the former reserves the authority to consecrate to the clergyman but attributes the consecratory efficacy of the words of institution to the fact that they are the creative word of the omnipotent Lord, while the latter asserts that the priest acts *in persona Christi* but attributes the consecratory power not only to the words but also to the power received by the priest in his ordination when the bishop says "Accipe potestatem offerendi in ecclesia tam pro vivis tam pro mortuis" (St. Thomas Aquinas, ST III, 82, ad 1).

When Luther seems to define the moment at which the real presence begins or ends, he is concerned about the efficacy of the word rather than the chronological issue as such. Luther repeatedly confessed his ignorance on this point (WA 6,510,32ff.; 18,166,10-11; 206,20; 23,87,32). In this Luther was in agreement with the church of the first 1200 years. "No one could think more highly [than Luther] of the consecration, no one could treat the consecrated elements more reverently, and no one could receive the true body and blood of Christ with deeper piety."

The Sacrament of the Altar and Its Implications: Statement Adopted by the 1960 Convention of the United Lutheran Church in America as a Guide to Its Congregations. New York: United Lutheran Church in America, n. d. (The following is condensed from paragraphs 17-25 and 40 of the "Basic Affirmations" and paragraphs 1 and 3 of "Matters of Liturgical Practice.")

In the sacrament the total risen Christ who shared with us our humanity and raised it into glory is present. The everywhere-present but unknown God is revealed and proclaimed as the God-for-man and actually is present to impart himself to man as such, giving the body that was broken and the blood that was shed on Calvary into the most intimate and restoring union with the believer and as a judgment on the unbeliever. He is present whether acknowledged or not. His presence is not produced by faith but acknowledged in faith. The word "real," added to "presence" to protect the sacrament against spiritualizing interpretations, adds nothing to the idea of the presence of the total Christ.

Christ is present and graciously imparts himself to the entire action. The precise moment of the beginning of his presence (for example, with the words of institution) or its ending (for example, with the oral reception) need not and cannot be specified.

Every meal at which Jesus is the invited guest is a celebration of his presence, but it is not a sacrament because it is not connected with the specific promise of Christ in connection with the giving of bread and wine for the remission of sins.

The use of earthly elements is essential to the sacrament in view of the total biblical witness. The presence, the masks, and the grace form a biblical triad that cannot be translated into philosophical categories without materializing the grace or magicizing the sacrament. Concentration on the elements and on the precise nature of the relationship between them and the presence and self-impartation of the total Christ marks a disastrous historical bypath.

The words of institution are not a formula which effects a change in the elements so that they are thereby removed from the realm of the profane to the sacred. These elements are to be treated with reverence but are not to become objects of veneration or adoration.

Placing the host directly into the communicant's mouth is a form of reception dictated by a material view of the relation of Christ to the elements. It has no support in Biblical theology. It is generally more appropriate to place the host in the communicant's hand.

No Lutheran theological description of how Christ is present among his people in the sacrament has ever suggested that this presence is one of material identity. Hence any reverent and convenient disposition of the elements remaining after a celebration is proper. The expenditure of grave theological reflection on such a point has covert pedagogical force and invites erroneous speculation.

Heinecken, Martin J. "An Orientation Toward the Lord's Supper Today," in Helmut T. Lehmann, editor, *Meaning and Practice of the Lord's Supper* (Philadelphia: Muhlenberg Press, 1961), 169-203. (This summary restricts itself to the sections "Memorial, Expectation, Real Presence" on pp. 180-191.)

The addition of the word "real" to "presence" is redundant. There is no presence other than that of the self-impartation of the total Christ.

The atoning death of Christ is a present reality and not just a memory. It is a present reality for faith, which is the only way it can be a reality for anyone.

The bread and wine mediate the presence of Christ, but these latter masks are not to be put on a par with the historical Jesus. The bread and the wine "share in that which they symbolize by virtue of the material order; but they are what they symbolize by virtue of the word of God" (Sittler). Hence there is no possible reason why these earthly elements should need somehow to be changed or transmuted to make way for, or give place to, the presence of Christ. This necessity is not suggested even remotely by the biblical witness. Bread and wine remain what they are, and no change in these elements themselves takes place at any point, either through an *epiklesis* or through the repetition of the words of institution. The words of institution are words of recollection, proclamation, and promise—God's creative word by means of which the promise once made brings about Christ's presence for us in and through the elements. Their use in the sacrament is inherently no holier than when a human life is saved and strengthened by means of them. Certainly the elements used in the sacrament are to be treated with due reverence, but why more so than the food that is served at the table upon which the blessing of God has been asked? Concern over the spilling of the wine, dropping of the host, etc., betray an orientation foreign to the one here espoused.

Verinus, Titus [ps.]. "The Moment at Which the Sacramental Union Begins," *Una Sancta,* Presentation of the Augsburg Confession, 1961, 11-18.

The Lutheran Reformers held that the sacramental union is accomplished in close temporal as well as causal connection with the recitation of the words of institution. At the same time they insisted on the integrity of the total sacramental action and denied sacramental reality as much to solitary masses as to the communion services of the "enemies of the sacrament."

Luther held that the body and blood of Christ were present at the time of the elevation (WA 6,524,21-35; 19,99-100; 54,163; WATR 5,308). He approved the prayer *Domine Jesus Christe,* with its reference to "this your most holy body and blood" prior to the celebrant's self-communion (WA 12,213). He holds that the hand of the priest who administers the host encloses the body of Christ (WA 30/3, 561). He states that the body of Christ clothes itself with the bread when the word is added to the element (WA 30/1, 53, see also WA 26,442,29-443,7; 445,8-15; 462,4-8; and 30/1,117, 34-35). He recommends that a host that has been put into the mouth of a communicant who dies before he can swallow it is to be consigned to the fire (WA 30/2,624; WABr 6,462). Wolfgang Musculus of Bern observes that in St. Mary's Church, Wittenberg, the celebrant diligently drained the chalice and afterward cleansed it with wine "that no blood might remain," and John Bugenhagen reprehends the practice of mixing consecrated hosts after the celebration with "profane" hosts as if the former themselves were "profane" (Kolde, *Analecta Lutherana*, 217,223).

The 1540 Church Order of Joachim II of Brandenburg called for the parish priest in a rochet, preceded by a sacristan with a bell and a lighted lantern, to take the venerable sacrament in both kinds to a dying parishioner (Sehling, *Evangelische Kirchenordnungen*, 3, 77-79). John Hachenburg of Erfurt reports that about 1542 a woman communicant in St. Mary's Church, Wittenberg, bumped against the chalice as she was kneeling down so that some of its contents spilled on her clothing. After the celebration Luther had the affected portion of her jacket lining cut out and burned, along with the wood that had had shaved from the part of the choir stall on which the contents of the chalice had been splashed (Kawerau, in *ZfPT*,25,293-294).

In the controversy at Eisleben between Wolfrum and Rauber in 1543, Luther called the practice of mixing consecrated elements remaining after the celebration with unconsecrated elements "a scandalous Zwinglian insanity" and defined the sacramental action as starting with the Our Father and continuing until the chalice had been drained and the hosts consumed (WABr, 10, 340-341, 348-349).

When in 1546 Adam Besserer dropped a consecrated host, administered an unconsecrated host to the last communicant, and after finding the dropped host put it with the unconsecrated hosts after the service Luther and Bugenhagen called for his banishment from the Lutheran community (WABr 11,259).

Martin Chemnitz disavows the position that the consecrated host becomes the body of Christ only when the communicants begin to eat it. When in the primitive church the deacons took the Holy Communion from the altar to the sick, or when the Eucharist was sent as a symbol of intercommunion by the bishop of a place to a visiting bishop, or when down into the fifth century the communicants took some of the consecrated elements home with them, Chemnitz holds that the *usus* or *actio* continued until the elements which had been consecrated for reception were consumed. (*Examen,* Part Two, Locus IV, sectio iii, paras. 9 and 13; sectio vii, 12-19.)

In the next century, John Gerhard describes the recitation of the words of institution as effecting a sacramental change of the bread (*sacramentalis panis mutatio*) (*Loci*, Locus XXI, cap. xii, paras. 136, 149, 153; cap. vii, para. 195).

The Conduct of the Service. Revised edition. St. Louis: Concordia Seminary Press, 1965. (The following is condensed from pp. 41-42.)

The General Rubrics of *The Lutheran Liturgy* prescribe that after the celebration the bread that remains shall be carefully removed from the paten and ciborium to a fit receptacle, there to be kept against the next communion, and the remainder of the consecrated wine be poured into the sacrarium or on the ground at a proper and convenient place outside the church. It is clear that the consecrated hosts are not to be mixed with unconsecrated hosts, but are to be carefully segregated in a fit receptable such as a special pyx or ciborium. If the celebration of the holy communion takes places in an inadequately equipped chapel or a private house, the celebrant should reverently consume what remains of the consecrated bread and wine.

(Note. The rubrics of the *Service Book and Hymnal* have no provisions for disposing of the elements remaining after the celebration.)

Brunner, Peter. "Zur Lehre vom Gottesdienst der im Namen Jesu versammelten Gemeinde," in Karl Ferdinand Müller and Walter Blankenburg (Editors), *Leiturgia: Handbuch des evangelischen Gottesdienstes,* I (Kassel: Johannes Stauda-Verlag, 1954), 83-361. (The following condenses in section C IV (d), "Das Heilsgeschen im Abendmahl," subsections 5, "Abendmahlsspeise und Realpräsenz," and 6, "Konsekration.")

The peculiar character of the holy communion is not merely that it couples the word with a dramatic action, although this is part of the anamnesis mystery. The difference between the eucharist and the *oth* of the Old Testament prophets is that the words that our Lord speaks with reference to the bread and wine interpret not his act of giving but that which he gives. The relation between bread and body and between wine and blood that Christ establishes is not "a combination through analogy but a combination through identity" (Lohmeyer). The broken bread and the wine offered to his disciples by virtue of his word are the body and blood of Christ given and poured out for them and for the multitude. 1 Corinthians 11,27-32 and 10,16-22 make it clear that St. Paul understood the words of institution in the sense of such an identity-combination *(Identitätsverknüpfung).* For him the communicant, in his communion with the body and the blood of Jesus given and poured out for us, has a share in the sacrificial death of Jesus on the basis of this sacramental participation and communion. The statements of St. John 6 are no less realistic and no more spiritualistic than the words of St. Paul about the real presence. Any attempt to play the Fourth Gospel off against St. Paul betrays a misunderstanding of the peculiarity of the former.

The New Testament puts special stress on the word about the bread, which has a relative independence as the constitutive element of the supper. In our ignorance of the Aramaic word that Christ used for "body," we cannot build a Eucharistic doctrine on it. Christ gives his body as his true corporeal incarnation (*Menschsein*) in its "for you" aspect. The body of Christ that Christ gives his disciples in the bread is he himself in his total obedience that climaxes in his death on the cross. His saving victory, his corporeal life lived for us, his death for us and his triumph for us, are in his body and it is his body that we receive with the bread.

The word about the cup interprets definitively the word about the bread by concentrating the saving event univocally on Christ's death on the cross. The blood is the covenant blood in which he himself becomes tangible for us.

The twoness of bread and wine, of the sacrificial body and of the sacrificial blood, identifies Our Lord's death with the Old Testament expiatory sacrifice. But his oblation on the cross is not dead, because the incarnate Christ is both God and man. The flesh of the incarnate Word is not separated from the vivifying divine Spirit. This sacrificial flesh and this sacrificial blood is as his flesh also *pneuma,* divine life even in the voluntary sacrifice of dying. Death does not destroy it, but it destroys death.

The risen and ascended Christ stands before God's throne as the eternal high priest, and his bloody sacrifice on Golgotha lives on there in pneumatic reality. Through the real presence the *repraesentatio* that takes place in the eucharist receives in a mode that is absolutely without analogy its really present concretion. In a mysterious fashion God communicates with the bread and wine the passion and death of Christ and his sacrifice on the cross with its eschatological *dynamis* that shatters all time and space. "It is the clear teaching of the New Testament that the holy communion is the making present of the sacrifice of Jesus Christ and the real bestowal of that which this offering has obtained" (Sasse).

Our celebrations of the holy communion have the originally instituted celebration in them and with them. The presence of

Jesus Christ in our celebrations is the presupposition of the fact that in our eucharists the bread is his body and the wine his blood.

The presence of Christ in our celebration depends on the gathering of two or three or whatever number they may be in his name as the *ekklesia* that baptism and the Gospel have constituted in order to do what he commanded his own to do in remembrance of him. There must be bread and wine in a cup. These are to be consecrated and thereby taken out of the purpose for which wine must then be received and eaten or drunk. Under such circumstances Christ imparts his active presence, by which he allows his supper to become a new event in our midst. The real presence is embedded in the holy supper; Augsburg Confession 10 emphasizes that the body and blood of Christ are truly present *in coena*. This does not preclude, indeed it demands, that we see the presence of the body and blood of Christ as a completed event that takes place at a specific place in the action. This event takes place when the Lord through his minister speaks these wonder-words with messianic authority. Distribution, reception, eating and drinking belong to the total anamnesis-action, but none of these create the real presence. When these words have been spoken, I can be as certain that the bread and wine are the body and blood of Christ as I am certain that they are when I receive them. This consideration should end any doubt about the propriety of a new consecration when the original supply of elements proves insufficient and new elements are brought to the altar.

The real presence ceases when the *actio* or *usus* as sacrament has come to an end. It contradicts the institution of Christ to affirm that the presence persists when the sacrament is reserved or carried about or exposed for adoration. Nevertheless the elements that remain *were* actually bearers of Christ's body and blood, creatures that Christ took up into the sacramental union. They thus have a right to be handled reverently. Luther had grave misgivings about mixing consecrated and unconsecrated elements and insisted that nothing remain after a celebration. If the Lutheran doctrine of the real presence is valid, the propriety of this procedure cannot be contested.

Brunner regards Luther's silence at the "Wittenberg Concord" negotiations of 1536 as evidence that he did not object in principle to Bucer's practice of returning surplus consecrated hosts to the pyx "with due reverence." Brunner holds that the procedure that Luther enjoins in connection with the contents of the chalice is the best. Brunner also holds that if there is surplus wine in the cruet—(Note: it is not clear if this is consecrated or unconsecrated wine)—there is no objection in principle to using it as a beverage provided that due reverence is exercised in every respect.

Grass, Hans. *Die Abendmahlslehre bei Luther und Calvin: Eine kritische Untersuchung*. Gütersloh: C. Bertelsmann Verlag, 1954. (What follows draws particularly on section II, of Part One, "Systematische Entfaltung," pp. 45-129.)

By 1526, Grass holds, the real presence had moved into the center of Luther's teaching about the sacrament of the altar; he had abandoned both the doctrine of transubstantiation and the doctrine of concomitance; and his emphasis lay on the real presence of the body and blood of Christ, although this presence was not without its personalistic aspects. The creative word of Christ in the recitation of the words of institution bring about a real consecration of the elements: "Ibi verba faciunt panem zum Leib Christi traditum pro nobis. Ergo non est amplius panis, sed corpus Christi hat das Brot an" (WA 30/1,53,23). Grass sees an ambiguity about the "thesaurus sacramenti," which Luther can describe in close context as the body and blood of Christ but also as the forgiveness of sins (WA 30/1,225,27-226,11; LC, Sacrament of the Altar, 30-32). Grass summarizes: The word constitutes and applies the real presence of body and blood in the holy communion. As constituting word it makes possible the bodily eating, as applicatory word it makes possible the spiritual eating. But the word does not exhaust itself in these two functions. It retains the additional character of *summa doctrinae evangelii*, which asserts itself along with the real presence as the treasure that the sacrament imparts. Apart from the special exegesis of the words, the presence of the *totus vivus Christus* accompanies the word as means-of-grace.

The combination of the real presence with the fruit of the sacrament (forgiveness of sins, life, and salvation) Grass sees as having in Luther only a positivistic, not a systematic foundation, since Luther concedes that mere bread and wine or, for that matter, anything else, could, if God so commanded, convey forgiveness of sins. He does concede that the gift of forgiveness as a consequence of the real presence of Christ's person is systematically developed by Luther, but this does not then specifically and exclusively characterize the holy communion. A systematic connection between the real presence of Christ's body and blood and everlasting life emerges only as Luther begins to develop the patristic idea that the body of Christ bodily received is a medicine of immortality.

Grass sees the real difference between the Lutherans and the Reformed in the *modus praesentiae*. The rule *Nihil habet rationem sacramenti extra usum* needs clarification. One explanation of the rule is "Denique quandocumque sacramentum transfertur ad usum alium extra institutum, non est sacramentum" (WA 39/2,147, 29). This, Grass holds, denies a real presence when the host is reserved or carried about or when a solitary mass is celebrated. It also denies the real presence to the communions of the "Sacramentarians," because they pervert the meaning of Christ's words of institution. The rule does not mean for Luther, for the early Lutherans, or for the Formula of Concord that the real presence occurs only in the reception; there is a real presence *ante sumptionem*. This real presence *ante sumptionem* was for Luther a prophylactic against the spiritualistic tendencies that he saw in the Zwinglian interpretation of the eucharist. While one cannot put Luther and the later Lutheran dogmaticians in opposition to one another, a shift in accent is perceptible, as when Leonard Hütter affirms the same position that Bucer had taken two generations before with reference to the elements left over after the celebration.

Luther prefers not to speculate about the relation of the body and blood of Christ to the elements. He uses a number of analogies, the unity of nature in the Trinity, the personal union of the two natures in Christ, the operational unity of an angel and the flame through which he stands revealed, the formal unity of the Holy Spirit and the dove, and the *unio mystica*. The *tertium comparationis* in each case is that two different essences can be and can be called one essence (WA 26,439,30). Ultimately, however, the sacramental union is unique.

Luther's positive assertions about the sacramental union are of two orders. Some are the vehement identifications of the body and the blood with the bread and wine that he affirms in his anti-Enthusiastic polemics, notably in his "Great Confession" of 1528. But even these are tempered by his refusal to affirm a local inclusion of the body and the blood in the bread and wine, both in the "Great Confession" and at Marburg in 1529. The mystery of the sacrament remains for Luther: "We do not want to fight about words, as long as it continues to be understood that it is not plain bread that we eat in Christ's holy communion but the body of Christ" (WA 23, 135,29ff.).

Kinder, Ernst. "Was geschieht im heiligen Abendmahl? Wirklichkeit und Dauer der Realpräsenz nach Luther und den Bekenntnisschriften," *Zeitwende/Neue Furche*, 30 (1959), 161-172.

The title question, "What happens in the holy communion?" must be asked within a double perspective: (1) The sacramental union exists because of the creative words of institution; (2) the sacramental union exists, as far as Christ's institution is concerned, to the end that the body and blood of Christ may be received and only to this end. Christ gives us his body and his blood through his word (and through nothing else) for us to eat and drink for the forgiveness of sins and for no other purpose. The teleological *terminus a quo* is *per verbum*, the *terminus ad quem* is *ad sumendum.*

The "real presence" is effected by the consecration. "The words are spoken through the mouth of the priest, but it is through God's might and grace, through the word that he speaks, 'This is my body,' that the elements that are set out in the communion are blessed" (St. John Chrysostom) (FC, SD, 7, 76).

"It is the command and institution of Christ that makes the bread his body and the wine his blood" (Luther) (para. 77).

If we base the "real presence" on the words of institution, we are compelled to use the words of institution to determine the end that the sacramental union has in view, that is, eating and drinking the body and the blood of Christ for the forgiveness of sins. The Lutheran symbolical books always combine the affirmation of the true and substantial presence of Christ's body and blood with the assertion that they are distributed and received. The consecration is the beginning of God's sacramental utilization of the elements through his creative word that extends through the eating and drinking. The "real presence" cannot be exhaustively contemplated by isolating the consecration and stopping at that point. It is not a static presence, but a real presence that is at work. The consecration in isolation is in a sense only half the sacrament; it is like a bridge that ends in midair. The thrust of the "real presence" that the consecration creates is toward an effect and finds its fulfillment only in this effect.

The "real presence" takes place only *in usu*. It is not a matter either of asking if the body and blood of Christ are present or alternatively of asking if they are communicated to the recipients. Neither the substance of Christ's body and blood nor the event of their reception exhausts the Lutheran concern. Presence and distribution, *adesse* and *exhiberi,* belong together. At the same time the Formula of Concord rejects both the spiritualists who make the "real presence" depend on the subjective faith of the communicant and the "actualists" who reduce the "real presence" to the momentary act of reception. The "real presence" exists independently of the reception as a result of the consecratory and creative word of God, but it exists in the interest of the reception. We can be certain of the "real presence" from the consecration to the reception within an action that has these terms. Beyond these limits that the words of institution define our practical behavior must be determined by our reverence for this salutary gift.

Between the consecration and the reception the elevation and adoration of the sacrament are appropriate expressions of our awed acknowledgement of the riches of this divine gift and our reverent, humble, and salvation-seeking thanksgiving that the body and blood of Christ are present for us to receive. In considering the treatment of the elements that remain after the celebration, we ought first of all to ask what has happened to the communicants who have received the body and blood of Christ. Since the words of institution make us certain of the "real presence" only with reference to their use, we cannot answer the question if the "real presence" persists with an unequivocal yes or no. At the very least we cannot treat the remaining elements as profane or irreverently. We can give an "interimistic" affirmative answer to our question and reserve them reverently *(würdig).* When they are distributed at a subsequent communion the words of institution should be repeated for their kerygmatic value. (Note: Although Kinder does not say so explicitly, he apparently does not think of such a repetition as "consecratory.") But it would be better to forestall this issue either by wholly consuming the consecrated elements at the celebration or reverently destroying them (*vernichten*).

Even though we may not have an unequivocal kind of certainty at this point, it would be better to go too far in a wordless confession of the salutary mystery of the "real presence" than to apocopate our confession by a profanation of the remaining elements. In our day the peril of casual profanation of that which is holy is an unquestionably greater threat than superstition.

Peters, Albrecht. *Realpräsenz: Luthers Zeugnis von Christi Gegenwart im Abendmahl.* Berlin: Lutherisches Verlagshaus, 1960.

(The following is a condensation of the final "summary and outlook.")

Luther's affirmation of the real presence of Christ in the sacrament of the altar is taken from the church's historic teaching. His doctrine of the omnipresence of Christ's human nature as united to the divine nature *("Ubiquitätslehre")* provides a dogmatic basis that supplements his exegetical basis. He incorporates the real presence of Christ in the holy communion into his Christology as well as into his pneumatic soteriology. His exegesis stresses that which the biblical witnesses have in common. The passages that point toward a real givenness of the body and blood of Christ under the bread and wine he thickens into univocal affirmations of the identity of the sacrificial body of Christ and the elements. This becomes apparent in his analysis of 1 Corinthians 10,16 and 11,24ff. By contrast the statements of St. John 6,53ff. are weakened.

We are driven to the real presence of Christ by a twofold opposite—on the one hand the prince of this world with his minions, the world, sin, death, the hostility of the "powers," and on the other hand, the divine law that beats upon our conscience. Union with Christ in the sacrament provided Luther with protection against the wrathful judgment of God and with freedom from a tortured conscience.

The gift of the sacrament is the same as that of the word, the *totus vivus Christus* in all the concentration of his resurrection body. Luther cannot separate Christ from his flesh and blood. Wherever the Lord is present he is present in his sacrificial body, which is simultaneously the glorified body of the resurrected and exalted One. The "real-and-material" (*dinglich-sachliche*) side of Christ's presence is accentuated in the sacrament. The *proprium sacramenti* is the concentration of the word on the *summa evangelii* and a bodily reception of the Lord in his sacrificial body under the elements of bread and wine as an immediate salutary contact of our mouths with him. The "condition" of the real presence under the elements is the same as it is in the word; the Lord binds himself to his promise to be present where his people act in his name and in obedience to him.

The Lord is really present in and under the elements, wherever the sacramental action accords with his institution. The association is so intimate that one can point to the bread and wine and say: "There is Christ's body and blood," or "The Lord is raised aloft at the elevation," or "His blood is poured into the mouths of the faithful." In spite of this profoundest condescension on his part, which can be compared only with his being offered up on the cross, he remains the Lord of life and of death, so that as we receive this material food the Lord of Lords personally encounters us in judgment and in grace. The confrontation of the external human person by the flesh and blood of Christ under the mask of the elements also involves a confrontation of the interior psychic man with the Lord in a listening to his word. The inner and outer events cannot be separated; the whole Christ comes to the whole human being.

For Luther the emphasis lies on the confrontation of the heart with Christ. This is especially true of the reception of the sacrament where the word of forgiveness strikes us in a particularly pregnant fashion. The Christ who is present in the heart effects sanctification in imparting forgiveness of sins. The freedom of the heart touches the body and works in it the new obedience. The eschatological renewal reaches out from the heart as center to touch the bodily person. The fruit of word and sacrament are identical.

The sacrament accomplishes its results immediately, for in the sacrament Christ's body touches our hands and our mouth immediately, but the sacrament has this result only in inseparable association with the union of the heart. Our bodily life receives the body of the Lord and is thus taken up into the body of Christ. This is the nexus between sacrament and ethos. In our reception of the sacrament the Lord takes possession of our bodily existence and conforms it to the sacrificial body of his obedience. The absorption of our bodily life into the body of Christ's sacrifice and obedience in our weekly reception of the sacrament becomes the source of power for our bodily activity during the week.

Thus we fleshly, sinful mortal men become spiritual, holy, and living men even upon this earth, but under the veil of faith and hope. This will break forth in glory only at the end of days, and then *levitas* and *hilaritas* will determine the form of our bodies.

Diestelmann, Jürgen. *Konsekration: Luthers Abendmahlsglaube in dogmatischliturgischer Sicht an Hand von Quellenauszügen dargestellt* (*Luthertum*, No. 22). Berlin: Lutherisches Verlagshaus, 1960.

(Fig. 1 reproduces a woodcut from the Bapst hymnal of 1567, and shows a kneeling communicant receiving the body of Christ from the celebrant's hand while two laymen hold a houseling cloth before the communicant.)

"If a person believes [that the body and blood of Christ are present] he cannot without sin withhold the reverence that is their due from Christ's body and blood. For I must ever confess that when his body and blood are there Christ is there." (WA 11,447) But formal adoration is neither to be commanded nor forbidden.

For Luther the consecration brings about the real presence in a marvelous manner, not because of the celebrant's ordination and anointing, but because Christ so ordained. Yet the mere eucharistic action without consecration does not achieve a sacrament. "As soon as Christ says, 'This is my body,' his body is there through the word and the power of the Holy Spirit. As long as the word is not there, it is plain bread; but when the words are added, they bring with themselves that about which they speak" (WA 19,491). Luther frequently uses the verb *wandeln* ("change, transform") for the consecration; he understands it as "bringing about the sacramental union of the body and blood of Christ with the elements." "*Eucharistia* est panis et vinum verbo conjunctum, mutatum in corpus et sanguinem Christi" (WA 30/1, 122,20-21).

The consecration takes place within the entire sacramental action ("prolatio verborum . . . est potissima et principalis actio in sacramento"). Luther strenuously differentiated consecrated from unconsecrated elements. His conception of the sacramental action did not preclude the communion of the sick in their homes with the sacrament consecrated at the parochial celebration.

There is no evidence of a change of heart on Luther's part that would distinguish the "young Luther" from the "mature Luther."

Philip Melanchton did not wholly share Luther's view, but opted for a stricter and more rigid application of the principle that the sacramental presence did not perdure beyond the immediate sacramental action. "Cum illae res sumuntur, simul adest Christus et est efficax. Haec sacramentalis praesentia est voluntaria; non est inclusio geometrica vel magica, qua cogatur Christus in pane manere . . . Cessante usu sacramenti cesset quoque sacramentum" (CR 7, 876-877). Note: Melanchthon shared this view with Bucer and the South German theologians; the Melanchthonian view and Luther's view have persisted side by side in the Lutheran churches ever since. Admittedly Melanchthon's "voluntary presence" theory was more acceptable to a John Calvin than Luther's rugged sacramental realism, but the charge that Melanchthon denied the objective presence of Christ's body and blood during the sacramental action cannot upon careful investigation be sustained.)

The "Heidelberg Roorback" *(Heidelberger Landlüge)*, which has Luther tell Melanchthon just before the former's death that he had been too rigid in his eucharistic doctrine and that Melanchthon should try to assuage the difference between the Lutherans and the Swiss on this point, is demonstrably a canard in the form in which it has been handed down. A possible kernel of truth in the account may be Luther's feeling that in the case of Adam Besserer he may have acted too hastily in recommending the latter's deposition and exile, in view of the subsequent investigations which may have come to Luther's hand and which showed that Besserer acted out of inexperience.

Luther's consecration doctrine is consciously pre-scholastic (WA 6,509). It is this consecration doctrine which underlies the definitions of the Formula of Concord. On the other hand the Arnoldshain Theses of 1957—which propose to set forth "the decisive content of the biblical witness concerning the holy communion" without a single positive reference to the consecration—are the logical working out of the Melanchthonian thrust.

(The appendix of sources reproduces 20 pages of documentation from Luther's works.)

Schanze, Wolfgang. "Die Konsekrationspraxis in der lutherischen Kirche," *Luthertum*, No. 25 (Berlin: Lutherisches Verlagshaus, 1961), pp. 27-48.

This essay addresses itself to the questions of the elevation, the consecration of a new supply of elements when the original elements have been insufficient for the number of communicants (*Nachkonsekration*), and the treatment of the consecrated elements.

The words of institution have consecratory force, but the consecration is the action of Christ, not of a human being. The consecration refers substantially to the elements, but it does not imply transubstantiation in the medieval sense. Luther's attitude in the Besserer and Wolfrum cases shows that he thought in categories that combined inseparably the ontological and the substantial. Neoprotestant theologians still tend to concur in Loofs' assertion: "Luther's eucharistic teaching, with reference to many elements that he regarded as important, is one of the most grandiose aberrations in the history of Christian reflection on the faith *(einer der grandios-*

esten Verirrungen christlicher Glaubensgedanken)." The Reformation warns us against an intellectualization of the divine mystery that takes place through the consecration. It was this that motivated Luther's rejection of the "scholastic subtlety" of transubstantiation. The consecration is not an isolated action, but it has meaning and effectiveness only in the framework of the entire sacramental action; conversely, the distribution is impossible without consecration.

The realistic Eucharistic theology that underlay the reformers' conception of the consecration long informed the liturgical practice of the Lutheran churches.

Luther's approving attitude toward the elevation was not share by all his associates; Guy Dietrich, Albert of Prussia, and John Bugenhagen abolished it in the 1540s because of its associations and where it did survive it became in most places a casualty of the Interimistic controversy. It has been restored here and there in connection with the liturgical revival; the Church of Hannover (1958) has officially recommended a modified elevation to the level of the celebrant's eyes.

The repetition of the consecration when the original supply of elements failed was universal through the 16th century. It was the particular target of the Neo-protestant theologians of the 19th and early 20th centuries, although it has survived widely and is rubrically prescribed in many Lutheran rites.

The early Lutheran community sought to (but could not) avoid the problem of what to do with elements left over after a celebration. Hence many church orders rubrically prescribed the consumption of all consecrated elements; others permitted the careful reservation against the next communion. Through the 17th century the church orders enjoin scrupulous care in this connection. The use of houseling-cloths to obviate the falling of any of the consecrated species on the ground has persisted in some places down to the present. The *ablutio calicis* was both commended and condemned.

Schanze concludes: "The contemporary church must . . . make its decisions in these questions on the basis of the profound awe that the mystery of the sacramental event demands from us."

Huhnke, Hans-Joachim. "Realpräsenz und Konsekration: Ein Beitrag zu Zentralpunkten lutherischer Abendmahlslehre," *Sanct Athanasius*, Vol. 15, No. 31 (June 28, 1964).

A propos the Arnoldshain Theses of 1957 and the literature elicited by them, Huhnke proposes to set forth the permanent content (*bleibenden Bestand*) of the Lutheran teaching about the holy communion.

This involves a substantial real presence. In the two Catechisms and the Smalcald Articles the Lutheran Church affirms the identity of the consecrated bread and wine and the body and blood of Christ. The "in, with and under" formula is already a kind of circumlocution. The adverbs *vere, realiter,* and *substantialiter* make it impossible for Lutherans to water down the corporeal-objective presence of the body and blood of Christ into nothing more than the personal presence of Christ in his body and his blood, although the former can never be divorced from the latter and the tension between the two is part of the mystery of the sacrament. "Substance" and its cognates, as well as other terms from the scholastic vocabulary, such as *materia,* in the reference to the body and blood of Christ as *materia coelestis,* are to be understood in the strict sense. The Lutheran symbols see in the doctrine of transubstantiation this element of truth that it secures the objective presence of Christ's body and blood. The idea of sacramental union is not intended to put the body and blood of Christ on a par with the bread and the wine; the "that" of the sacrament refers (in the words of David Hollazius) to the body and blood of Christ *principaliter, sive in casu recto, sub ratione generalissima huius rei,* whereas the elements are referred to only *minus principaliter, sive in obliquo.* (A footnote cites the observation of Friedrich Brunstäd's *Theologie der lutherischen Bekenntnisschriften* that with reference to Apology 10 "in a certain sense one can stand on Lutheran ground and talk about a transformation of the elements.") Both the medieval doctrine of transubstantiation and the Lutheran doctrine of the sacramental union are logically complicated efforts to explain the sacramental mystery with a view to protecting it against distortions. Both have their strengths and their weaknesses. Both are concerned about the same point, the objective presence of the body and blood of Christ.

Consecration is the achievement of the substantial presence of the body and blood of Christ through the reference to the bread and wine of Christ's essential declaration (*Seinsaussage*), "This is my body," "This is my blood," since thereby the elements are "consecrated (*geweiht*)" to be the body and the blood of Christ. The efficacy of the consecration depends on the command of

Christ to repeat his action. The words of consecration are immediately efficacious, without an interval between speech and action. Thus Luther can say in a sermon on December 19, 1528: "Quando accedit verbum ad elementum, tunc fit sacramentum" (WA 30/1, 117,34-35).

The consecration is intrinsically complete in the recitation of the words of institution, but it must always take place within the frame of a distribution and reception of the sacrament. This becomes clear in the consecration theology of the Formula of Concord, which sees the omnipotent creative Word of the Incarnate God binding itself in its pristine power to his ministers' recitation of the words of institution over bread and wine in the context of the divinely ordained corporate celebration and bringing about the substantial presence of Christ's body and blood even before the reception.

Schöne, Jobst. *Um Christi sakramentale Gegenwart: Der Saligersche Abendmahlsstreit* 1568/1569. Berlin: Evangelische Verlagsanstalt, 1966.

This study is the first monographic inquiry into the "Saliger Controversy" in over a century. The activities of John Saliger (Beatus), presumably Lübeck-born, can be traced only from 1566, when he transferred from Woerden to Antwerp, to 1580, when he was banished from the Lowlands and disappears. The Lübeck phase of the controversy extended from April to July 1568, the Rostock phase from December 1568 to October 1569. Both phases ended with Saliger's dismissal, from a curacy in St. Mary's Church in Lübeck and from the pastorate of St. Nicholas' Church in Rostock.

The controversy is important (1) because it involved such important Lutheran theologians of the period as Martin Chemnitz, John Wigand, and David Chytraeus; (2) because it is an integral part of the prehistory of Article 7 ("Of the Holy Communion") of the Formula of Concord, into which a portion of the final decision in the controversy was written; and (3) because the controversy has generally been misinterpreted. The common impression given by modern references to the controversy is that Saliger was twice dismissed because of his eucharistic views, chiefly his assertion that the body and blood of Christ are truly present before the reception *(ante sumptionem).* Schöne demonstrates that there was no fundamental difference in the eucharistic doctrine actually professed by the participants in the controversy, and that Saliger's dismissals were occasioned by his intemperate contentiousness.

Note may be taken of common insights that the controversy brought out: (1) the careful distinction between *usus* or *actio* (the total eucharistic action) and *sumptio* (oral reception); (2) the rejection of the speculation that the consecration of the already consecrated elements (specifically the wine) communicated itself to unconsecrated elements added thereto; (3) the attribution of consecratory efficacy to the repetition of the words of institution when spoken in the context of a corporate celebration of the holy eucharist; (4) the practice of consecrating only as many hosts and only as much wine as the number of intending communicants required; (5) the practice of consecrating the new supply of elements if that initially set aside proved insufficient; (6) the emphasis on the rule that consecration is for the purpose of reception and the care exercised to insure that none of the elements remained after the celebration; (7) the stress on the objectivity of the presence of the body and blood of Christ in terms of the *manducatio oralis* (oral reception of Christ's body and blood) and the *manducatio indignorum* (reception of the body and blood of Christ by "unworthy" communicants); (8) the assertion that the minister who distributes the sacrament has in his hands the body and the blood of Christ; (9) the equation of the consecrated elements and the body and the blood of Christ (*praedicatio identica*); (10) the presence of the body and blood of Christ before the reception; (11) the stress on the integrity of the total sacramental action; and (12) commitment to the Reformation rule that *nihil habet rationem sacramenti extra usum a Christo institutum*.

Negatively the thesis that the "sacrament exists before the use" is rejected as misleading because of terminological ambiguity. Also rejected are such opinions as: (1) that "the communion of the body of Christ" in 1 Corinthians 10,16 refers to the sacramental union of bread and body rather than the communion of communicant and the bodily present Christ; (2) that the consecration in itself confects a complete sacrament without any reference to subsequent reception; (3) that the body of Christ is not in the bread but in the eating; and (4) that the body and blood of Christ are not present prior to the reception (described as an opinion which "no one in our churches" entertains).

Roser, Helmut. "Zur lutherischen Lehre von der Konsekration," in *Lutherische Blätter*, 6 (1954), No. 39, 173-195.

The author begins with a liturgicohistorical survey of the

roots out of which the question of the consecration grow. Then he fixes the *status controversiae*: Is the bodily presence of Christ's body and blood in the bread and wine (*leibliche Gegenwart des Leibes und Blutes Christi im Brot und Wein*), about which there can be no difference of opinion among Lutherans, realized only in the moment of reception (*sumptio*), or is the body and the blood of Christ upon the altar even before the reception, so that the minister of the communion has the body and blood of Christ in his hand? Roser commits himself to the latter position. At the hand of materials cited in previous summaries Roser shows that this was the position of Luther, the consistency of whose eucharistic theology Roser defends against those who would play off the "reforming Luther" against the "Luther who was unable to transcend the remnants of Roman thinking." Roser holds that Luther's view is reflected in early Lutheran liturgies, in an important segment of Lutheran theological tradition, and in the Lutheran symbolical books. He sees the idea of *species* reflected in the definition of Apology 10, "quod . . . corpus et sanguis Christi . . . vere exhibeantur cum illis rebus *quae videntur,* pane et vino, his qui sacramentum accipiunt" (emphasis original). Roser observes that in general only the secret adherents of the Calvinian view ("Cryptocalvinists") forbade the consecration of the elements brought to the altar to supplement a failing species. Roser holds that the Sacred Scriptures do not resolve the question at issue directly or indirectly, but that a rigorous application of the Reformation principle which stresses God's salvific action *extra me* and *pro me* in the area of Christology (soteriology) to the question of the consecration requires the view that the real presence is achieved prior to the reception and depends wholly on the words of institution. He also holds that this view is essential to a proper appreciation of the holy communion as a corporate rather than a purely individualistic experience.

(In a response by Hans Kirsten, "Einige Ergänzungen 'Zur lutherischen Lehre von der Konsekration,'" in *Lutherische Blätter*, 7 [1955], No. 41, 28-33, Kirsten agrees that Roser has accurately reproduced Luther's position. Kirsten also agrees that the sacramental action (and the sacramental union) cannot be limited to the reception *(sumptio)*. He expresses doubt that the Formula of Concord intended to commit itself to Luther's position *in toto*. The minimum Lutheran requirement is the conviction that every communicant receives the body and blood of Christ when he receives the consecrated elements. One cannot affirm with certainty that the sacramental union takes place only during the distribution and reception. Nor can one affirm with certainty that the sacramental union is a reality before or after the distribution and reception. The possibility that the sacramental union may begin before and continue after the distribution and reception requires that the consecrated elements be treated with due reverence. This reverence must not become a cult of adoration of the elements. The pious opinion that the sacramental union begins before and continues after the distribution and reception cannot be made a *discrimen ecclesiae*. The view that the sacramental union takes place only during the distribution and reception is a pious opinion that Lutherans must tolerate as long as no exclusive claim for its correctness is made.)

CONTEMPORARY ROMAN CATHOLIC THEOLOGY OF THE EUCHARISTIC SACRIFICE

By Thomas E. Ambrogi, S. J.

It shall be our purpose in this paper to develop, at least in outline, some of the more significant areas of contemporary Roman Catholic theology which might be relevant to a Lutheran-Catholic confrontation on the question of the Eucharist as sacrifce. Before proceeding, however, a preliminary observation concerning methodology may be in order.

How can a Lutheran theologian determine with confidence the precise content of the faith of the Catholic Church today when it affirms that the Mass is a sacrifice? To be sure, there exists a body of dogmatic statements on the question, principally from the Council of Trent, and these are binding on the faith of the contemporary church. It must be seen, however, that this Tridentine corpus of doctrinal formulations by no means exhausts the total consciousness of the church concerning the sacrificial dimension of the eucharistic celebration. The fathers at Trent had no intention of developing an articulated theology of eucharistic sacrifice. The original meaning of their canons and decrees, of the dogmatic affirmations which they did in fact make within the context of the Reformation situation, is binding today on a Catholic theologian. But it is precisely the task of the theologian both to accurately determine what the context of those affirmations is, and to bring to bear upon them the total theological consciousness of the church today. A contemporary theology of eucharistic sacrifice will therefore both safeguard the heart of the faith which was enunciated at Trent and also integrate this into a far broader and more penetrating theological synthesis, which synthesis itself is made possible by the continuing evolution of the church's total awareness of the mystery of salvation which has been committed to her.

We do not intend here to pose the theoretical questions of the nature and authority of a dogmatic statement, or of the development of dogma. When, however, Lutherans and Catholics are discussing their respective church positions on the Eucharist as sacrifice, the Catholic "position" cannot be exhaustively found in the canons and decrees of the Council of Trent. What the Catholic Church holds on eucharistic sacrifice will not only include those dogmatic propositions of Trent, but will necessarily also involve various legitimate theological explanations of the central body of doctrine in question. E. Skibbe has criticized James F. McCue's recent study of "Luther and Roman Catholicism on the Mass as Sacrifice" on the grounds that McCue is merely reading later, "more ecumenical" interpretations into certain texts of Luther and into the formulations of Trent.[1] Skibbe sees this as a faulty methodology, since he is convinced that "only official confessional statements can provide a basis for agreement between churches." Only these official statements—i.e., the Book of Concord, and not Luther's private writings; the canons of Trent together with papal interpretations, and not Professor McCue's theologizing—can possibly possess an authority sufficient to ground real confidence in any consensus which might be achieved in the dialogue.

This is admittedly a thorny question, and one which perhaps should be discussed in depth before the contemporary Lutheran-Catholic dialogue proceeds much further. At the outset of this paper, however, we take the position that the purpose of this particular group is not primarily comparative symbolics, but theological exchange on the faith of our churches in the mid-1960's. Our mutual theologizing will necessarily be within a confessional tradition. It will therefore not obscure the fact that genuine conflict on the meaning of sacrifice has existed in the past and continues to exist. Historical research and respect for historical fact will be the presuppositions which have formed the confessional attitudes and positions which are brought into contact in the dialogue. But the focus of our common search is primarily on the theological question: is the Eucharist a sacrifice, and, if so, in what sense is this to be understood? Since the church is a living organism with a history, the stuff of our discussion on this question will indeed be grounded in and faithfully represent the official doctrinal statements of each

---

[1] E. Skibbe, "Roman-Lutheran Dialogue: a question of method," ***Una Sancta*** **23 (1966) 75-85. McCue's study can be found in** ***Journal of Ecumenical Studies*** **2 (1965) 205-233.**

of our churches, but our approach to one another must be on the level of theological understanding of the Christian mystery, within the total context of the two theological systems which have evolved since the Reformation.

Consequently, to the question: "What is the precise doctrinal position of the Catholic Church on the Mass as sacrifice?" an adequate answer can only be attempted in terms of both doctrinal statements of the magisterium and theological interpretation of those statements. We shall first simply summarize the major doctrinal points affirmed by the Council of Trent. Then we shall elaborate certain newer insights and directions of contemporary Catholic theology which may facilitate a more penetrating understanding of the total Catholic position. To mistrust in principle the authority of theology in explaining a dogmatic position seems to us to be an illusory search for the absolute doctrinal formulation which the pilgrim People of God can by its very nature never achieve. Both because the church is the pilgrim church of sinners and because the eucharistic mystery is infinite in its richness and depth, there can be no one totally exhaustive and authoritative statement of the "Catholic position" on eucharistic sacrifice. We shall attempt to present what with confidence we believe to be a legitimate Catholic understanding of the matter.

SUMMARY OF THE DOCTRINE OF TRENT ON SACRIFICE

From the decrees and canons of Session XXII of the Council of Trent,[2] the following doctrinal affirmations on the sacrifice of the Mass can be stated:

1. "In the Mass there is offered to God a true and proper sacrifice." (DS 948)

2. "Since his priesthood was not to be terminated with his death," Christ established in his church an order of priests, "the apostles and their successors in the priesthood," through whom he would continue his sacrifice for all time. (DS 938)

3. The sacrifice of the altar is one with the sacrifice of the cross. "The victim is one and the same, and he who now offers through the ministry of priests is the selfsame as he who then offered himself on the cross." (DS 940)

4. The difference from the sacrifice of Calvary "is only in the manner of offering." The Mass is an "unbloody immolation,"

---

[2]Denzinger-Schonmetzer, *Enchiridion Symbolorum.* Freiburg: Herder, 1965, ed. 33. 937a-956.

a mystical sacrifice, in which "the church through her priests immolates Christ through visible signs." (DS 938)

5. The sacrifice of Calvary is all-sufficient to atone for all the sins of all mankind. The Mass-sacrifice in no way implies that anything is wanting in that sacrifice of Calvary, nor does it "in any way detract from that sacrifice." (DS 940)

6. The Mass is not an absolute sacrifice, but was instituted at the Last Supper as a relative sacrifice, by which that "sacrifice in blood, accomplished but once on the cross, was to be represented, so that the memory thereof should remain until the end of the world." (DS 938)

7. Nevertheless, the Mass is not merely a "sacrifice of praise and thanks," or only a "mere commemoration." (DS 950) In it Christ himself is really contained, and "his body and blood are offered to the Father under the appearances of bread and wine." (DS 938)

8. All the efficacy of the Mass flows from the sacrifice of Calvary. It "applies the saving force of the sacrifice of the cross for the remission of sins which we daily commit." (DS 938) "It is also offered for the faithful departed in Christ who are not yet fully cleansed." (DS 940) Therefore, "this sacrifice is in truth a propitiatory sacrifice." (DS 940)

9. This propitiatory application of Christ's sacrifice does not justify the wicked without their repentance. It can bring it about that, "if with a sincere heart and a true faith, with fear and reverence, in contrition and repentance we draw near to God, 'we may receive mercy and find grace to help in time of need' (Hb 4,16). Appeased by this offering, the Lord, granting grace and the gift of repentance, forgives sins, even the greatest crimes." (DS 940)

It is clear from the above statements, especially from No. 7, that the Catholic doctrine on the Mass-sacrifice is intimately related to the doctrine of real sacramental presence. The Eucharist is both sacrament and sacrifice; it is the re-presentation to the Father of Christ's unique saving sacrifice on the cross precisely because the body and blood of Christ are substantially present under the elements of bread and wine. It is true that these two dimensions of the eucharistic mystery, sacrament and sacrifice, cannot be simply identified. They involve certain irreducible formal differences which must be respected. And yet, it is of the essence of the Eucharist that it is a sacramental sacrifice, that is, a sacrifice with a sacramental structure.

In its concern for pedagogical clarity, Catholic textbook-theology has often had the unfortunate tendency to overstress the distinction between the sacramental and the sacrificial aspects of the Eucharist. But Christ does not first become present in order to then become a victim. The sacrament in the technical sense of the term comes into being as the result of an action which is of its nature sacrificial, viz., the double consecration, and the sacrament cannot be adequately understood except as the completion of the sacrifice. In other words, Christ becomes present and remains present after the sacrificial action proper, precisely in order that through his live-giving, victim flesh he may communicate to men the union with God which his sacrifice achieved for them.

Post-tridentine theology of the real presence has tended to statically focus its attention on problems of the manner of Christ's presence here and now in this physically located host lying upon this altar, neglecting adequate attention to the further sacrificial and sacramental finality of this presence. At the same time, theologians have frequently developed elaborate theories of sacrifice which have little explicit reference to the reality of sacramental presence. Much contemporary theology of the real presence is attempting to right this imbalance, and is thereby discovering new meaning in its integrated consideration of the Eucharist as a sacramental sacrifice. It will therefore be helpful for our purposes to examine some of the general lines of this "new" theology of the real presence.

BACKGROUND OF THE NEW THEOLOGY

The renewal of eucharistic theology can be seen to be the product of the convergence of several streams of thought over the past few decades. We can do no more here than sketch, under four general headings, some of these major influences.

1. Within the last twenty years, Catholic theology has experienced a general reawakening to the notion of sacramental sign. "*Sacramentum est in genere signi*" had been, of course, one of the leading ideas of the great scholastics of the 13th century. In their concern to counteract the excessive physical realism which was current in the period from the 8th to the 11th century, men like Peter Lombard, Bonaventure and Thomas had become acutely sensitive to the sign structure of the sacramental order. It is instructive to observe how the reaction of Catholic theology to the problematic of the 16th century Reformation had the unfortunate effect of distorting this cardinal insight of the medieval scholastics. Trent's

rejection of the Reformers' presence "in sign or figure only," the empty symbol of Zwingli (*tantummodo in signo vel figura*: DS 883), led to a deep-seated Catholic distrust of symbolism, the very essence of sacramental reality. Post-tridentine theology, with its antithetical preoccupations, got bogged down in an analysis of real presence almost exclusively according to physical rather than sacramental categories of thought. It was only in this century that the work of men like Beauduin, Casel, Masure, Billot, de la Taille and Vonier gradually began to restore the insight that the proper mode of the real presence can only be appraised within the category of "*sacramentum-signum*," and that physical theories, as such, go beyond the framework of sign, placing us in the realm of the extra-sacramental.

This whole movement was greatly aided by modern phenomenology's accent on man as "symbol-maker." When symbol-making activity is analyzed from an anthropological point of view, a symbol can be seen to be much more than a mere cognitive medium, the symbol somehow containing in itself something of the reality of the maker.

2. A second influential factor has been neo-scholasticism's reconsideration of the aristotelian notion of "substance." This philosophical development has been forced by the impact of modern physical science on cosmology, but it has had important consequences for the traditional theology of transubstantiation. One result was a relatively quiet but significant controversy which raged during the 1950's between two Italian theologians, F. Selvaggi, of the Gregorian University, and Carlo Colombo, then professor at the major seminary in Milano. For Colombo, modern physics makes it imperative to say that transubstantiation involves not a physical, but an ontological change in the elements. Selvaggi, on the other hand, continued to identify the dogma of Trent with a real physical, even chemical change. Colombo's reaction to the physical change theory has been shared by many others, and it is an important background piece to the so-called new theology.

Related to this debate was the much-discussed question of whether, in defining the dogma of transubstantiation, Trent had also definitively canonized the aristotelian categories in which the dogma is expressed. We shall have to return below to a brief discussion of this question.

3. A third important influence on the new theology is the greater prominence now being given to the ecclesial character of the

eucharistic presence of Christ. We are returning to the scriptural, patristic and medieval emphasis upon the *res sacramenti*, the *communio ecclesiastica*, viz., the real presence of Christ in the eucharistic community and in the souls of each member of the church. Post-tridentine theology had heavily emphasized the *res et sacramentum*, viz., the real presence of Christ in the host, presence being seen almost as an end in itself. We are now returning to an awareness of the purpose for which the Lord renders himself present under the elements: his growth in the heart of the Christian and in the Christian community.

4. Perhaps the most immediately fruitful influence upon the new theology has been the developing awareness of the personalist dimension of the sacramental system. The ground-breaking synthesis here has been E. Schillebeeckz, *Christ the Sacrament of the Encounter with God.*[3] F. Durrwell, *La Résurrection de Jésus, mystère de salut*[4] and K. Rahner, *Kirche und Sakramente*[5] have also exercised a very formative influence upon this new direction. For Schillebeeckx, sacraments are not things, but personal encounters of men on earth with the living and glorified man Jesus by way of a visible form. "What takes place in the sacraments is the immediate encounter in mutual availability between the living *Kyrios* and ourselves. The sacraments are this encounter."[6] In other words, the sacraments are, in ecclesial visibility, Christ's eternally–actual act of redemption as personally affecting a particular man; they are the redemptive act in sacramental visibility.[7]

It is in the light of this whole rich development that one must view current discussion of the real presence in terms of "transignification" and "transfinalization." The recapturing of a sense for sign, the reappraisal of theories of real physical change, the emphasis upon the ecclesial and the personalist character of sacramental presence–all of this is intimately related with the contemporary attempts to express the truth of transubstantiation in personalist phenomenological categories which are radically other than those of a scholastic philosophy of nature.

---

[3]New York: Sheed & Ward, 1963. Originally published as *Christus, Sacrament van de Godsontmoeting*. Bilthoven: Nelissen, 1960.

[4]Paris: Editions Mappus. English translation: *The Resurrection*. New York: Sheed & Ward, 1960.

[5]Freiburg: Herder, 1961. English translation: *The Church and the Sacraments* (Quaestiones Disputatae 9). New York: Herder & Herder, 1963.

[6]*Op. cit.*, 62.

[7]*Ibid.*, 74.

The convergence of these many influences has recently begun to find expression in formal magisterial documents. The *Constitution on the Liturgy's* description of the various modes of presence of Christ in the liturgical celebration is the most significant of these:

> To accomplish so great a work, Christ is always present in His Church, especially in her liturgical celebrations. He is present in the sacrifice of the Mass, not only in the person of His minister, . . . but especially under the Eucharistic species. . . . He is present in His word, since it is He Himself who speaks when the holy Scriptures are read in the church. He is present, finally, when the Church prays and sings, for He promised: "Where two or three are gathered together for my sake, there am I in the midst of them" (Mt 18,20).[8]

In the Mass, therefore, the Lord is seen to be "really" present in manifold ways. He is present in the person of the celebrant; present in his word when it is proclaimed; present under the elements, as our sacrificial food and drink; present in the prayers and song of the rite, in the celebrating community. The recent encyclical *Mysterium Fidei* also details these and a number of other ways in which Christ is "really" present to his church: present in her works of mercy, present in the church's power to govern the People of God, present in all the sacraments insofar as they are actions of Christ, etc.[9] All of these awakened insights into the multiple presences of Christ have cast the whole theological consideration of "presence under the species" into a much broader context, thus helping to restore to perspective a rather exclusive focus upon a mechanical physical presence in this host on this physically located altar.

THE ESSENCE OF THE TRIDENTINE DOGMA OF REAL PRESENCE

Before outlining the main thrust of the newer theories of transignification and transfinalization, it will be helpful to give the essence of the dogmas of real presence and transubstantiation as they are defined in Trent. These can be summed up for our purposes as follows: "After the consecratory action in the eucharistic celebration, Jesus Christ is truly and substantially present where formerly there had been bread and wine. The essential reality of bread and wine no longer exists. The change which has taken place in the conse-

[8] ***Constitution on the Sacred Liturgy*, par. 7.**

[9] ***Mysterium Fidei*, par. 35-38.**

crated species is total: transubstantiation describes it fittingly enough."[10]

The key point here, the heart of the Catholic faith which is being expressed, is that the change which takes places in the elements is a radical, ontological change. What was bread and wine becomes not merely a sign pointing to, or a figure calling to mind, the body and blood of Christ. By this total and remarkable conversion, the species of bread and wine contain a new "reality," which we may justly term an "ontological reality."

In the tradition, this truth has been aptly expressed and interpreted in terms of a scholastic philosophy of substance. It seems clear from recent investigation, however, that the term "substance" as used by the fathers at Trent was not intended to be taken in a technical philosophical sense, and therefore that the dogmatic definition does not include the necessary identity of the dogma with its expression in an aristotelian-scholastic dialectic of substance and accidents. The *Acta* of the Council give no indication that the fathers understood the term *substantia* in any other way than it had been understood in previous declarations of the magisterium. Besides the fact that no definition of the term is given, the Council insists that its declarations be understood in a traditional manner, on those points where previous magisterial statements existed. Moreover when it was proposed that a change be made in Canon 2[11] from "*manentibus speciebus*" to "*manentibus accidentibus,*" the fathers rejected such a change because "*species*" (and not "*accidens*") was the traditional term of the councils and the fathers. When one sees that the terms *substantia* and *transubstantiatio* are current in magisterial usage at least as early as the anti-Berengarian writings of the eleventh century,[12] i.e., at a date prior to the influence of aristotelianism on eucharistic theology, it becomes clear that the origin of the Tridentine "substance" is to be found not in medieval theology and philosophy, but in the traditional faith of the church.

In Tridentine usage, therefore, "substance" means the radical reality of a thing, as opposed to what a thing appears to be. When Canon 2 speaks of the "conversion of the total substance of the bread into the body," it means that what was in reality bread is no longer bread, and has become the body of Christ, by a real ontologi-

[10] Cf. DS 874, 877, 883, 884.

[11] DS 884

[12] The use of the word "substance" in a eucharistic connection goes back even earlier to the fifth or sixth century, the first instance being the sermon "Magnitudo" by an unknown author.

cal change. This profoundly real change, of course, is within the framework of the *sacramentum-signum,* a fact which must never be lost sight of.

TRANSIGNIFICATION, TRANSFINALIZATION

A thorough-going reappraisal of the scholastic explanation of the dogma of transubstantiation first began to appear publicly about ten years ago, with theological debate finding its principal focus in the Netherlands and in England. The fact that theologians like Schoonenberg, Smits and Schillebeeckx were publishing their research in relatively unavailable Dutch journals contributed greatly to the confusion and misrepresentation which marked the earlier phases of the discussion outside of Holland.

The first serious study to appear in English was an article by Charles Davis, discreetly published in 1964 in the Australian review *Sophia.*[13] After stating his personal disaffection for the Thomist theology of the real presence, Davis termed his own essay "a tentative effort at a solution, offered here for criticism and discussion." In his argumentation one can detect many of the currents of thought which we have already noted in Catholic eucharistic theology, as well as certain indications of future directions. The lead which Davis offered in that article has since been taken up by an increasing number of English-speaking theologians. A brief analysis of his argument should therefore claim our attention at this point.

As background to his investigation, Davis first lists two preliminary principles. The first is that real presence and transubstantiation are not knowable by anyone who does not know the *purpose* of the consecrated elements, viz., to be for man's union with Christ. Transubstantiation is an action by which Christ establishes a new relation with us through the use of bread and wine, giving himself to us through them. It is but one moment in the total process of Christ's self-giving. It does not statically have its own meaning and purpose, something which the Thomist theology, considering transubstantiation as an event in the material world, often saw it to have. Transubstantiation is therefore a religious event, not a material event. The species are now used for a new purpose; they become the sacramental means of Christ's self-giving. Only in this religious context can the event of transubstantiation be known for what it truly is.

---

[13]"The Theology of Transubstantiation," *Sophia* 3(1964), 12-24. *Sophia* is the journal of philosophical theology of the University of Melbourne.

A second principle then follows. "A knowledge of the material world that did not include a knowledge of man as man and of distinctly human activities would not reveal the existence of bread, however exhaustive the knowledge might be. . . . Bread as bread is knowable only in relation to man, and that is because it exists as bread only in relation to man."[14]

After then developing at some length the inadequacy of the scholastic notion of substance, traceable to an inadequate physical science of the time, Davis then returns to his point with the question: "What is bread?" In the world of artifacts, he argues, things have neither meaning nor existence apart from their relation to man. Bread is a conglomeration of many substances. It is a reality of human life, a material thing with a human significance. It is true, a limited range of substances must be present before man can make bread; we cannot make something bread simply by treating it as if it were bread. And yet, making bread involves no more than the accidental juxtaposition of various components and their accidental modification. The unity and intelligibility of bread comes from the finality imposed on it by man, and not from any substantial change in the order of physical reality.

This analysis is then applied to transubstantiation as an event in the religious order. Davis suggests that at the consecration the bread ceases to be bread because the significance of this matter for man and its relation to him is changed. . . . The bread becomes the body of Christ because the bread is now an outward manifestation of Christ and because the reality of Christ's body as a life-giving reality can be reached by man through this form. What stood to man in relation of bread now stands to him as the body of Christ. Instead of bread we have the sacrament of the body of Christ.[15]

This consecrated element continues to look like bread. The non-believer would call it still bread, and would say that the new significance and finality which we give it have no reality outside of our imagination. The man of faith, however, believes on the word of God that in treating it as the body of Christ, he is recognizing its objective significance in the real order. Bread simply means more than the sum-total of its material ingredients, and Christ has made this bread his body, has given it a new meaning for us. Davis insists that he is not saying that transubstantiation means only that we treat the bread as the body of

[14] *Art. cit.*, 16.

[15] *Ibid.*, 20.

Christ, that we only act as if it were such. It is not we who decide to alter the status of bread and give it a new meaning. "Christ alone can make the bread his body. He does so by the efficacious words of consecration. These do not merely tell us of the change, but they bring it about in the real order."[16]

SOME PROBLEMS FOR CATHOLIC THEOLOGY

Now a number of serious problems are raised by this new attempt to express the mystery of eucharistic presence. Not the least of these concerns the possibility of a legitimate "development" of dogma. The encyclical *Mysterium Fidei* at least states the problem when it says that a Catholic theologian is not allowed to "discuss the mystery of transubstantiation without mentioning what the Council of Trent stated about the marvelous conversion of the whole substance of the bread into the body and of the whole substance of the wine into the blood of Christ, speaking rather only of what is called 'transignification.'"[17] The most responsible proponents of the new theology are in fact not speaking *only* of "transignification," but are also seriously concerned with both mentioning and preserving at the same time that essential element of the Catholic faith which was enunciated in the declarations of Trent. But the question arises as to how one can legitimately speak of a "development" here. A theologian expressing himself in the context of a personalist phenomenology would seem to be operating in such a radically other thought-world from that of a scholastic philosophy of nature, that one must ask whether his first "mentioning what the Council of Trent stated about the marvelous conversion" of substance can possibly be anything more than a filial doffing of his cap to the tradition, while he is in fact then proceeding off on another, radically new line of theological development. As *Mysterium Fidei* no doubt shows, this is a question of serious concern for Catholic theology, and one which has not yet been fully probed.

But the real neuralgic point in this new theory itself, the question which immediately agitates Catholic theology antecedent to the problem of doctrinal "development," is whether the profound ontological change which is demanded by Catholic tradition is in fact clearly being maintained when the change is seen to be in the meaning of the bread for man and its purpose for man. Is this not

---

[16] *Ibid.*, 21.

[17] *Mysterium Fidei*, par. 11.

tantamount to saying that the bread remains bread, but that Christ simply uses the bread for a higher purpose? Does not transignification really mean that the bread is in fact not changed into the body of Christ, but rather used as a vehicle for the body of Christ? In other words, is this not a theory of consubstantiation rather than transubstantiation? It is precisely in the being forced to ask this question in this totally new context that we believe the new theology of real presence can render a vital service to ecumenical dialogue, particularly between Lutherans and Catholics.

We would suggest that the theory of transignification, as it has been so far developed in its most responsible expression, neither denies nor contradicts the dogma of transubstantiation. It simply places the event of total eucharistic conversion on the level of sacramental reality, where it should indeed be placed. A number of points in the theory, it is true, still remain to be worked out in detail. But the misunderstanding and general malaise which is the initial reaction of many Catholics on first contact with the theory, are fundamentally a result of our deep-seated fear of the word "symbol" in reference to the Eucharist. In reality, however, a sacrament is only a certain kind of symbol, one which effects what it signifies. Davis has pointed this out very well when he says: "A symbol need not mean something that points to another thing that is absent in reality; it can mean something that manifests the presence of a reality distinct from itself but mediated through it. A sacrament is such a symbol."[18]

SOME QUESTIONS FOR LUTHERAN-CATHOLIC DIALOGUE

At this point we have arrived, it seems to us, at a critical point of confrontation between the Lutheran and the Catholic traditions. The first question to arise would concern the nature of the sacramental order as such. What precisely does the Lutheran tradition mean by the mediation of grace through a visible sacramental sign? To what extent can a Lutheran accept the Catholic understanding of the mediation of salvation through created means: through the humanity of the glorified Christ, through the church which is his fullness, and through the sacraments which are his actions and the focal point of personal encounter with him? In other words, are we really communicating meaningfully when we both use the term "sacrament"? Or is it indeed true, as has been

[18] *Art. cit.*, 23.

frequently maintained, that Lutheran "solafideism" necessarily implies the implicit rejection of Catholic "incarnationalism" and the entire order of grace as understood by the Catholic tradition?[19] These questions admittedly involve broad christological, soteriological and ecclesiological horizons. But they all come to a burning focus in our search for mutual understanding on the precise nature of eucharistic presence and on the intimately related question of eucharistic sacrifice. The sacramental structure of the church is therefore a primary point of confrontation which must be faced by both Lutherans and Catholics in the contemporary dialogue.

The second question would focus directly on the problem of the eucharistic "presence" of Christ. As we have seen, the Catholic understanding is that the Eucharist is both sacrament and sacrifice, in one indivisible moment. Any Lutheran-Catholic discussion of sacramental sacrifice must therefore first determine the exact nature of our agreement when we both affirm the "real" presence of Christ in the Sacrament.

Is this agreement in reality anything more than verbal? It is no doubt true that Lutherans and Catholics stand together in rejecting what has been understood to be the "empty sign" of the Reformed tradition. But is Luther's rejection of Zwingli here anything *more* than an antithetical position? A Catholic theologian might be able to muster a good deal of sympathy for 16th century Lutheranism's rejection of Roman theories of transubstantiation. As theological explications of the limits of the mystery, these theories as they have been historically elaborated might well seem to be blasphemous sophistry, rationalistic attempts to contain the *mysterium tremendum* in explainable formulas. But theology need not necessarily be sophistry, and the Catholic theologian is somewhat non-plussed by a Lutheran's strong affirmation of the "real presence" of Christ and then his absolute refusal to discuss theologically the nature of that presence or the manner in which a change is effected in the elements. The Lutheran insists that he is not defending a theory of consubstantiation, that the traditional formula of presence "in, with and under" the elements is an antithetical, "de-limiting" position only, and not a positive theological affirmation. But in order to determine the extent of our agreement or disagreement on the fact of *real* eucharistic presence, it seems to us that the Catholic theologian must challenge the Lutheran to express himself some-

---

[19]See, e.g., F. Clark, *Eucharistic Sacrifice and the Reformation*. Westminster: Newman, 1960. 103-112; 156.

how in terms which confront the Catholic tradition's insistence on the profound, ontological nature of the change effected in the elements.

Intimately related to our agreement on "real" eucharistic presence is the position of each tradition on the question of the reserved sacrament. It is a curious historical fact that the Lutheran tradition has no real theological position as to the reserved sacrament. It would seem not altogether unfair to say that Lutherans in general have contented themselves with polemical attacks against Roman devotional abuses of the reserved sacrament, without ever articulating a positive theology either for or against the perduring presence of the eucharistic Lord beyond the time of the sacramental celebration. The Lutheran elaboration of just such a theology would seem to be highly desirable in determining the degree of consensus which we share as to precisely what happens at the moment of consecration during the eucharistic celebration itself.

We submit that this inadequately resolved question of real presence is at the heart of the Lutheran-Catholic controversy on eucharistic sacrifice. If we can presume to sort out the most fundamental difficulty which the Lutheran Church has had with Roman Catholic sacrifice, it is that the Mass is considered by Catholics to be a "good work" offered by man to God, instead of purely a testament and a promise of God's favor to men. The heart of this objection is then amplified by the reproach that the Roman Catholic "sacrifice of the altar" derogates from the sufficiency of that of the cross.

Here, it seems to us, we are involved in a problematic with a double thrust: one having to do with the nature of the sacramental order in general, and the other dealing with the sacramental manner in which the sacrifice of the cross is actualized in the Mass. Both questions bear directly on just what is being affirmed when we each insist on the "real" presence of Christ in the Supper.

In order to open up the first of these two questions, it would appear profitable to discuss together the relation of the Last Supper to the sacrifice of Calvary. The Catholic tradition does indeed see the Last Supper as a sacrifice, but as a sacramental sacrifice, offered in a sacramental manner by Christ in anticipation of the historically unique sacrifice which would be offered the following day on Calvary. In order for there to be any Lutheran-Catholic understanding of positions on this crucial point, our discussions would necessarily take us into the precise nature of sacramental reality and its distinction from the order of physical, historical reality.

The more obvious area of discussion, however, will involve the relation of the sacrifice of Calvary to that of the Mass. And it is here that the nature of the "presence" of Christ in the species is crucial.

As the Roman Catholic understands it, the Mass is the celebration of the paschal mystery of the Lord by the Christian community. By the consecratory action of the minister, acting in the person of Christ and according to the institution of Christ, the victim flesh and blood of the Redeemer in his humanity is rendered truly present under the symbol of bread and wine. The *transitus Domini*, that entire passage to the Father which the Redeemer Christ, and we in him, achieved by his love and obedience on earth, is once again made present to men in the Mass. The sacrifice by which we were redeemed, involving the entire mysterious upward movement to the Father which was the life, passion, death and resurrection of Christ the Mediator, is re-presented to the Father by Christ in his mystical body. It is the entire church, i.e., both Christ the head in his glory and we the members of his mystical body, who offers this sacrifice in a sacramental manner. The celebration of the paschal mystery in the liturgical assembly, therefore, is the church's continual self-offering in Christ. When the church celebrates the eucharistic sacrifice she participates in the unique and all-sufficient sacrifice of Calvary, according to the degree of faith and charity which she in all her members possesses at any given moment in the history of salvation. These are not two sacrifices, one of the cross and one of the Eucharist, but rather one work and one sacrifice: accomplished by Christ and participated in sacramentally by the church.

The Eucharist is in a unique way "the redemptive act in sacramental visibility." The special and central position which the Catholic tradition accords the Eucharist among all the sacraments comes from the fact that the reality of Christ's victim body as a life-giving force can be encountered by man through the sacramental form of bread and wine. The real presence of the glorified Christ in his victim *humanity* is of capital importance, because it is as *man* that the Son is mediator of grace. He is mediator in his humanity, according to the ways of humanity, and it is precisely in his eucharistic presence formally in his humanity that man continues to find the possibility of encounter with the saving power of his redeeming sacrifice.

It should be clear, then, that any Lutheran-Catholic agreement on eucharistic sacrifice will depend essentially on a common understanding of "real" presence. We have attempted to phrase the central issues within the integrated context of sacramental sacrifice, in order to avoid as much as possible the formulations of ancient and dead-end *Kontroversfragen.* Contemporary theology situates our traditions on a horizon of discourse in which our historical confrontations can be viewed and discussed in a fresh new light, quite different and radically more creative than anything which our forefathers ever knew. Our responsibility for entering into informed dialogue, and for drawing the practical consequences of this dialogue in the life of our churches, is therefore all the more urgent.

CONTEMPORARY LUTHERAN THEOLOGY AND THE EUCHARISTIC SACRIFICE

By Kent S. Knutson

THE purpose of this brief is to describe current Lutheran thinking regarding the role of sacrifice in the Eucharist in such a way as to provide the right setting for dialogue with Roman Catholics. This is an unusually difficult task because the Lutheran situation concerning the eucharistic sacrifice has certain peculiarities which do not apply to other doctrinal questions. Four should be mentioned. 1) The discussion of sacrifice at the time of the Reformation was carried on in such a polemical fashion and in such a restricted way that it provides a much smaller platform for launching than do other Reformation themes. 2) The official documents of Lutheran theology, the Confessions, continue this narrower base and do not provide us with a clear, consistent and sufficient treatment of sacrifice for purposes of discussion with a Catholic. 3) Current discussion is spotty and incomplete and has been, at least up to now, carried on in the context of the Faith and Order Movement rather than in an environment which does service to the necessary questions raised by a Lutheran-Catholic dialogue. 4) The Lutheran understanding of eucharistic sacrifice is so intertwined with other theological commitments such as relationship of Word and Sacrament, christology and ecclesiology that to raise it as an isolated inquiry tends to present a distorted picture.

It is my intention to explain the first three items briefly and then to move on to a treatment of point 4.

I.

McCue has given us the material for a discussion of Luther and this need not be repeated here. Luther research continues to inform Lutherans and others and certainly re-opens the question of eucharistic sacrifice for Lutherans. I suspect that both Lutherans and Catholics are willing to agree that responsibility for the

16th century controversy rests on both sides and Lutherans interested in dialogue with Catholics recognize both the possibility and the necessity of re-evaluation of their position. This arises not only because of the willingness of Catholics to talk but for the integrity of Lutheran theology as well. It should be added, however, that the results of Luther research are not authoritative for a Lutheran nor are they restrictive for a construction of a contemporary Lutheran theology.

The material from the Lutheran Confessions is a bit puzzling.[1] Luther does not use sacrifice in either the Small or Large Catechism in his exposition of the Lord's Supper. Since the Small Catechism is the chief teaching instrument in the Lutheran Tradition, this means that Lutheran laymen are not acquainted with sacrifice as a way to speak of the meaning of the sacrament. The word sacrifice still has a very unfamiliar ring in this context and those acquainted with it at all think of it as a "Catholic" word. The Lutheran liturgy, however, by its never-failing use of the Words of Institution and the *Agnus Dei* and by the emphasis upon Body and Blood, indirectly remind the participant of the place of sacrifice in the sacrament. And the name of the Lord in the Lutheran mind is still identified with expiatory sacrifice.

Nor is sacrifice used in the articles on the Lord's Supper in the Augsburg Confession. Melanchthon explains in the Apology that this was done deliberately because it was an ambiguous term.[2] The Article on the Mass (XXIV), however, speaks of the "abominable error" "according to which it was taught that our Lord Christ had by his death made satisfaction only for original sin, and had instituted the Mass as a sacrifice for other sins."[3] It goes on to say that "this transformed the Mass into a sacrifice for the living and the dead, a

[1] The attitude of Lutherans toward the confessions waries somewhat both as character of commitment and the relative authority of the various confessions. The Lutheran World Federation, for example, claims only the Small Catechism and the Augsburg Confession as the basis for membership. The reason for this is the somewhat ambiguous situation among the Scandinavian churches regarding the Formula of Concord. The Formula was not accepted among all Lutherans in Germany even in the 16th century and was considered by many non-German Lutherans as a "German affair"— let the Germans raise and answer their own questions! This has created some problems for American Lutherans involved in church mergers consolidating the German and Scandinavian backgrounds. In general this has been solved by the acceptance of the whole Book of Concord but with the reservation that the Small Catechism and the Augsburg Confession are the chief confessions.

[2] T. G. Tappert, ed., *The Book of Concord*, (Philadelphia, 1959), p. 251.

[3] Ibid., pp. 58ff.

sacrifice by means of which sin was taken away and God was reconciled." The result, says the confession, is a multiplication of masses for the individual, loss of faith and true service to God, the notion that grace is obtained through the performance of this work, and a lack of emphasis on the requirement of faith to receive the benefits.

The tone here, therefore, is completely negative. Even the sacrifice of thanksgiving and praise is not mentioned. The conclusion is rather that the Mass is a communion in which the Priest and others receive the sacrament for themselves and it is claimed that this right use of the Mass is observed among Lutherans in continuity with the church from ancient times.

Luther does not attack sacrifice in the Smalcald Articles, even in the Article on the Mass[4] and the Formula of Concord confines itself to the statement ". . . we also reject and condemn all other papistic abuses of this sacrament, such as the abomination of the sacrifice of the Mass for the living and the dead."[5] The reasons for this lack of concern are not important here.

It is Melanchthon in the Apology who offers the discussion which has become the basis for the classic Lutheran position. His view can be summarized this way.

1. The Mass does not confer grace *ex opere operato*, nor does it merit for others the forgiveness of venial or mortal sins, of guilt or of punishement.[6]

2. A sacrament is a ceremony or act in which God offers us the content of the promise joined to the ceremony. By way of contrast, a sacrifice is a ceremony or act which we render to God to honor him.[7]

3. There are only two types of sacrifice. One is the propitiatory sacrifice; this is a work of satisfaction for guilt and punishment that reconciles God or placates his wrath or merits the forgiveness of sins for others. The other type is the eucharistic sacrifice; this does not merit the forgiveness of sins or reconciliation, but by it those who have been reconciled give thanks or show their gratitude for the forgiveness of sins and other blessings received.[8]

---

[4] Ibid., pp. 293ff.

[5] Ibid., p. 588

[6] Ibid., p. 251

[7] Ibid., p. 252

[8] Ibid., p. 252

4. There has really been only one propitiatory sacrifice in the world, the death of Christ. . . .[9]

5. Worship is the offering of praises, prayer, thanksgiving and confession and is valid because of faith, and only because of faith.[10]

6. Among the praises of God or sacrifices of praise we include the proclamation of the Word.[11]

7. The only Priest who sacrifices for sin is Christ.[12]

8. Lutherans retain the daily sacrifice in the proclamation of the Gospel and the proper use of the sacraments.[13]

9. The sacraments are not only signs among men but signs of God's will toward us.[14]

The object of Melanchthon's comments in addition to *The Confutation* is a quotation from Thomas: "The body of the Lord, once offered on the cross for the original debt, is daily offered on the altar for daily offenses so that in this the church might have a service that reconciles God."[15]

I have not made a special investigation of the 150 years following this Confessional period, but I think it is safe to say that this period, so formative for Lutheran thinking, does not venture beyond Melanchthon's position. The compendium of this period which is widely used in Lutheran Seminaries does not deal with the question of sacrifice and the sacrament at all.[16]

The revival of interest in the topic in our century can most likely be traced to Yngve Brilioth's seminal work *Eucharistic Faith and Practice Evangelical and Catholic* of 1926. [17] This was written

---

[9]Ibid., p. 254

[10]Ibid., p. 254

[11]Ibid. p,. 256

[12]Ibid., p. 260

[13]Ibid., p. 258

[14]Ibid., p. 262

[15]Ibid., p. 260 quoted from Thomas Aquinas, *Opuscula*, 58; *The Venerable Sacrament of the Altar*, c. 1. This work was actually written by Pseudo-Thomas. Cf. *Die der Evangelisch-Lutherischen Kirche*, 5th ed. (Gottingen, 1964), p. 93, note 1 and F. Clark, *Eucharistic Sacrifice and the Reformation* (Westminster, Md., 1960), pp. 472-493.

[16]Heinrich Schmid, *The Doctrinal Theology of the Evangelical Lutheran Church*, Third Edition, revised, Charles A. Hay, Henry E. Jacobs, trs. (Mpls, 1961)

[17]Yngve Brilioth, *Eucharistic Faith and Practice Evangelical and Catholic* A. G. Hebert, tr. (London, 1956)

with special attention to the relationships between the Church of Sweden and the Church of England. Brilioth felt that Luther had recovered the highest conception of the eucharistic sacrifice in the early church in his teaching of the self-oblation of the church to God in union with the one sacrifice but that unfortunately he did not work out this idea fully and became lost in his rejection to the "awful example" of the Roman Mass, rejecting the Mass not only as *Werkopfer* but *Deutopfer* as well. It was impossible for him to retain the idea of the act of memorial. This made it difficult for him to view favorably even the constructive attempts made to purify the medieval practices. Brilioth quotes from the *Liber Ratisbonesis* of 1541 to illustrate one of the attempts at *rapprochement*. Here eucharistic sacrifice is summarized under four heads:

> 1. It is the church's ever-renewed presentation, *repraesentativo nomine,* of the one sacrifice, which can never be repeated, but which has an eternal efficacy, and still avails for those who in faith show it forth before God.
>
> 2. It is the church's self-oblation to God, as Christ's mystical body; in thankfulness for the sacrifice of the cross, whereby alone man is saved from perdition, the church dedicates herself to God.
>
> 3. It is a sacrifice of praise.
>
> 4. It includes the material offerings of bread and wine and other gifts to the poor. . . .[18]

This satisfied neither Wittenberg nor Rome but Brilioth proposed that the discussion could be picked up at this point today for he believed that it expressed evangelical doctrine. He urged a re-evaluation of the whole matter. His greatest interest, however, was in the restoration of the communal character of the sacrament which had been de-emphasized in favor of a strident individualism. His recommendation of the latter point was picked up immediately and has become one of the more important re-emphasis in contemporary Lutheran sacramentology, but his request for a new view of eucharistic sacrifice lay dormant until the Faith and Order Conference in Edinburgh.

Edinburgh became the occasion for the surprising discovery that real progress could be made in the ticklish doctrine of eucharistic sacrifice. The trigger for this agreement was the book *The Fulness*

---

[18]**Ibid., p. 139**

of Sacrifice by F.C.N. Hicks, Bishop of Gibraltar.[19] He maintained that Medieval theologians speculated concerning the kind of sacrifice in the Mass without having a clear conception of the Jewish background of the ideas of the sacrifice in the ancient church. He claimed that it was too readily assumed that sacrifice consists solely in the death of the victim. It was then an easy step to the idea that any idea of sacrifice in the mass must be a repetition of the death on Golgotha. The protest of the reformers to this was justified. Hicks proposed to break this deadlock by a careful study of the Old Testament concept of sacrifice and use this as the pattern for an interpretation of the sacrifice of our Lord.

Hicks makes his own summary of his proposal:

> The offerer, then, makes his own approach to the presence of God: it is his own free act. He identifies himself with the victim in the pressing on its head of his hands: what happens thereafter to the animal happens symbolically to himself. He kills the animal: "the soul that sinneth, it shall die.": the death is his own death, accepted by him as the consequence of sin. The life is now set free; it is for this that the death is effected: and as set free it is taken by the priest into the presence of God. The atonement–at-one-ment–has been made; and the substance of the offering, the flesh, can now be offered, and, so offered, God accepts it by his fire, and accepting, transforms it. In the common meal on the flesh of the victim, now that atonement has been effected, the life of the offerer has been brought before the face of God, and his offering made and accepted, God and man become at one, and man finds his fellowship with man.[20]

Hicks applies this interpretation to Christ. The sacrifice of Christ begins with the incarnation. He makes himself one with us. We crucify him. He then takes his blood, that is, his life, which by identification with the incarnation is our life, and brings it to God, that is, he *atones* for us. His manhood is thus offered to God in service forever and God transforms this offering as he accepts it. Through Christ's resurrection and ascension the body of His humiliation becomes exalted. The sacrifice is thus a name for the whole action from incarnation to exaltation and is continuous. He is still obedient at the right hand of God, as man, but now we, the church, obey in him. When we "offer him" we offer ourselves. The

---

[19]F. C. N. Hicks, The Fulness of Sacrifice, (London, 1930)

[20]Ibid., p. 13, 14

offering is received and transformed and although imperfect is accepted because it is offered in union with the whole body whose head is Christ. Our offering thus results in communion. Without the communion, the offering is meaningless. This, Hicks insists, does not permit any kind of repetition and does not require any kind of materialism in the presence.

Edinburgh is remembered in the Ecumenical Movement as the "exciting" Conference because so many points of old disagreement seemed to fall. The delegates put a summary of Hicks' argument into the appendix of their report, probably too enthusiastically, because the unity was less substantial than it appeared. But it had the effect of opening the question in a new way and the discussion continued in the preparations for the Lund Conference of 1952, especially in the two preparatory volumes, *Intercommunion* and *Ways of Worship*.[21]

A spate of volumes, especially by Anglicans, now appeared. Some of the more influential were Gregory Dix's *The Shape of the Liturgy*,[22] Arthur M. Ramsey's *The Gospel and the Catholic Church*,[23] Eric L. Mascall's *Corpus Christi, Essays on the Church and the Eucharist*[24] and a smaller but important volume *The Catholicity of Protestantism*, edited by R. Newton Flew and R.E. Davis.[25] Two Roman Catholic books, Eugene Masure's *The Christian Sacrifice*[26] and Joseph Pascher's *Eucharistia, Gestalt and Vollzug*[27], also command much attention. The deadlock was broken, especially for Scandinavian Lutherans,[28] and the discussion began in earnest. The interest was much less in Germany but there was influence in America, although rather scattered. The *United Testimony of Faith and Life*[29] which became

---

[21] Donald M. Baillie and John Marsh (eds.), *Intercommunion*, (New York, 1952) Pehr Edwall, et al. (eds.), *Ways of Worship*, (New York, 1951)

[22] Gregory Dix, *The Shape of the Liturgy*, (London, 1945)

[23] Arthur M. Ramsey, *The Gospel and the Catholic Church*, (New York, 1936)

[24] Eric L. Mascall, *Corpus Christi, Essays on the Church and the Eucharist*, (New York, 1953)

[25] R. Newton Flew and R. E. Davies (eds), *The Catholicity of Protestantism*, (Philadelphia,)

[26] Eugene Masure, *The Christian Sacrifice*, (New York, 1944)

[27] Joseph Pascher, *Eucharistia, Gestalt und Vollzug*, (1953)

[28] The most prominent example is Gustaf Aulen, *Eucharist and Sacrifice*, (Philadelphia, 1958) Eric Wahlstrom tr.

[29] The American Lutheran Church "United Testimony on Faith and Life," Handbook of the American Lutheran Church (Minneapolis, 1965).

the basis for the merger of three Lutheran bodies into the American Lutheran Church of 1960 shows no interest but *The Sacrament of the Altar and its Implications*[30] adopted by the 1960 convention of the United Lutheran Church in America discusses sacrifice in relation to the Eucharist at some length. Although it retains the customary Lutheran emphasis on the sacrifice of thanksgiving and praise and the sole initiating activity of God in the sacrament, it does give a new emphasis to the act of memorial.

> The memorial aspect of the sacrament is, however to be understood not in sheer chronological concepts as mere recollection of a past event which becomes dimmer as time goes on. Only the believer (or he who is offended) may become contemporary with the saving events of Calvary at any age. Just as faith beholds in the son of Mary the Immanual of God, so faith alone can perceive this memorial as more than a memory of a past event devoutly recalled and symbolically reenacted. What *was*, is; he who *was, is present;* what was given in self-sacrifice is at every moment of need newly available.[31]

The eucharistic sacrifice also became an important part of the Lutheran-Reformed conversations. It was here agreed that the atoning sacrifice of Christ becomes contemporary in the sacrament. Christ lives as our eternal high-priest ever making intercession for us. The emphasis is still on the self-giving of God in Christ but sacrifice is "necessarily associated with the celebration of the sacrament."[32]

It is clear that new winds are blowing.

II.

How shall a contemporary Lutheran sympathetic to a re-evaluation of the eucharistic sacrifice structure his argumentation? He must proceed with some care because he is on unfamiliar ground and admits to the need for further dialogue which he must not unduly prejudice at the beginning while at the same time he remains committed to basic categories which inform his whole thinking. But he must begin.

1. A Lutheran is uneasy about beginning with a definition of sacraments in general. He feels that he has no right, aside from spec-

---

30 United Lutheran Church in America, *The Sacrament of the Altar and its Implications*, (New York, 1960).

31 Ibid., Section 14.

32 U.S.A. National Committee of the Lutheran World Federation, *Christology, The Lord's Supper and Its Observance in the Church* (New York, 1964)

ulation, to erect a structure into which an act of God must fit, or design a need of man which God might reasonably be prepared to meet. He rather prefers to see the acts of God as functions which he examines *aposteriori*, giving them names, such as sacraments, if it seems helpful, and regulating his theology by their giveness rather than by their inferred characteristics.

This leads him to say that the sacraments are Gospel, that is, they are acts by which God moves to offer and impart his grace. The sacraments are the events in which God acts on men, not on elements. The validity of a sacrament is thus inescapably related to their use, to the participation of men in receiving their benefits or their judgment. This in no way detracts from their objectivity, for they are God's acts, but retains the wholeness of the activity and their purpose, that of the communication to men of life and salvation.

We understand this talk best in the context of the language of Word and Sacrament. There is no communication of grace separable from the Word of God and no Word of God which cannot also be designated sacrament. The Word of God is God himself in his creative, judging, redemptive, gracious activity. It is God's reality made present to men. This reality, this gift, is made present through various forms—the forms of words of proclamation, the form of events, such as absolution, or worship, or events with defined elements and acts such as Baptism and the Eucharist.

These events of grace all have the same purpose—that of imparting God's gracious dispensation toward men to man. A Lutheran resists the idea of hierarchies of grace or kinds of grace, but he understands that the various forms of grace display particular characteristics. Thus the preached word employs ideas, and their reception is through the understanding, while sacrament is a name for the forms of grace which employ words-with-water or words-with-bread-and-wine and are directed to the whole man in a more dramatic way. The words-with-water emphasize the aspects of grace which are initiation, incorporation, forgiveness, and impartation of the Spirit and is unrepeatable. The words-with-bread-and-wine emphasize the aspects of grace which are renewal, unification, strengthening, intimacy, remembrance, hope, forgiveness and growth in the Spirit and is repeatable.

We have difficulty in ascribing to the Eucharist the term "centrality" or "heart of the faith." Each sacramental action has all the elements of God's gracious activity. Each is central, each is capable of accomplishment of the fulness of God's gift. Each has its place and does not displace another or complete another. Each is dependent on the other, yet complete in itself, yet no one can be neglected or pitted against the other.

2. A Lutheran turns to christology for the delineation of various themes applicable to an understanding of the Eucharist. In classical Lutheran theology, the events from incarnation to and including the death of Christ are termed the "state of humiliation." God became man for us. In Christ God identified with and participated in the fulness of the predicament of man, yet without sin. The restoration of the word sacrifice for this state is one of the current proposals which is very helpful, as Hicks had suggested, for we believe it correctly describes the whole self-giving of God at tremendous cost.

The term "state of exaltation" is assigned to the period from the descenus on. The descensus, resurrection and ascension are all interpreted as the events by which God exalts his Son, that is, places him at his right hand in glory, honor and power. There is a continuity between the state of humiliation and exaltation because it is the same Christ who died and rose again, who was born of Mary and sits at the right hand, the one who is both God and man forever. But there is also a radical discontinuity because the exalted Christ exists in a state of being which is no longer confined by space and time, which is no longer a state of suffering and shame, which is the beginning of an age which is a reign of victory and which occurred only after the completion of the acts of sacrifice in the humiliation.

This radical discontinuity is of great importance for the doctrine of the real presence. It is the exalted, the glorified and powerful Christ who comes in the sacrament. He is at once the one who suffered and died, who was God's sacrifice, and the one who has completed his sacrifice, and whom God raised to a new status. He is *both* the crucified and the risen Lord. And he has both completed and continues his work, but he now continues his work *because* he has *completed* his work in humiliation.

The sacrifice is especially related to his death because here the sacrifice is so clearly exemplified and its goal accomplished. We cannot agree with Hicks' description of the atonement as only union between God and man. The atonement is too complex to describe here. The contemporary Lutheran sees it in a wider context than some of his predecessors, however, although not exceeding Luther's richness of understanding. The atonement is described in the picture of a conflict through which God in Christ overcomes evil—death, devil and the flesh—at great sacrifice, in the picture of suffering love whereby he reveals the depth of his grace, in the picture of propitiatory sacrifice whereby he satisfies his own wrath and frees man from his condemnation. Any concept of the role of sacrifice in the sacrament must encompass all of these facets. The simple identification of sacrifice with his death, the narrowing of the atonement to a placation of God's wrath as an object by another subject, a separated God-man, or the identification of atonement with a union in love alone, harbors many dangers which leads the seeker after understanding either to deprive the work of God of its magnificance or define the sacrament in such a way as to distort its real intent.

3. The doctrine of the real presence is of crucial importance at this juncture. Lutherans are aware that they have sometimes emphasized the presence out of proportion to other aspects of the Eucharist because of the apologetic demands but this in no wise should deter us from giving the doctrine its proper due. We are also aware that the intricacies of argumentation in the Formula of Concord (Articles VII and VIII) are easily misunderstood or at best are complex beyond necessity. But this does not mean that it is easier at this moment to produce final clarity!

a. Our Lord is present among his people in many ways—in the worship, in prayer, in the preached Word, when two or three are gathered, in Baptism—indeed in his exercise of Lordship over the whole world he is everywhere present. But the Eucharist focuses special attention upon his presence in *this* event.

b. The mode of his presence must be understood with the christological background described. He comes to us as both God and man *from* his exalted state. Lutherans have attempted to define the possibility of this in the *communicatio idiomatum* and *genus majestaticum* doctrines. These doctrines teach that the divine attributes of the risen Lord are communicated to the human nature of the risen Lord without destroying or transforming the human nature. The human nature is thus able to be omnipresent. Whether this language is any longer viable for a modern man is debatable but its intention is clear. The Christ who is present is the "whole" Christ, not the Lord as Spirit only, or divine nature only. Christ comes to man where man is with the promise that in this activity, through eating and drinking, he gives to us his body and blood, that is, himself, his life and being. In saying this, Lutherans separate themselves from the Zwinglian tradition and probably also from the Calvinist, depending in the latter upon the interpretation which is made of Calvin.

c. In the Eucharist, the Lord is both the giver and the gift. He is the host and that which is eaten and drunk. He is not confined to or limited to the elements of bread and wine. The Lutheran phraseology if "in, with and under" is easily misunderstood. Rather than limiting his presence, it seeks to characterize his presence as non-spatial. The presence is not well described as consubstantiation, that is, *along with* only, or as impanation, that is, *within* only, but rather in a dynamic sense of being present in the whole activity of the sacrament as well as imparted by means of the bread and wine. In recent times, Lutherans have spoken more freely of a "personal presence" or in "total presence" rather than only of his "real" or "true" presence, the latter being tautologies at best.

d. The relation of the mode of the presence to nature is not well delineated in Lutheran theology. We find Paul Tillich's discussion interesting but have not absorbed these suggestions to a degree that presents a position.[33] The transformation of nature by God's presence seems to us to close the gulf between God and his creation. This is true of the idea that man is ontologically transformed or changed as well as the idea of bread and wine being changed. Indeed, the two are bound in Catholic thought as we see it. Classical Catholic theory, especially the transubstantiation doctrine, seems to us to be more a destruction of nature, or displacement of nature, than an elevation of nature. We can admit of nature being the bearer of grace, not because of its own intrinsic capacity or receptivity, but because God chooses to so use nature.

It is still a grave problem for us to be sympathetic to the word "change" in almost any sense as a word which is applicable to the relation of the presence to the bread and wine. We say "almost any sense" because there is the possibility that one could speak of a change in the use of the bread and the wine, the change in "vocation" of these elements as Leenhardt suggests.[34] But we cannot derive from the given Biblical account any basis for a necessity for an ontological change. This, of course, obviates for us any idea of a permanent presence in the bread and the wine. The sacrament is the activity of God in which he comes to us in the form of bread and wine, not the activity of God whereby he changes nature in a fixed way.

3. Our understanding of the sacrament is inseparable from

---

[33]**Paul Tillich, *The Protestant Era*, J. C. Adams, tr. (Chicago, 1957) Chp. VII.**

[34]**Oscar Cullmann and F. J. Leenhardt, *Essays on the Lord's Supper* (Richmond, 1958.)**

our understanding of the church. God comes to his people, binding them to one another as well as to himself. His presence is a gift of fellowship as well as forgiveness and life. In this way we would understand "union" with God rather than in an ontological sense. The Eucharist is a sacrament of unity. It is a sign or mark of the church whereby the church is both created and made known. The church is both "before" the sacrament, for the sacrament is always celebrated "in" the church and "by" the church, but the church is always as well the recipient of the sacrament and therefore "under" and "after" the sacrament.

III.

What does this say to our dialogue about eucharistic sacrifice?

1. We are prepared to re-evaluate our traditional vocabulary and understanding in an attempt to remove the ambiguity surrounding the eucharistic sacrifice. By this we mean that the term sacrifice should not be confined only to the sacrifice of thanksgiving and praise, an emphasis which should not be diminished, but should also be applied to the character of God's gift and activity.

2. We want to emphasize that the Lord who is present in the Supper is both the crucified and risen Lord, who at great cost gave himself for us, who continues to intercede for us, and who comes to us with his benefits.

3. That which makes the sacrament sacrament is God's activity according to his gracious promise, and that which makes possible our reception of his benefits is faith, The term sacrifice should rightly be used both of God's activity on our behalf in the sacrament and of our giving of ourselves to him in the sacrament.

4. What words should be used to communicate and yet safeguard this meaning is not yet clear. The word "representation" provides problems for us. Wrongly interpreted, and easily so, it can imply a "doing over" in some symbolical sense of the sacrifice once made. Aulen has suggested that we say the sacrifice is "actualized," that is, its benefits made present and appropriable. He also suggests "self-impartation of suffering love."

This discussion raises questions we need to address to Roman Catholics.

1. How does a Catholic react to the continuity—radical continuity of the relation between the death and resurrection of our Lord?

2. What is the meaning of "offer up the victim to God" as it occurs in the Constitution of the Church?

3. Is there any sense in which the Catholic understands the eucharistic sacrifice to produce a change in God?

4. How does the Catholic derive his various theories of "change" in the elements from the Biblical text?

5. What place do individual Masses have in the present Catholic interpretation of eucharistic sacrifice? Do they not destroy the communal aspect and imply that the sacrifice is the work of the priest?

6. What ideas are involved in the word sacrifice as used for the atoning work of Christ?

8. What is the meaning of the centrality of the Eucharist in the context of the proclaimed Word as a means by which God confronts us?

9. What is the Catholic understanding of the "change" in man wrought by the sacrament?

This has been an attempt to open up the possibility for dialogue on the basis of some fundamental themes in Lutheran thought. Some aspect of Lutheran sacramentology, such as concept of sign, have not been treated. Such themes need to be investigated in subsequent papers or conversation.

SACRAMENTAL REALITY, SIGN, AND PRESENCE

By Thomas E. Ambrogi, S. J.

THE place where Schillebeeckx comes closest to treating these notions is in *Christ the Sacrament of the Encounter with God* (New York: Sheed and Ward, 1963), pp. 54-65. The following is part summary, part interpretation of Schillebeeckx' ideas.

I *SACRAMENTAL REALITY*

According to Schillebeeckx, there are two aspects to Jesus' redemptive acts: they take place in history, yet they have a perennial character. *(Ibid.*, p. 55) Jesus' actions, as "historically past" facts, are over and done with; as such, they cannot be made once more actually present, not even by God himself. To deny this is Docetism, for it means denying the genuine historicity of Jesus' existence as man: human history is essentially irreversible. Yet Jesus' acts, as the deeds of the God-man, have a trans-historical element about them. As personal acts of God, the sacrifice of the Cross and all the mysteries of the life of Christ are eternally actual and enduring. This enduring reality consists in the relationship of loving obedience between the Son incarnate and the Father. "The perennial element in Christ's historical acts is thus identical with the enduring character of the Incarnation." *(Ibid.*, p. 58)

Sacramental reality is ultimately nothing but the reality of Christianity itself—of the Incarnation, understood not simply as a once-and-for-all event but as something eternally actual. It is a *present* reality: human existence itself, as transformed and elevated by the redemptive love of God. Since Christ's death and resurrection, the world and man are forever intrinsically other than they would have been had God not become man, had the God-man not been "obedient unto death."

So understood, Christianity is not primarily a doctrine about certain past events or about human nature in the abstract, but is the sacrament (gesture and word, reality *and* interpretation) of what human life in the concrete now forever is. It is a *present* fact, not an idea or a historical memory—the substance of human life as it actually exists. Christianity is not merely the record of certain past facts in their implications for the present, but is the expression of everything that man—real man, existing man, graced man—always already is. Sacramental reality is simply the reality of the new relationship which is present, potentially or actually, wherever a human being exists. (This is the meaning of the *res sacramenti:* the unity of the people of God, the *communio ecclesiastica,* the Church herself as the gathering of the dispersed children of God.)

To speak of Christ, the Church, Christianity itself as sacramental is to indicate a twofold reality: interpretation and being, sign and signified, expression and thing expressed. As underlying reality, Christianity is the dwelling of God with man, God's acceptance of man in merciful love. As interpretation of that reality, Christianity is doctrine and rite, message and sign—the expression in word and symbol of the underlying truth, the new meaning of life brought about by Christ. Christ is the sign and sacrament of human life as a life towards God: both its explanation and the cause of what it explains. He is the symbol of man: not merely a "typical representation" or empty sign, but the efficacious cause of what man's life now is—*signum efficax gratiae.* His life, his teaching, his Church express and clarify the meaning they confer. Sacramental reality is essentially the reality of the New Being, of man's union with God which Christ achieved once and for all, but expressed and made tangible here and now in concrete ritual acts.

II *SACRAMENTAL SIGN*

Schillebeeckx notes that one of the major factors in the renewal of Catholic eucharistic theology has been the recovery and reappraisal of the scholastic notion that *sacramentum est in genere signi*—that sacraments are *signs* rather than physically present things. To speak of the Eucharist (or any sacrament) as a sign is to introduce a certain duality into our thinking—a distinction, which is precisely not a separation, between the reality of the sacrament and its visible form.

Now to acknowledge a difference of some kind between what is expressed and the expression itself already implies a measure of withdrawal from the context of liturgical worship. It implies a reflective pulling-back from the sphere of immediate action to the plane of abstract analysis. Phenomenological description gives way to conceptual reflection.

The difference can be illustrated by the duality between word (as uttered sound) and idea. When we speak or listen to others speaking, we use words without attending to the difference between the sound-patterns and the thought which they communicate: we grasp both together in an indissoluble unity. We do not attend, in other words, to word-sound as such—as *sign*, conveying that which is not itself—but simply to the meaning it expresses. It is only in a moment of reflection that we become directly conscious of the "distance" between word and thought—by considering, for example, the fact that the same idea can be conveyed by a different set of sounds (e.g., horse, *cheval*, *pferd*, *equus*, etc.). At the level of action, we have unity—identity of sign and signified; at the level of reflection, we have duality—the recognition of sign as sign, i.e., as somehow not simply the same as the reality it expresses. These two levels are psychologically distinct: to attend to words as sounds means that one will not hear language, but noise. Just so, the uninhibited and spontaneous use of words excludes any but a subsidiary and, so to speak, peripheral awareness of words as sound-signs. Notice, for instance, the breakdown of fluency which occurs when we suddenly discover that we are unsure of the correct pronunciation of some word we have begun to use.

This mysterious unity-in-duality which characterizes all of human symbolic activity (language, gesture, art, etc.) has a special relevance to sacramental theology. In the sacraments, the new relationship between God and man which Christ has brought about is expressed and made tangible in visible actions and concrete objects. The Christian believer by his faith "dwells in" and uses such signs in a manner similar to the way all men use language to convey thought. The external signs are absolutely indispensable for man in his historical and corporal reality. Physical signs are not themselves "meanings," and yet without them "meanings" could not be communicated—indeed, could not exist. For meaning to be actualized there must be the word; for grace to be actualized and rendered accessible to man's consciousness, there must be preaching and sacrament. The visible form of the sacrament is something "other" than pure sacramental reality. That reality itself—transformed human existence, the dwelling of God with man—requires the visible form and calls it into being in order to actualize itself at a particular time and place.

Thus at the level of sacramental action there is identity of sign and signified: the Eucharist *is* the Body and Blood of Christ. At the level of reflective analysis, there is duality: the sacred species is the *sign* of Christ's sacrifice and of the eternally actual mystery of redemption. The sign points to a reality which is distinct (though inadequately distinct) from itself. Yet to imagine this distinction as the distinction of two *things* quite external to each other—as, say, the curving arrow on the sign is distinct from the curve in the road—is to eliminate the unity which is an intrinsic element of the sacramental action. It denies something which is *given* in the experience of the worshipful reception of the sacraments. To be conscious, at such a moment, of the distinction between the sign and what it signifies is to frustrate the very purpose for which sacramental activity exists; it is to eliminate the essential difference between the preached word and the sacramental symbol. To be conscious, at the moment of receiving the host, that the wafer is not Christ, but bread which represents Christ, is to receive "not Christ, but bread." In such a case, the sacrament ceases to be sacramental—the actual presence of redemptive grace in historical tangibility—and becomes doctrinal, pedagogical, didactic: a concrete image serving as a reminder of what took place in the past, a present object representing, but not actually *presenting*, an "absent" person. (Not that Christ, on such an understanding of the sacraments, would have to be totally absent: but he would be *no more* present in the host than in any other object—e.g., a picture—one chose to make represent him.)

Only the Church, with her faith, can guarantee the substantial identity of sacramental sign and sacramental reality. For this reason (and to this extent) Christian sacramentalism goes beyond a general psychological analysis of symbolism. The "real presence" of Christ in the sacraments cannot be verified merely in terms of the description of symbolic activity suggested above. But the Church's faith in the reality of sacramental presence is not something added on to her faith in the Christ-event; it is simply her belief in the Incarnation, expressing itself in the domain of ritual action. If God in Christ has become one with man, then the sacraments *are* what they signify. If not, they are "mere signs," external to the reality they indicate, a reality which itself becomes somewhat obscured by this way of viewing it. The sacraments are signs in any case, but for them to function as *sacramental* signs a fundamental identity between sign and reality must be acknowledged, *prior* to the distinction and including it—an identity analogous to the unity of the one human person, which comprises the duality of soul and matter.

Perhaps the kiss of love is the nearest human analogy to the sacramental encounter. The kiss is first of all a sign. It is not simply the same as the love which it expresses. For the love may be present without finding this particular expression at a given moment, or the kiss may be there when the love is gone, as in Judas' kiss of Christ. Yet love depends on such expressions to actualize itself, and without them it would wither and die. In order to be, to make itself present and knowable, love must realize itself in signs which are "other" than love itself. At the moment when lovers kiss, however, no distinction between sign and signified is psychologically possible, much less desirable. The kiss simply *is* their love manifesting itself in action. By the kiss love is strengthened and increased. It does not simply remain what it was before, but grows through further experience. The kiss, in short, does not merely *express* a given reality, the reality itself lying unchanged somewhere behind it, in a domain apart. It is an efficacious sign, causing to be and to be *more* the very thing which it expresses. The sacramental sign, like the kiss, is always both identical with and yet other than the reality it renders present. But the distinction is secondary to, and can only be understood in terms of, the original unity.

III *SACRAMENTAL PRESENCE*

How does the "real presence" of Christ in the Eucharist differ from his no less real presence in the Christian community, in the Word of preaching, in the other six sacraments? Clearly it is a qualitative rather than an absolute difference, a matter of intensity rather than of kind. Sacramental reality is always the enduring reality of the Incarnate God. It differs internally according to the mode of its realization.

The Eucharist is the bringing-together of the various "presences" of Christ: in word, in community, in the other sacraments. It is the focussing of his reality in its most intensely personal expression. As love between a man and a woman finds expression in all the dimensions of their life together (many of which allow for only a minimum of conscious affectivity), but tends naturally to its fullest, most conscious, most personal consummation, so the reality of God's love needs expression in a variety of forms but tends to its fullest and most direct realization in eucharistic communion.

According to Schillebeeckx, in every sacrament we have a personal presence of Christ, but the principle of presence differs. In the other six sacraments Christ is present only in virtue of his redemptive *act* sacramentally embodied, where in the Eucharist Christ *himself* is present by the power of transubstantiation. (*Ibid.*, p. 60)

The difference may be suggested by the distinction between the lover's presence in the gift to his beloved, and his presence in the kiss. The gift is a sign by which his enduring devotion is made present to his beloved. She does not merely reason to that devotion through the gift, she experiences it as present, she *feels* it. This is the justification for speaking of the gift as a form of personal presence, in spite of spatial separation. But, in the intensity of realized presence, the gift can hardly compare with the kiss—which is no less a sign, but so much more powerfully expressive.

The eucharistic celebration is just such a focussing, just such a climactic realization of the ever-present reality of redemption. In it God presents himself to the man who makes himself present to God. In terms of the movement "up" to God, it means that the permanent meaning of human life—God's Ex-sistence in matter and time—is given archetypal expression at a specific time and place. What man, through Christ, "always already is" before God, is ritually realized: this is the eucharistic sacrifice. At the same time, the union of man with God which Christ brought about, and which alone makes the sacrificial attitude possible, is deepened and strengthened through Communion: this is the movement "down" to man. The Mass is the effective sign of what man in Christ now forever is; it *realizes* God's presence among us—by expressing the very reality it brings about.

THE EUCHARIST: A LUTHERAN-ROMAN CATHOLIC STATEMENT

As a result of our conversations on the eucharist, we Roman Catholic and Lutheran theologians wish to record, chiefly and first of all, our profound gratitude to God for the growing unity on this subject which we see in our day.

Our responsibility is to try to articulate and explain this increasing agreement to the people and leadership of our churches, so that they may test for themselves what we have discussed and draw whatever conclusions in thought and action they find appropriate.

What we have to report is not so much original with us as simply one manifestation of a growing consensus among many Christian traditions on the Lord's supper.[1]

Ours, however, is a specifically Roman Catholic-Lutheran contribution. It attempts to go beyond the more general ecumenical discussion of the eucharist to an examination of the particular agreements and disagreements of our two traditions. While we have considered the biblical and patristic sources of eucharistic doctrine and practice in our preparatory conversations, this statement deals with problems that have become particularly acute for Lutherans and Roman Catholics as a result of the sixteenth-century controversies. It does not try to treat the sacrament of the altar comprehensively.

Our attention has focused on two issues: the eucharist as sacrifice, and the presence of Christ in the sacrament. These issues have been especially divisive in the past and are involved in most

---

[1]Various terms are current in the different Christian traditions for this sacrament: e.g., eucharist, holy communion, sacrament of the altar, mass. We shall use them interchangeably. Further, in order to mark the way our statement shares in the growing ecumenical consensus, we shall, on occasion, use language from the documents of the ecumenical movement to express our own convictions.

of our historical disagreements on eucharistic doctrine and practice. For this reason it seems to us important to enunciate our growing agreement on these two points, even though there are other aspects of the sacrament of the altar we have not yet discussed.

I
THE EUCHARIST AS SACRIFICE[2]

With reference to the eucharist as sacrifice, two affirmations have not been denied by either confession; four aspects of the problem have been major points of divergence.

1. *a*) Lutherans and Roman Catholics alike acknowledge that in the Lord's supper "Christ is present as the Crucified who died for our sins and who rose again for our justification, as the once-for-all sacrifice for the sins of the world who gives himself to the faithful."[3] On this Lutherans insist as much as Catholics, although, for various reasons, Lutherans have been reticent about speaking of the eucharist as a sacrifice.

   b) The confessional documents of both traditions agree that the celebration of the eucharist is the church's sacrifice of praise and self-offering or oblation. Each tradition can make the following statement its own: "By him, with him and in him who is our great High Priest and Intercessor we offer to the Father, in the power of the Holy Spirit, our praise, thanksgiving and intercession. With contrite hearts we offer ourselves as a living and

---

[2]Scripture and the history of theology contain many ways of describing Christ's sacrifice and therefore also the sacrificial character of the memorial of that sacrifice which is the eucharist. The most general meaning of "sacrifice" is broader than any current in contemporary usage—or in that of the sixteenth century. Thus, according to the Second World Conference on Faith and Order (Edinburgh, 1937), "If sacrifice is understood as it was by our Lord and His followers and in the early Church, it includes, not His death only, but the obedience of His earthly ministry, and His risen and ascended life, in which He still does His Father's will and ever liveth to make intercession for us" (L. Vischer, ed., *A Documentary History of the Faith and Order Movement, 1927-1963* [St. Louis: Bethany Press, 1963] p. 57). In what follows, however, no particular theory of "sacrifice" or of related terms such as "propitiation" is presupposed.

[3]*Consultation on Church Union: Principles* (Cincinnati: Foreward Movement Press, 1967) p. 50. See also the Montreal Faith and Order affirmation: the Lord's supper is "a sacrament of the presence of the crucified and glorified Christ until he come, and a means whereby the sacrifice of the cross, which we proclaim, is operative within the church" (P. C. Rodger, ed., *The Fourth World Conference on Faith and Order: Montreal, 1963*, p. 73).

holy sacrifice, a sacrifice which must be expressed in the whole of our daily lives."[4]

2. Historically, our controversies have revolved around the question whether the worshiping assembly "offers Christ" in the sacrifice of the mass. In general, Lutherans have replied in the negative, because they believed that only thus could they preserve the once-for-all character and the full sufficiency of the sacrifice of the cross and keep the eucharist from becoming a human supplement to God's saving work, a matter of "works-righteousness."

a) First of all, we must be clear that Catholics as well as Lutherans affirm the unrepeatable character of the sacrifice of the cross. The Council of Trent, to be sure, affirmed this, but Lutheran doubts about the Catholic position were not resolved. Today, however, we find no reason for such doubt, and we recognize our agreement in the assertion that "What God did in the incarnation, life, death, resurrection and ascension of Christ, he does not do again. The events are unique; they cannot be repeated, or extended or continued. Yet in this memorial we do not only recall past events: God makes them present through the Holy Spirit, thus making us participants in Christ (I Cor. 1:9)."[5]

b) Further, the Catholic affirmation that the church "offers Christ" in the mass has in the course of the last half century been increasingly explained in terms which answer Lutheran fears that this detracts from the full sufficiency of Christ's sacrifice. The members of the body of Christ are united through Christ with God and with one another in such a way that they become participants in his worship, his self-offering, his sacrifice to the Father. Through this union between Christ and Christians, the eucharistic assembly "offers Christ" by consenting in the power of the Holy Spirit to be offered by him to the Father.[6] Apart from Christ we have no gifts, no wor-

---

[4]Rodger, *op. cit.*, pp. 73-74. See also the *Apology of the Augsburg Confession* XXIV, 30-88, esp. 33, 35, 74-75, 87. References to the Lutheran Confessions are based on *Die Bekenntnisschriften der Evangelisch-Lutherischen Kirche* (5th ed.; Gottingen, 1964.)

[5]Rodger, *op. cit.*, p. 73.

[6]Luther says: "not that we offer Christ as a sacrifice, but that Christ offers us"; but he also holds that this involves a sense in which "we offer Christ": "Through

ship, no sacrifice of our own to offer to God. All we can plead is Christ, the sacrificial lamb and victim whom the Father himself has given us.

c) Another historically important point of controversy has been the Roman Catholic position that the eucharistic sacrifice is "propitiatory." Within the context of the emphases which we have outlined above, Catholics today interpret this position as emphatically affirming that the presence of the unique propitiatory sacrifice of the cross in the eucharistic celebration of the church is efficacious for the forgiveness of sins and the life of the world. Lutherans can join them up to this point.[7] They reject, however, what they have understood Trent to say about the mass as a propitiatory sacrifice "offered for the living and the dead,"[8] even though the Apology of the Augsburg

---

it (faith), in connection with the sacrament, we offer ourselves, our need, our prayer, praise and thanksgiving in Christ, and thereby we offer Christ. . . . I also offer Christ in that I desire and believe that he accepts me and my prayer and praise and presents it to God in his own person" (*A Treatise on the New Testament*, in *Luther's Works* 35 [Philadelphia: Fortress Press, 1961] 98-101). This agrees with the testimony of the Second Vatican Council, which, quoting St. Augustine, says that the "aim" of the sacrifice offered in the eucharist is that "the entire commonwealth of the redeemed, that is, the community and the society of the saints, be offered as a universal sacrifice to God through the High Priest who in His Passion offered His very Self for us that we might be the body of so exalted a Head" (*Decree on the Ministry and Life of Priests*, no. 2; tr. W. M. Abbott and J. Gallagher, eds., *The Documents of Vatican II* [New York: Guild Press, 1966] pp. 535-36; quotation from Augustine's *City of God* 10, 6). The continuation of this quotation is paraphrased in the 1947 encyclical *Mediator Dei*, no. 125: "in the sacrament of the altar which she [the church] offers, she herself is also offered." The contemporary Catholic theologian Karl Rahner explains this point by saying that the eucharistic offering of Christ inseparably involves "the believing, inner 'yes' of men to the movement of loving obedience of Christ to the Father." He goes on to speak directly to the fears which Protestants have expressed regarding the notion of the "sacrifice of the mass": "The sacrifice of the mass creates no new gracious and saving will in God vis-a-vis the world which did not already exist through the cross (and only through the cross!)." "We can speak of 'moving' God to forgiveness, reconciliation, mercy and assistance through the sacrifice of the mass only in the sense that the gracious will of God, founded exclusively on the reconciliation of the cross, becomes visible in the sacrifice of the mass, comes to man . . . and takes hold of him"—producing, Rahner goes on to suggest, manifold effects in the worshipers and, through their actions and prayers, in the world ("Die vielen Messen und das eine Opfer," *Zeitschrift fur katholische Theologie* 71 [1949] 267 and 288).

[7] A question can still be raised whether the word "propitiatory," given its usual connotations, correctly describes the Father's action in Christ on Calvary. Cf. C. F. D. Moule, *The Sacrifice of Christ* (Philadelphia, Fortress Press, 1964) pp. vi-viii, 33 f., and the literature cited on p. 46.

[8] Denzinger-Schonmetzer 1753 (950).

Confession concedes with respect to prayer for the dead that "we do not forbid it."[9] We have not discussed this aspect of the problem; further exploration of it is required.

d) In addition to the growing harmony in ways of thinking about the eucharistic sacrifice, there is a significant convergence in the actual practice of eucharistic worship. Doctrine is inevitably interpreted in the light of practice, as well as vice versa, and consequently oppositions on this level can negate apparent doctrinal agreement. For example, the Reformers and later Lutherans have believed that the multiplication of private masses and the associated systems of mass intentions and mass stipends are evidence that Roman Catholics do not take seriously the all-sufficiency of Christ's sacrifice, and this suspicion has been reinforced by such statements of Catholic theologians as "the sacrificial worth of two Masses is just double the sacrificial worth of one Mass."[10] Now, however, the Second Vatican Council in its Constitution on the Sacred Liturgy has declared that the nature of the mass is such that the communal way of celebrating is to be preferred to individual and quasi-private celebrations.[11] As the liturgical renewal progresses in this and other respects, each group in these discussions finds it increasingly easy to understand and approve what the other says about the eucharist in general and its sacrificial aspects in particular.

The question of eucharistic sacrifice is closely related to other issues. The problem of the "real presence" has been the first to claim our attention. Do we, in the eucharist, genuinely encounter Christ in the full reality of his person and sacrificial action? It is therefore to this subject that we now turn.

II
THE PRESENCE OF CHRIST IN THE LORD'S SUPPER

Here, too, there are areas in which this group believes that Roman Catholics and Lutherans can make the same affirmations, and others in which our agreement is not yet complete.

---

[9] XXXIV, 94.

[10] A. Vonier, *Collected Works* 2 (London, 1952) 343. It should be noted that Vonier does not regard such a statement as irreconcilable with his own insistence on the uniqueness and sufficiency of Christ's sacrifice.

[11] Cf. *Constitution on the Sacred Liturgy*, nos. 26 and 27.

1. *a)* We confess a manifold presence of Christ, the Word of God and Lord of the world. The crucified and risen Lord is present in his body, the people of God, for he is present where two or three are gathered in his name (Mt. 18:20). He is present in baptism, for it is Christ himself who baptizes.[12] He is present in the reading of the scriptures and the proclamation of the gospel. He is present in the Lord's supper.[13]

b) We affirm that in the sacrament of the Lord's supper Jesus Christ, true God and true man, is present wholly and entirely, in his body and blood, under the signs of bread and wine.[14]

c) Through the centuries Christians have attempted various formulations to describe this presence. Our confessional documents have in common affirmed that Jesus Christ is "really," "truly" and "substantially" present in this sacrament.[15] This manner of presence "we can scarcely express in words,"[16] but we affirm his presence because we believe in the power of God and the promise of Jesus Christ, "This is my body. . . . This is my blood. . . ."[17] Our traditions have spoken of this presence as "sacramental,"[18] "supernatural" and "spiritual."[19] These terms have different connotations in the two traditions, but they have in common a rejection of a spatial or natural manner of presence, and a rejection of an understanding of the sacrament as only commemorative or figurative.[20] The term

---

[12]Cf. *Constitution on the Sacred Liturgy*, no. 7; St. Augustine, *Treatise on the Gospel of John* 6, 1, 7 (PL 35, 1428).

[13]Cf. *Constitution on the Sacred Liturgy*, no. 7; *Instruction on Eucharistic Worship* (May 25, 1967) no. 9; FC (= *Formula of Concord)* SD (= *Solid Declaration)* VIII, 76-84.

[14]1 Cor. 11:27. Cf. Denzinger-Schonmetzer (hereafter DS) 1636, 1640 f., 1651, 1653. Writing of the eucharistic presence, E. Schlink states: "The divine nature of Christ is not without the human nature and the human nature is not without the divine nature" *(Theology of the Lutheran Confessions* [Philadelphia, 1961] p. 158.) See also FC SD VII, 60; VIII, 76- 84.

[15]Cf. DS 1636; Ap (= *Apology of the Augsburg Confession)* X, 1, 4; FC Ep (= Epitome) VII, 6, 34; SD VII, 88, 126.

[16]DS 1636. Cf. FC SD VII, 38.

[17]Cf. DS 1636; FC Ep VII, 16 f.; SD VII, 97-103, 106.

[18]DS 1636. Cf. FC Ep VII, 15; SD VII, 63.

[19]FC Ep VII, 14 f. In the context of the *Formula of Concord*, it is clear that "spiritual" here is not opposed to "real." Cf. SD VII, 94-106, 118.

[20]Cf. AC (= *Augsburg Confession)* X; Ap X, 1 ff.; FC Ep VII, 6 f., 26 ff., 34; SD VII, 2-11, 38, 48 f.; DS 1636, 1651.

"sign," once suspect, is again recognized as a positive term for speaking of Christ's presence in the sacrament.[21] For, though symbols and symbolic actions are used, the Lord's supper is an effective sign: it communicates what it promises; ". . . the action of the Church becomes the effective means whereby God in Christ acts and Christ is present with his people."[22]

d) Although the sacrament is meant to be celebrated in the midst of the believing congregation, we are agreed that the presence of Christ does not come about through the faith of the believer, or through any human power, but by the power of the Holy Spirit through the word.[23]

e) The true body and blood of Christ are present not only at the moment of reception but throughout the eucharistic action.[24]

2. In the following areas our historical divergences are being overcome, although we are unable at present to speak with one voice at every point.

a) In reference to eucharistic worship:

a. We agreed that Christ gave us this sacrament in

---

[21]Cf. DS 1651; FC SD VII, 7, 49, 116; *Constitution on the Sacred Liturgy*, nos. 33, 59; *Instruction on Eucharistic Worship*, no. 6.

[22]*Consultation on Church Union: Principles*, p. 49.

[23]Cf. LC (= *Large Catechism*) V, 9 f., 14; FC Ep VII, 9, 35; SD VII, 73-82, 89, 121; DS 1636 f., 1640. See also DS 1612; FC Ep VII, 8; SD VII, 16, 32, 89; LC IV, 52, and V, 4 ff., 15-18. Catholics see in these affirmations of the Lutheran Confessions the essential content of the Catholic doctrine of the *exopere operato* working of the sacraments. In some of the pre-Tridentine Confessions, Lutherans rejected a concept of *opus operatum* which Catholics do not recognize as their own. Cf. DS 1606 ff., 1612.

[24]Cf. AC X, 1; FC SD VII, 14; Ep VII, 6: "We believe . . . that in the holy supper the body and blood of Christ are truly and essentially present and are truly distributed and received *(wahrhaftig ausgeteilet und empfangen werde)*. . . ." In his *Sermon on the Sacrament of the Body and Blood of Christ* (1526; WA [= Weimar edition] 19, 491, 13), Luther declared: "As soon as Christ says: 'This is my body,' his body is present through the Word and the power of the Holy Spirit" (tr. F. Ahrens, American edition 36, 341). Cf. WA 30/1, 53, 122.—Trent (DS 1654) refers to Christ's presence before reception as "ante (usum)." For Trent *usus* means the actual reception by the communicant: "in usu, dum sumitur" *(ibid.)*. Lutherans speak of the whole liturgical action as *usus*: the consecration, distribution and reception *(sumptio)* of the sacrament (FC SD VII, 85 f.). If, therefore, Lutherans do not speak of Christ being present before or apart from "use," this is not to be understood as contradicting Trent; for the Lutheran Confessions agree that Jesus is present *(adesse)* in the sacrament before he is received *(sumi)*, that is, *ante sumptionem*. It is "the body and blood of Christ" which "are distributed to us to eat and to drink. . . ." (SD VII, 82).

order that we might receive him and participate in his worship of the Father.[25]

b. We are also agreed that the Lord Jesus Christ is himself to be worshiped, praised and adored; every knee is to bow before him.[26]

c. We are further agreed that as long as Christ remains sacramentally present, worship, reverence and adoration are appropriate.[27]

d. Both Lutherans and Catholics link Christ's eucharistic presence closely to the eucharistic liturgy itself. Lutherans, however, have not stressed the prolongation of this presence beyond the communion service as Catholics have done.

e. To be sure, the opposition on this point is not total. Following a practice attested in the early church, Lutherans may distribute the elements from the congregational communion service to the sick in private communion, in some cases as an extension of this service, in some cases with the words of institution spoken either for their proclamatory value or as consecration.

f. Also in harmony with a eucharistic practice attested in the early church, Roman Catholics have traditionally reserved the consecrated host for communicating the sick, which, according to the Instruction of May 25, 1967, is the "primary and original purpose" of reservation.[28] The adoration of Christ present in the reserved sacrament is of later origin and is a secondary end.[29]

---

[25]DS 1643: "(sacramentum) quod fuerit a Christo Domino, ut sumatur, institutum."

[26]CF. Phil 2:10.

[27]Cf. DS 1643, 1656; FC SD VII, 126: one must not "deny that Christ himself, true God and man, who is truly and essentially present in the Supper when it is rightly used, should be adored in spirit and in truth in all places but especially where his community is assembled" (ed. T. G. Tappert). See also Luther, WA 11, 447 (Amer. ed. 36, 294); St. Augustine, *On Psalm 98*, 9 (PL 37, 1264).

[28]*Instruction on Eucharistic Worship*, no. 49.

[29]Cf. *ibid.* As Dom Lambert Beauduin has expressed it, the eucharist was not reserved in order to be adored; rather, because it was reserved, it was adored (cf. *Melanges liturgiques . . . de Dom L. Beauduin* [Louvain, 1954] p. 265). It should be noted, however, that adoration of the reserved sacrament has been very much a part of Catholic life and a meaningful form of devotion to Catholics for many centuries.

The same Instruction repeats the insistence of the Constitution on the Sacred Liturgy that any adoration of the reserved sacrament be harmonized with and in some way derived from the liturgy, "since the liturgy by its very nature surpasses" any nonliturgical eucharistic devotion.[30]

b) In reference to the presence of Christ under both species, a divergence of practice concerning the cup for the laity has been one of the most obvious signs of disunity between Roman Catholics and other Christians. Catholics of the Eastern rites in union with the Roman See have always retained the practice of communion under both species. The Lutheran confessions emphasize the desirability of communion in both kinds in obedience to "a clear command and order of Christ,"[31] but do not deny the sacramental character of communion administered to a congregation in one kind only. At Vatican II the Roman Catholic Church reintroduced, to a modest but significant extent, communion under both kinds for the Western church.[32] The Council thereby recognized that this practice better expresses the sign of the mystery of eucharistic presence. Recent liturgical directives have explicitly acknowledged this principle and have extended this usage.[33]

c) Lutherans traditionally have understood the Roman Catholic use of the term "transubstantiation" to involve:

a. An emphatic affirmation of the presence of Christ's body and blood in the sacrament. With this they are in agreement.

b. An affirmation that God acts in the eucharist, effecting a change in the elements. This also Lutherans teach, although they use a different terminology.[34]

---

[30]*Instruction on Eucharistic Worship*, no. 58; cf. *Constitution on the Sacred Liturgy*, no. 13.

[31]AC XXII, 1.

[32]Cf. *Constitution on the Sacred Liturgy*, no. 55. It should be noted that some scholars hold that communion under both kinds has not always been the practice within the church even in ancient times. For example, J. Jeremias (*The Eucharistic Words of Jesus* [New York, 1964] p. 115) suggests that "the breaking of the bread" in the New Testament refers to communion under one species. Other scholars disagree.

[33]Cf. *Instruction on Eucharistic Worship*, no. 32.

[34]Lutherans traditionally speak of the change that takes place in the elements as

c. A rationalistic attempt to explain the mystery of Christ's presence in the sacrament. This they have rejected as presumptuous.

d. A definitive commitment to one and only one conceptual framework in which to express the change in the elements. This they have regarded as theologically untenable.

It can thus be seen that there is agreement on the "that," the full reality of Christ's presence. What has been disputed is a particular way of stating the "how," the manner in which he becomes present.

Today, however, when Lutheran theologians read contemporary Catholic expositions,[35] it becomes clear to them that the dogma of transubstantiation intends to affirm the fact of Christ's presence and of the change which takes place, and is not an attempt to explain how Christ becomes present. When the dogma is understood in this way, Lutherans find that they also must acknowledge that it is a legitimate way of attempting to express the mystery, even though they continue to believe that the conceptuality associated with "transubstantiation" is misleading and therefore prefer to avoid the term.

Our conversations have persuaded us of both the legitimacy and the limits of theological efforts to explore the mystery of Christ's presence in the sacrament. We are

---

involving a sacramental union with the body and blood of Christ analogous to the hypostatic union of the human and divine natures in Christ; cf. FC SD VII, 36 f. Coupled with this affirmation is the statement that the bread and wine are essentially untransformed *(unvorwandelten)*; cf. SD VII, 35 ff. In Ep VII, 22 the Roman Catholic affirmation of transubstantiation is understood to involve an annihilation *(zunicht werden)* of the bread and wine. It should be noted, however, that Trent's understanding of transubstantiation has nothing to do with the idea of annihilation of the elements. Catholic theologians emphasize today that the substantial change of bread and wine is a sacramental change which involves no change in "the chemical, physical or botanical reality of bread and wine" (E. Schillebeeckx, "Transubstantiation, Transfinalization, Transignification," *Worship* 40 [1966] 337). Further, on the basis of Ap X, 2, which cites with approval the Greek tradition that the bread is truly changed into the body of Christ ("mutato pane"; "panem . . . vere mutari"), there is a certain sense in which "one can stand on Lutheran ground and talk about a transformation of the elements *(Verwandlung der Elemente)*." Cf. Fr. Brunstaed, *Theologie der lutherischen Bekenntnisschriften* (Guetersloh, 1951) p. 156.

[35]Cf. K. Rahner, "The Presence of Christ in the Sacrament of the Lord's Supper," in *Theological Investigations* 4 (Baltimore, 1966) 287-311; E. Schillebeeckx, "Christus tegenwoordigheid in de Eucharistie," *Tijdschrift voor Theologie* 5 (1965) 136-72.

also persuaded that no single vocabulary or conceptual framework can be adequate, exclusive or final in this theological enterprise. We are convinced that current theological trends in both traditions give great promise for increasing convergence and deepened understanding of the eucharistic mystery.

CONCLUSION

There are still other questions that must be examined before we Catholic and Lutheran participants in these conversations would be prepared to assess our over-all agreements and disagreements on the doctrine of the sacrament of the altar. To mention two important omissions, we have not yet attempted to clarify our respective positions on the roles of the laity and the clergy, the "general" and "special" priesthood, in sacramental celebrations, nor have we discussed the pressing problem of the possibilities of intercommunion apart from full doctrinal and ecclesiastical fellowship.

On the two major issues which we have discussed at length, however, the progress has been immense. Despite all remaining differences in the ways we speak and think of the eucharistic sacrifice and our Lord's presence in his supper, we are no longer able to regard ourselves as divided in the one holy catholic and apostolic faith on these two points. We therefore prayerfully ask our fellow Lutherans and Catholics to examine their consciences and root out many ways of thinking, speaking and acting, both individually and as churches, which have obscured their unity in Christ on these as on many other matters.

PARTICIPANTS

Catholics:

The Most Rev. T. Austin Murphy, Auxiliary Bishop of Baltimore, Maryland

The Rev. Thomas E. Ambrogi, S.J., Professor of Sacramental Theology and Ecumenics, Woodstock College, Woodstock, Maryland

The Very Rev. Msgr. Joseph W. Baker, Vice-Chairman of the Ecumenical Commission of the Archdiocese of St. Louis, Missouri

The Very Rev. Msgr. William W. Baum, Chancellor of the Diocese of Kansas City-St. Joseph, Missouri

The Rev. Raymond E. Brown, S.S., Professor of Sacred Scripture, St. Mary Seminary, Baltimore, Maryland

The Rev. Walter Burghardt, S.J., Professor of Patristics, Woodstock College, Woodstock, Maryland

The Rev. Godfrey Diekmann, O.S.B., Professor of Patristics, St. John's Abbey, Collegeville, Minnesota

The Rev. Maurice C. Duchaine, S.S., Professor of Dogmatic Theology, St. Mary's Seminary, Baltimore, Maryland

The Rev. John F. Hotchkin, Assistant Director, Bishops' Committee for Ecumenical and Interreligious Affairs, Washington, D. C.

Professor James F. McCue, School of Religion, University of Iowa, Iowa City, Iowa

The Rev. Harry J. McSorley, C.S.P., Professor of Ecumenical Theology, St. Paul's College, Washington, D. C.

The Rev. Jerome D. Quinn, Professor of Old and New Testament, St. Paul Seminary, St. Paul, Minnesota

The Rev. George Tavard, A.A., Department of Religious Studies, Pennsylvania State University, University Park, Pennsylvania

Lutherans:

Dr. Paul C. Empie, General Secretary of the U.S.A. National Committee of the Lutheran World Federation, New York, New York

Dr. Arnold Carlson, Executive Secretary, Division of Theological Studies of the Lutheran Council in the U.S.A., New York, New York

Dr. Bertil E. Gartner, Professor of New Testament, Princeton Theological Seminary, Princeton, New Jersey

Dr. Kent S. Knutson, Professor of Systematic Theology, Luther Theological Seminary, St. Paul, Minnesota

Dr. Fred Kramer, Professor of Dogmatics, Concordia Theological Seminary, Springfield, Illinois

Dr. George Lindbeck, Associate Professor of Historical Theology, Yale University Divinity School, New Haven, Connecticut

Dr. Paul Opsahl, Associate Executive Secretary, Division of Theological Studies of the Lutheran Council in the U.S.A., New York, N.Y.

Dr. Arthur Carl Piepkorn, Graduate Professor of Systematic Theology, Concordia Seminary, St. Louis, Missouri

Dr. Warren Quanbeck, Professor of Systematic Theology, Luther Theological Seminary, St. Paul, Minnesota

Dr. John Reumann, Professor of New Testament at Lutheran Seminary, Philadelphia, Pennsylvania

Dr. Joseph Sittler, Professor of Systematic Theology, University of Chicago Divinity School, Chicago, Illinois

Dr. Krister Stendahl, Professor of Biblical Studies, Harvard University Divinity School, Cambridge, Massachusetts

$2.95

Augsburg Publishing House • Minneapolis, Minnesota 55415

10